LEGENDARY LOCALS

OF

FORT LAUDERDALE

FLORIDA

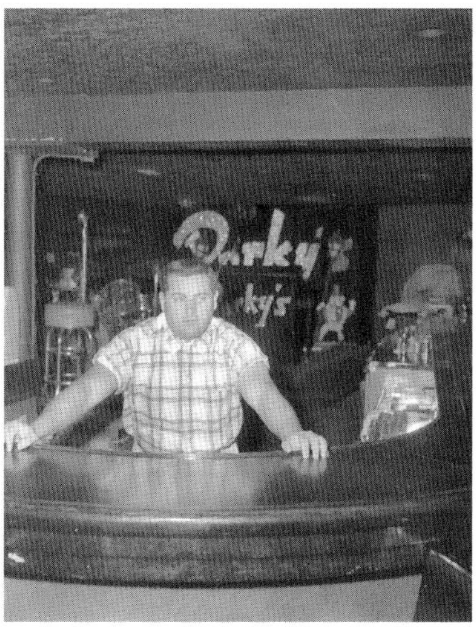

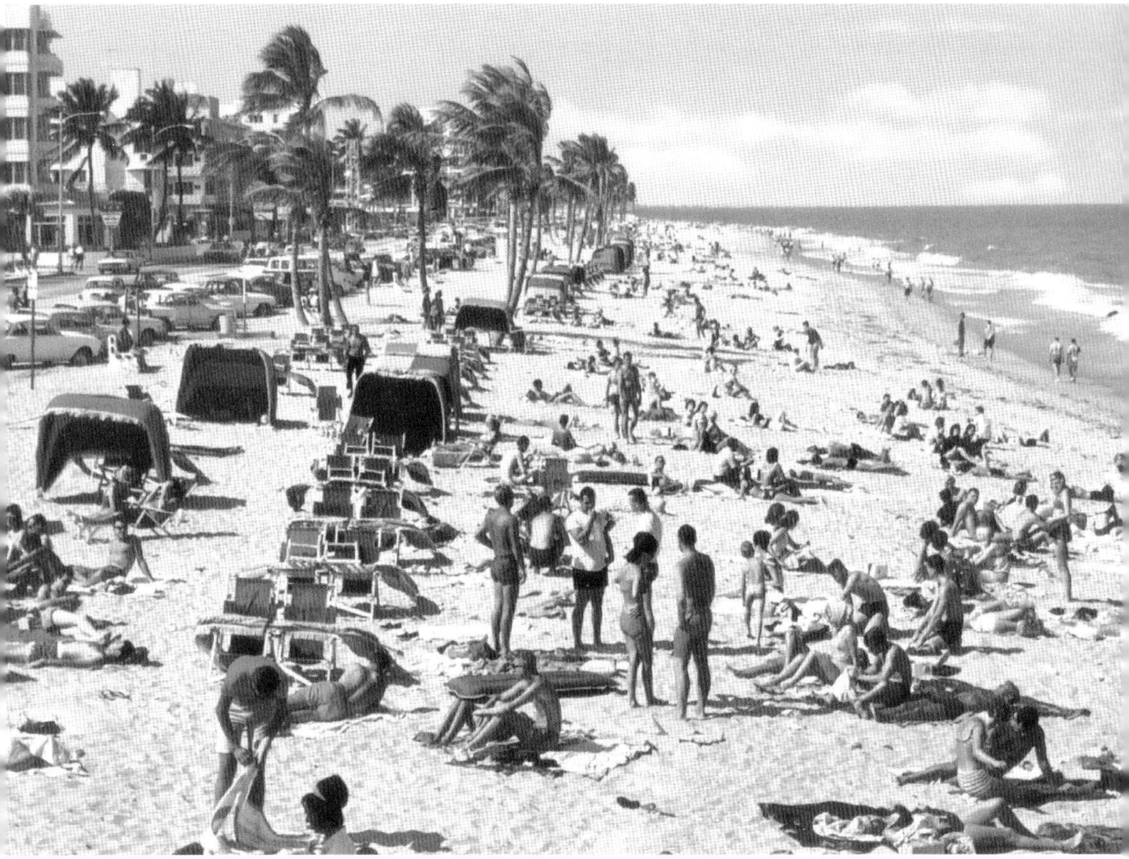

Fort Lauderdale Beach

Although the beach was not the initial draw to Fort Lauderdale, it has been a favorite destination of locals and tourists since the 1930s. A spring-break destination of college students until 1985, the beach has remade itself into a first-class, family-friendly resort area. (Courtesy of the Fort Lauderdale Historical Society.)

Page 1: Donald "Porky" Baines, Owner of Porky's Hide Away

Porky's was a 1950s and 1960s roadhouse that featured live music. It was popular with the spring break crowd, as students could drink all day for $1.50. The movie *Porky's* is loosely based on the nightclub. (Courtesy of the Fort Lauderdale Historical Society, Gene Hyde Collection.)

LEGENDARY LOCALS

OF

FORT LAUDERDALE

FLORIDA

TODD L. BOTHEL

LEGENDARY LOCALS

ISBN 978-1-4671-0220-9

Legendary Locals is an imprint of Arcadia Publishing
Charleston, South Carolina

Printed in the United States of America

Library of Congress Control Number: 2015936408

For all general information, please contact Arcadia Publishing:
Telephone 843-853-2070
Fax 843-853-0044
E-mail sales@arcadiapublishing.com
For customer service and orders:
Toll-Free 1-888-313-2665

Visit us on the Internet at www.arcadiapublishing.com

Dedication
I dedicate this book to my mother, Muriel J. Chappell, for her lifetime of support and belief in me.

On the Front Cover: Clockwise from top left:
Shirttail Charlie, Seminole Indian (Courtesy of the Fort Lauderdale Historical Society; see page 21), William Verity, seafarer (Courtesy of the Fort Lauderdale Historical Society; see page 125), Wayne Huizenga, entrepreneur (Courtesy of the Fort Lauderdale Historical Society; see page 48), Chris Evert, tennis player (Courtesy of Todd Bothel; see page 98), Ed Stone Jr., architect (Courtesy of the Fort Lauderdale Historical Society; see page 31), Francis Abreu, Cuban architect, (Courtesy of the Fort Lauderdale Historical Society; see page 27), George Burrows, master electrician (Courtesy of *Sun-Sentinel*; see page 45), Eula Johnson, civil rights activist (Courtesy of the Fort Lauderdale Historical Society; see page 83), Commodore Brook, publicist (Courtesy of the Fort Lauderdale Historical Society; see page 50).

On the Back Cover: From left to right:
Tony Tommie, Seminole Indian (Courtesy of the Fort Lauderdale Historical Society; see page 22), Junior League moving the King-Cromartie House (Courtesy of the Fort Lauderdale Historical Society; see page 84).

CONTENTS

ACKNOWLEDGMENTS

When pulling together the information and images for a book like this, invariably, some interesting individuals are left out of the final product. Like most major cities in the United States, Fort Lauderdale has enough legendary locals to fill three or four books. Finding the contacts to get appropriate materials is sometimes difficult, and winnowing down the inclusion list is a painstaking process. I have tried to include individuals from all walks of life, race, and gender. Of course, the famous and noteworthy people are represented, but so are the everyday folks that make a community thrive.

This book would not be possible without the repository of historical images and archival material located at the Fort Lauderdale Historical Society. Executive director Patricia Coyle-Zeiler allowed me access to the collections to conduct my research and to select and scan the images. Curator Chris Barfield and research associate Cherie Thompson aided in preparing the list of potentials and in the scanning of some images.

Other individuals who assisted in providing photographs and biographical information include the following:

Myrka Don Fred, Special Collections, African-American Research Library and Cultural Center
Jessica Savage, media relations director, Greater Fort Lauderdale Convention & Visitors Bureau
Sherri DeBlasio, athletic office, St. Thomas Aquinas High School
Minerva Bloom, museum coordinator, Naval Air Station Fort Lauderdale Museum
Denyse Cunningham, curator, Bonnet House Museum and Gardens
Phillip Colhouer, senior designer-marketing, Stiles Corporation
Mary Whyte, communications & community relations manager,
Broward Center for the Performing Arts
Jason Leidy, photographer, Middle River Arts
Cayia family
Louise Crocco
Betsy Buntrock
Mr. and Mrs. William Crawford
Blaine Rogers, development specialist, Westminster Academy

I would also like to thank Steve Harmon, executive director of the *Paul and Young Ron Show*, for arranging the interview with the guys and Jacqueline Goldstein, curator of the Jewish Museum of Florida-FIU, for proofreading and editing the draft.

Unless otherwise noted, all images appear courtesy of the Fort Lauderdale Historical Society.

INTRODUCTION

For at least 5,000 years, people have been drawn to the Fort Lauderdale area. The prehistoric peoples of South Florida (the Glades culture) and the early peoples of the area (the Tequesta) enjoyed the abundance of natural resources available along Fort Lauderdale's New River. The Spanish controlled the region from 1513 until 1763, when Florida was ceded to the British under the terms of the Treaty of Paris, following the Seven Years' War. By 1763, the last of these aboriginal peoples had left the area, and except for a few white settlers (the Lewis and Robbins families in the 1790s), Fort Lauderdale was devoid of population. The British controlled Florida until 1783, when it was ceded back to Spain at the end of the Revolutionary War. The Seminole Indians first appeared in what is now Broward County in the 1820s and were joined by approximately 70 white farmers, led by William Cooley, along the river. Florida was ceded to the United States by Spain in 1821 through the Adams-Onis Treaty.

The city of Fort Lauderdale is named for a Second Seminole War (1835–1842) fortification built on the banks of the New River in 1838. In that year, Maj. William Lauderdale led a detachment of Tennessee Volunteers south along the east coast of Florida to capture Seminole agricultural lands. Lt. Robert Anderson, later commander of Fort Sumter at the start of the Civil War, was part of the detachment. Altogether, three forts named "Fort Lauderdale" would be constructed: the first at the fork of the New River; the second near Tarpon Bend; and the largest on the beach, at the site of today's Bahia Mar Yachting Center.

After the war, southeastern Florida remained a virtual wilderness due to the lack of transportation into the region, even after statehood in 1845. A wagon road from North Miami to New River was constructed in 1857 under the command of Capt. Abner Doubleday. It was abandoned at the end of the Third Seminole War (1855–1858). In 1892, however, the Dade County government authorized a rock road to be built between Lantana (central Palm Beach County) and Lemon City (North Miami). An overnight camp and ferry crossing was established on New River, and a young Ohioan, Frank Stranahan, arrived in 1893 to take charge of the facilities. He soon established a flourishing trading post with the local Seminoles, and by 1895, Stranahan's Trading Post was a South Florida landmark.

In 1896, Henry Flagler's Florida East Coast Railway was extended south through Fort Lauderdale and on to Miami, providing rapid transportation from all parts of the nation to South Florida. The little village increased in size. In 1910, there were 143 residents, but the Bolles Land Lottery brought 3,000 people to the area. The city incorporated in 1911 as a result. In 1915, Broward County was created out of parts of Dade and Palm Beach Counties.

The new county was named for Napoleon Bonaparte Broward, who, as governor of Florida, had begun a massive project in 1906 aimed at dredging the Everglades. The draining of the Everglades opened up new, fertile farmland, and the canals that were constructed provided an efficient means for agricultural produce to be shipped to market. Fort Lauderdale became a major center for the shipping of winter fruits and vegetables north via the railroad.

As Fort Lauderdale moved into the 1920s, it began to change from an agricultural community to a resort town. Tourists came for the sportfishing and the Everglades experience. New hotels and businesses sprung up, centered on the downtown railroad, not the beach. Population doubled and tripled in the early years of the decade, and many of the city's finest residential developments (Rio Vista, Sailboat Bend, and Isle of Venice) date from this era. However, hopes for continued prosperity came to an abrupt end on the evening of September 18, 1926, when a deadly hurricane struck the South Florida coast; hundreds were killed and thousands of structures were destroyed in Fort Lauderdale, Hollywood, and Miami. In the aftermath, many residents left, never to return. South Florida plunged into economic depression three years ahead of the rest of the nation.

Except for the completion of Port Everglades in 1928, the next decade and a half were quiet times for Fort Lauderdale. It was not until World War II that the local economy was revived. The war brought tens of thousands of servicemen to the region, since the South Florida climate was deemed suitable for training facilities. Torpedo bomber pilots, such as George H.W. Bush, trained at today's Fort Lauderdale–Hollywood International Airport, and submarine hunters ventured out of Port Everglades to do battle with German U-boats. Beach hotels were used for training schools and housing servicemen. Local boatyards produced minesweepers, aircraft rescue boats, and submarine chasers. A manufacturing plant made projectiles and shells, and an electronics company made radio parts.

After the war, many servicemen returned to Fort Lauderdale to resume their lives. This influx spurred a second land boom, and for the next 40 years, the city experienced unprecedented growth. New subdivisions, such as Coral Ridge and Galt Ocean Mile, expanded the boundaries of the city. Suburbs like Plantation and Coral Springs developed in the former agricultural lands of western Broward County. Fort Lauderdale's annual College Swim Forum grew into the phenomenon of "Spring Break" that brought as many as 350,000 college students per year to the area at its peak in 1985.

By 2013, the city had achieved a population of over 172,000, making it the eighth largest city in the state; Broward County's over 1.78 million residents make it Florida's second largest county. Demographically, the city is 52 percent white, 31 percent black, and 14 percent Hispanic. Today, Fort Lauderdale has become the regional governmental and commercial center for a major metropolitan area and is world famous as a tourist destination (12 million annually). Not too bad for a city that recently celebrated its centennial.

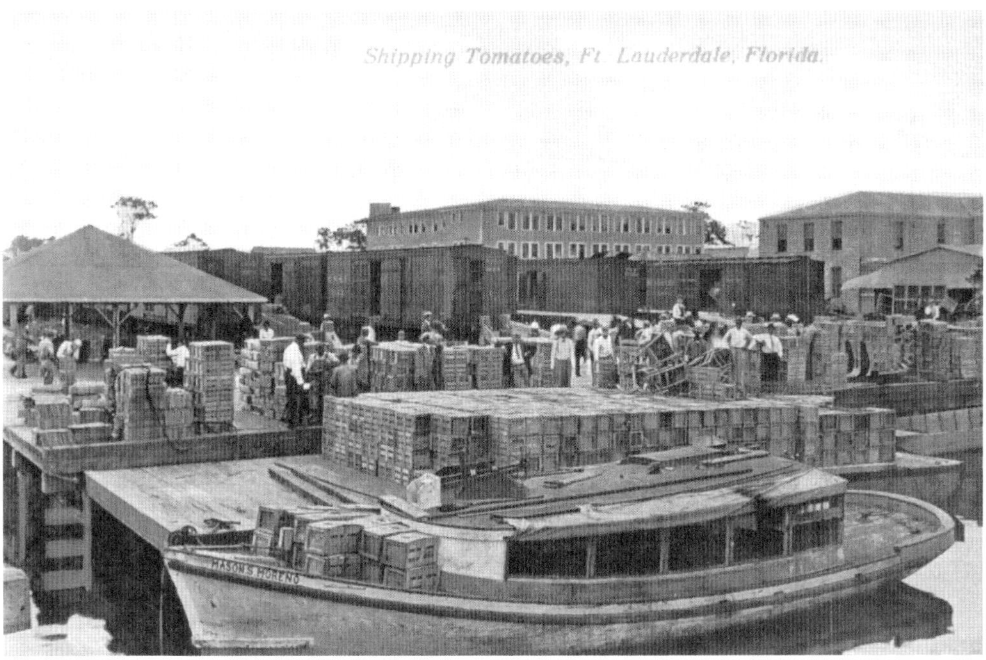

Shipping Tomatoes via the Florida East Coast Railway
In the early 20th century, the major economic activity of the Fort Lauderdale area was the growing of fruits and vegetables. The railroad allowed farmers to send their products to northern markets.

CHAPTER ONE

Early Settlers

Until the mid-1890s, the settlement of the New River/Fort Lauderdale area was sporadic. Native Americans had lived in the area for thousands of years. The first nonnative settlers were the Surles and Frankee Lewis family, who arrived in 1789 and established a farm on the south bank of the New River. They remained until the 1820s. By 1793, Capt. Joseph Robbins and his family were also living along the river. During the early years of the 19th century, the Seminole Indians moved into South Florida. In 1830, after buying Frankee Lewis's land interests at New River, Richard Fitzpatrick introduced a plantation style development. The New River settlement was comprised of approximately 70 individuals, including the William Cooley, David Williams, Mary Rigby, and Howe families and their slaves. Following the Seminole Indian attack on the Cooley family in 1836, the New River settlement was abandoned. US Army troops were stationed in the area during the Second and Third Seminole Wars, but "Fort Lauderdale" was also eventually abandoned.

Besides some local Seminole camps, the New River area was basically devoid of settlers until 1893. Union supporter Isaiah Hall and his family lived on the river during the Civil War after leaving pro-Confederate Miami. By 1870, John "Pig" Brown and his family were living on the barrier island along New River Sound. They remained in the area, raising hogs, until John was elected to the state legislature in 1876, never to return. That same year, the United States Life-Saving Service built House of Refuge No. 4 on the beach, and Washington Jenkins was appointed keeper. Additional keepers that served there until 1893 were Edwin Bradley, John Peacock, Charles Coman, and Dennis O'Neill. William "Cap" Valentine arrived in 1891 as the first postmaster.

In 1893, Frank Stranahan arrived to operate the overnight camp and ferry for the overland stage line. Stranahan eventually built a trading post and traded with the Seminoles. By 1895, he had been joined by Andrew Jackson Wallace, Philemon Bryan, Ed and Richard King, Frank Oliver, and a small African American community, including Bob McCullough and Jeff Lockhert. They had all come to the area to farm. In 1896, the first Florida East Coast Railway train arrived, allowing for produce shipments to northern markets. The small town at the crossroads of the New River and the railroad continued to grow. Early pioneer families such as the Cromarties, Berryhills, TenBrooks, Powers, Aldridges, Reeds, and Jacksons arrived during this time. Gov. Napoleon Bonaparte Broward was elected in 1904 with the promise of draining the Everglades. Construction of dredges in 1906 and the cutting of canals from New River to Lake Okeechobee opened up parcels of farmland in the former swamp. This new land tantalized many Americans. The Bolles Land Auction brought 3,000 people to the small village of 143 inhabitants in 1911. This led to the incorporation of Fort Lauderdale on March 27, 1911.

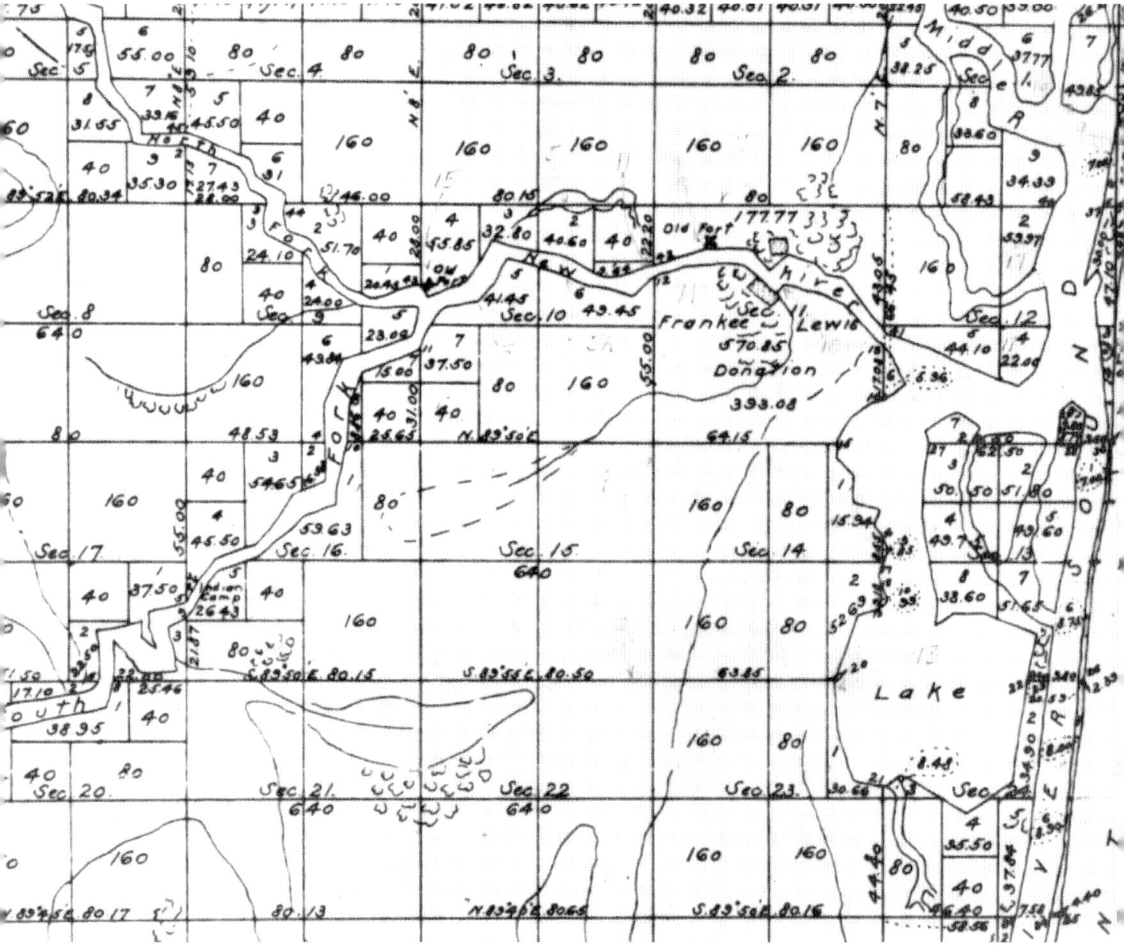

Surles and Frankee Lewis, First Known Settlers

The first permanent nonnative residents of the area, Surles and Frankee Lewis and their three sons, arrived on the New River around 1789. Their farm included a cabin and several outbuildings, and they raised limes, oranges, sugar apples, coconuts, and guava. The Lewises remained until 1824. In 1825, Frankee, then a widow, received a land donation from the US government for one square mile (640 acres), much of which today are the Colee Hammock and Rio Vista neighborhoods. In 1830, she sold the land to Richard Fitzpatrick for $400.

William Cooley's Family Massacred at Start of Second Seminole War

Born in Maryland, William Cooley arrived in Florida in 1813 and settled on the New River in 1824. He had a 20-acre farm and a mill where he processed arrowroot from the coontie plant. Arrowroot was a starch that was used to make bread dough, wafers, and biscuits. Cooley was also in the wrecking business (salvage of cargo from shipwrecks) and served as an appraiser of shipwrecks, property, and slaves. In 1831, he was appointed the justice of the peace of the New River settlement (around 50 white residents at the time). Cooley had always maintained friendly relations with the Seminoles and traded with them. However, in his capacity as justice of the peace, he was blamed for the acquittal of white settlers who had killed a Seminole chief. On January 6, 1836, while Cooley and other men were at Lighthouse Point salvaging the *Gil Blas*, the Seminoles attacked the Cooley homestead, killing Nancy Cooley, their three children, and the children's tutor. The remaining New River settlers fled to the Cape Florida Lighthouse in Miami. This attack, coupled with the earlier Dade Massacre near Tampa on December 28, 1835, started the Second Seminole War. After burying his family, Cooley remained in the Florida Keys before eventually moving to the Tampa area.

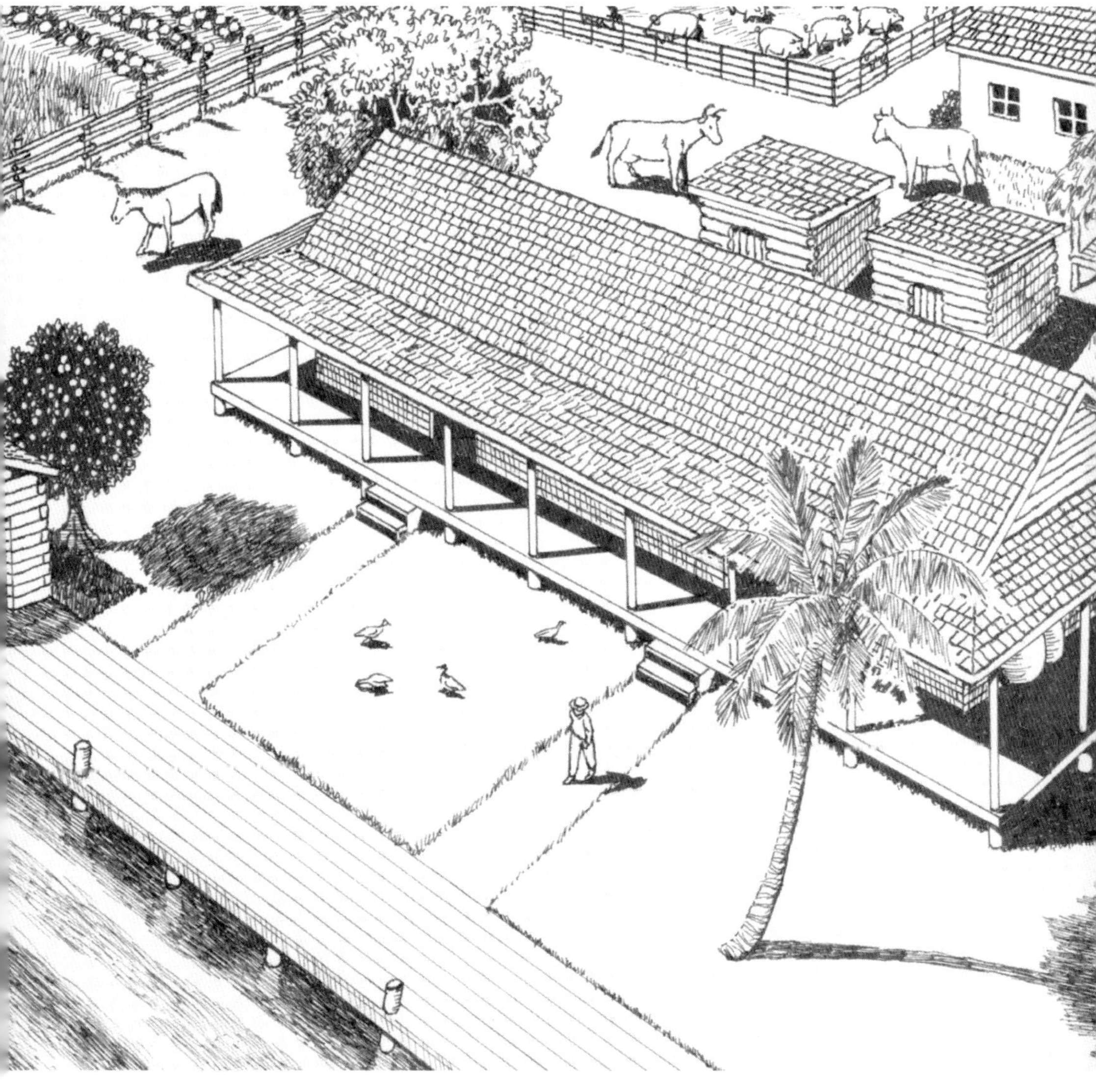

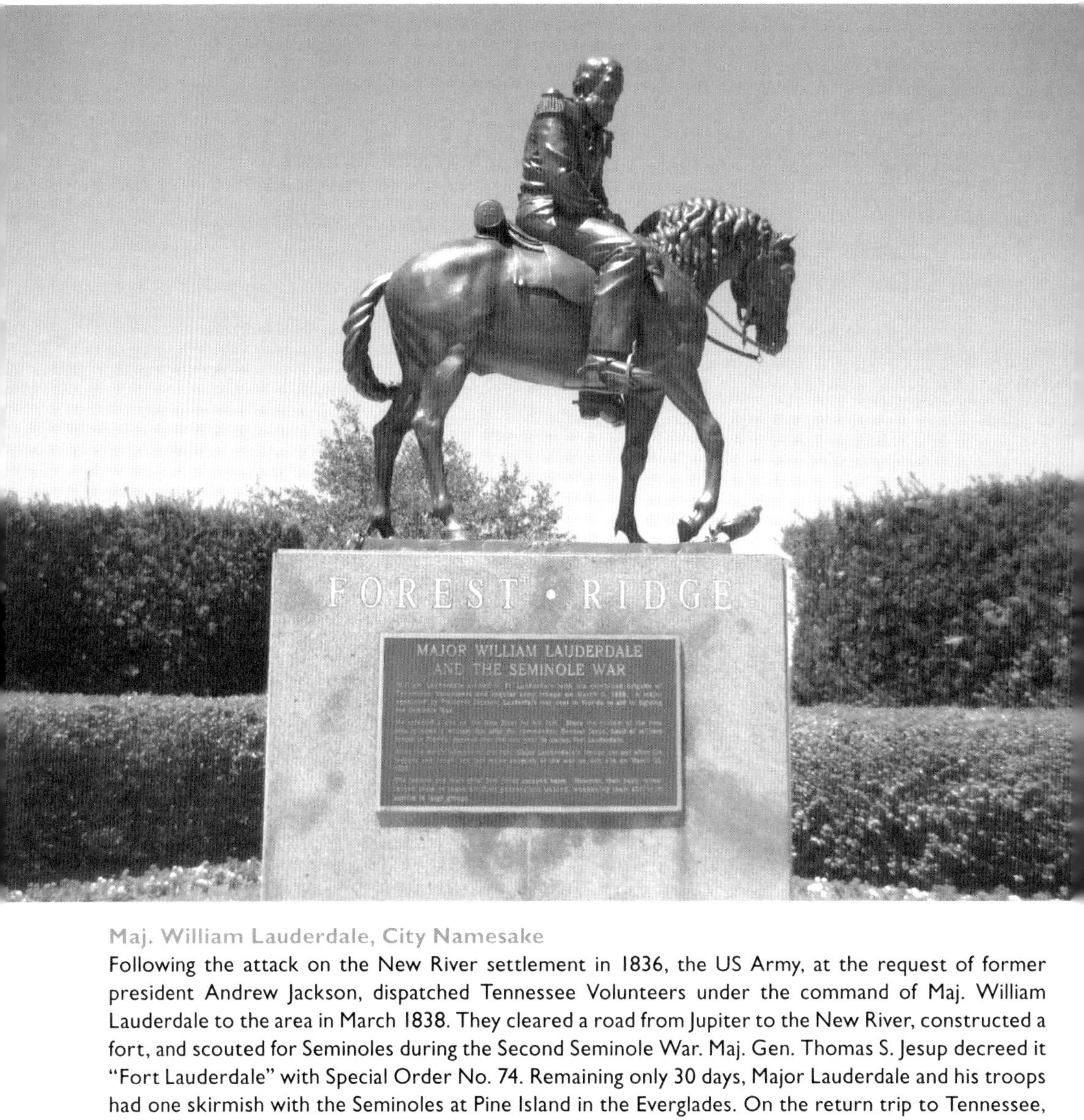

Maj. William Lauderdale, City Namesake

Following the attack on the New River settlement in 1836, the US Army, at the request of former president Andrew Jackson, dispatched Tennessee Volunteers under the command of Maj. William Lauderdale to the area in March 1838. They cleared a road from Jupiter to the New River, constructed a fort, and scouted for Seminoles during the Second Seminole War. Maj. Gen. Thomas S. Jesup decreed it "Fort Lauderdale" with Special Order No. 74. Remaining only 30 days, Major Lauderdale and his troops had one skirmish with the Seminoles at Pine Island in the Everglades. On the return trip to Tennessee, Major Lauderdale passed away in Baton Rouge, Louisiana. This nine-foot statue by Luis Montoya stands at Pine Island Ridge in Davie. (Photograph by the author.)

Washington Jenkins, First Keeper of House of Refuge No. 4

Washington Jenkins was appointed the first keeper of the House of Refuge at Fort Lauderdale beach in 1876. He was a 25-year-old South Carolinian who left his farm on the New River to take the keeper's post. The Houses of Refuge were stations operated by the US Life-Saving Service to shelter shipwrecked sailors. Ten were built along the east coast of Florida. Jenkins lived at House of Refuge No. 4 with his wife, Mary, and their four children. As part of his duties, Jenkins was to record high water marks, beach descriptions, tidal rise and fall, water depth, and sand bar measurements. He served as keeper until 1883.

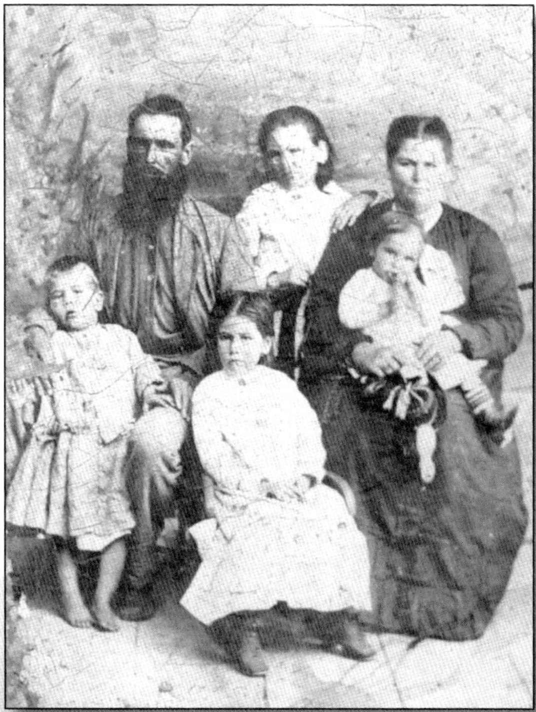

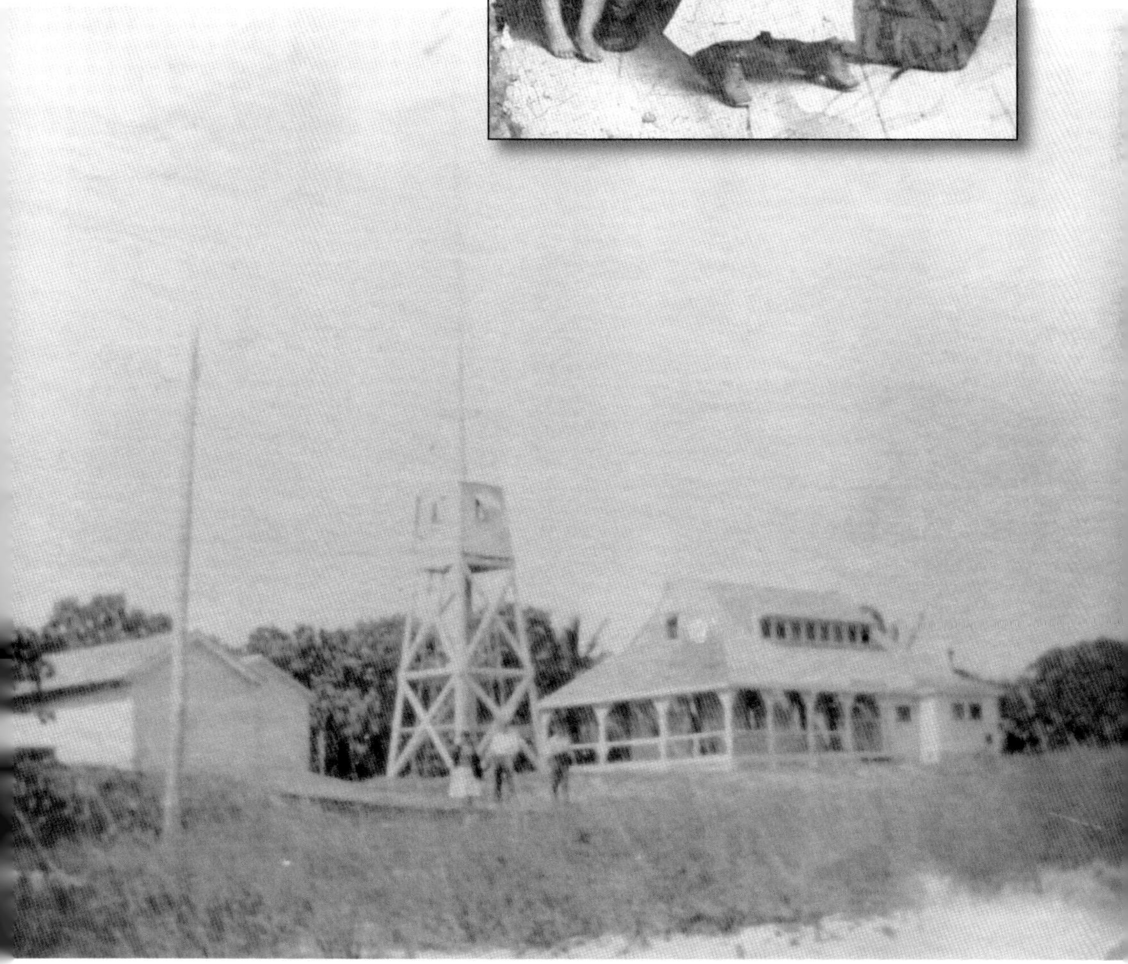

Frank and Ivy Stranahan, Father and Mother of Fort Lauderdale

Ohio native Frank Stranahan came to Fort Lauderdale in 1893 to manage the overnight camp and New River ferry for the overland stage line. He established a trading post with the Seminole Indians and became postmaster. In 1899, 18-year-old Ivy Cromartie arrived to become the first schoolteacher. After a short courtship, Frank and Ivy married on August 16, 1900. The following year, Frank constructed a larger trading post building, which quickly became a post office, community center, and town hall. By 1906, the business had expanded to include a general store and bank, and he constructed a new building closer to the railroad and turned the trading post building into his residence. The Stranahans became substantial landowners and were involved in almost every aspect of Fort Lauderdale community life. They donated many parcels of land, including the sites of the memorial hospital, Stranahan Park, Dillard (Colored) School, and Lauderdale High School. Ivy was active in the Woman's Christian Temperance Union, served as president of the Woman Suffrage Association, and founded both the Fort Lauderdale Woman's Club and the Friends of the Seminoles. Following two hurricanes in 1926 and 1928, the Florida land boom collapsed and Fort Lauderdale's economy fell into depression. The Stranahan bank failed, and, reeling from his own financial problems and concerns for his fellow citizens, Frank committed suicide in 1929. After Frank's death, Ivy continued to be involved in civic affairs. She started the movement that led to the Florida Homestead Exemption law, helped to establish a hospital for the black community and housing for the elderly, served on the planning and zoning board, and championed the Camp Fire Girls. Following Ivy's death in 1971, the Stranahan House was renovated and opened as a historic house museum in 1984.

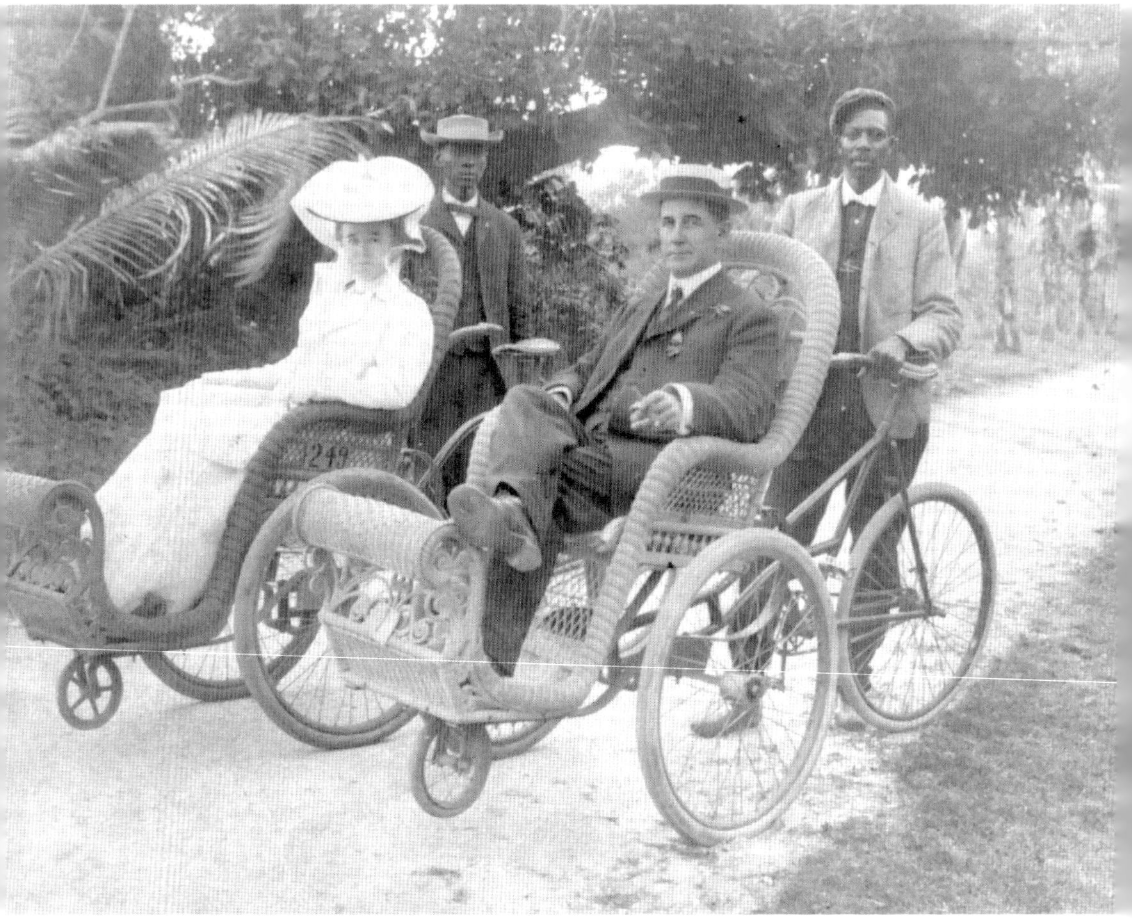

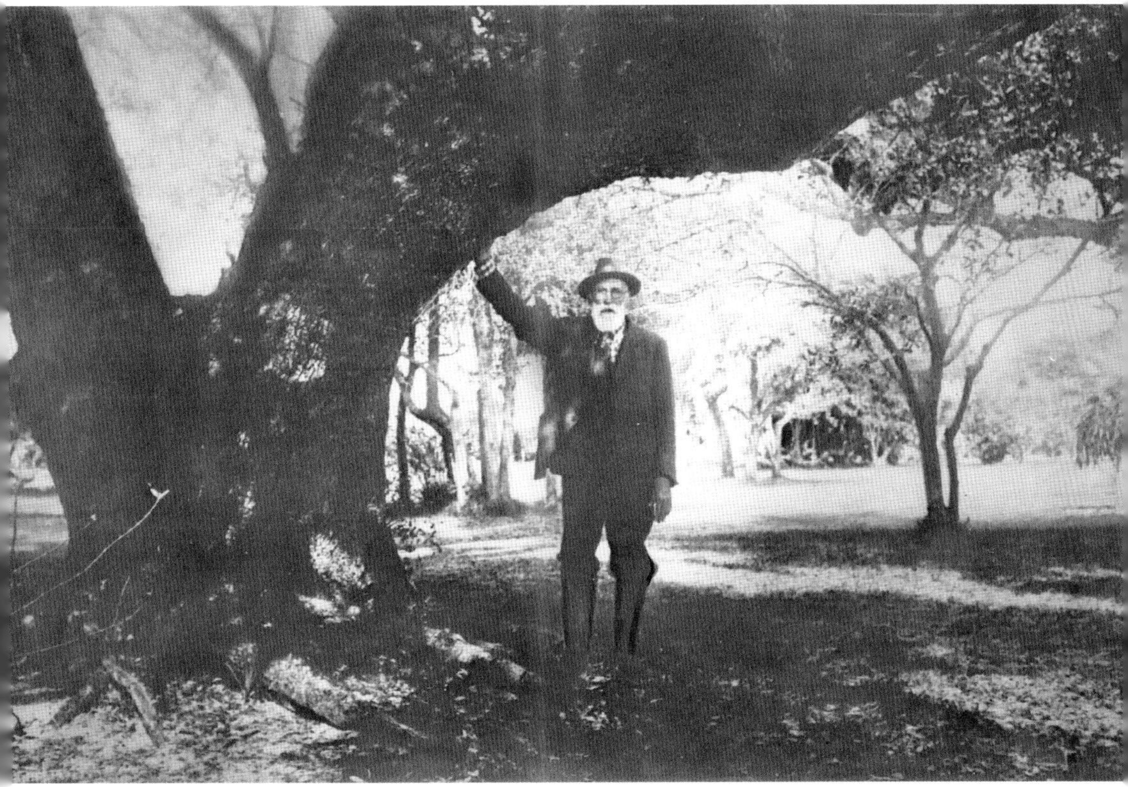

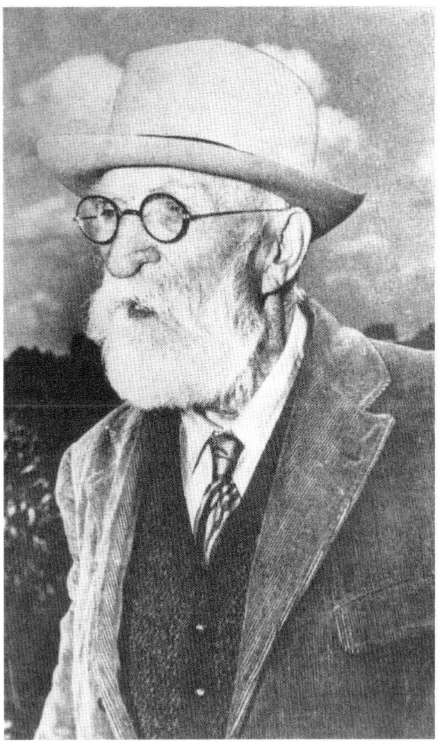

Hugh Taylor Birch, Natural Preservationist
Born in 1848 and attending Antioch College in Ohio before going to Chicago and studying law, Hugh Taylor Birch became a successful attorney and was legal counsel for Rockefeller's Standard Oil. In 1893, during the Columbian Exposition in Chicago, he wanted to escape the bustle of the city and a houseful of relatives; so he headed south. Birch rented a sailboat and made his way down Florida's east coast. A storm forced him ashore at the Fort Lauderdale inlet. Here is where Birch found what he labelled as "the most beautiful [land] that I have seen on all of my travels." In 1894, he and business partner McGregor Adams began purchasing oceanfront property for about $1 an acre. Eventually, they owned about 3.5 miles of beachfront. In 1919, Birch gifted his daughter, Helen, and her new husband, Frederic Clay Bartlett, 35 acres as a wedding present (now the Bonnet House Museum and Gardens). Birch continued to winter in Fort Lauderdale until his death in 1943. To preserve the subtropical paradise from encroaching development, he donated the remaining 180-acre estate to the State of Florida as a public park, which is still used by the community today.

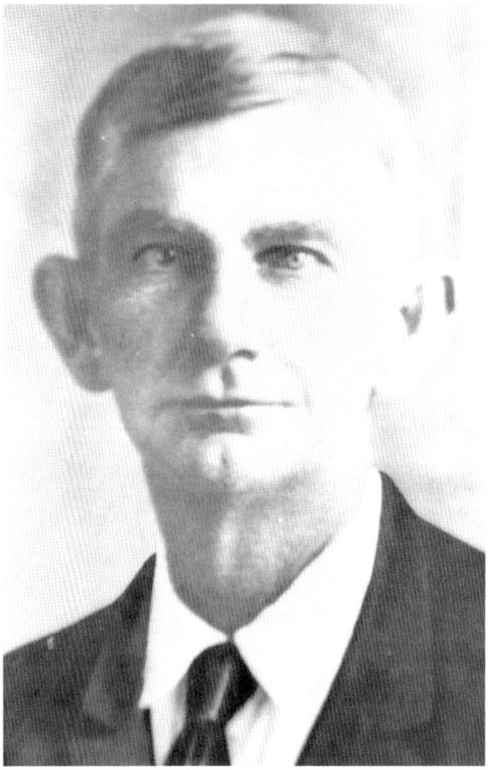

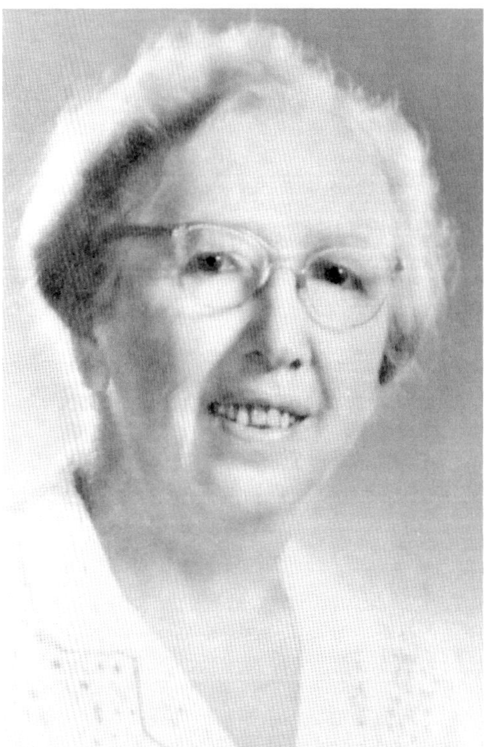

Frank and Eva Oliver, First Town Wedding

Frank Oliver arrived in town in 1895 and began farming. Eva Bryan visited in 1900 and married Oliver in 1902. They were wed standing in a rowboat, presided over by justice of the peace and postmaster William "Cap" Valentine. Oliver became partners with Frank Stranahan and later bought the Stranahan Company, renaming it the Oliver Brothers Company. Oliver was the first president of the first bank, Fort Lauderdale State Bank, and built the Keystone Hotel, the first hotel east of the railroad tracks. Bryan was the first president of the Woman's Civic Improvement Society (later the Woman's Club) and helped to organize the Garden Club and the First Baptist Church. She was also the first woman in town to drive an automobile. Her daughter Margaret was the first white girl born in Fort Lauderdale.

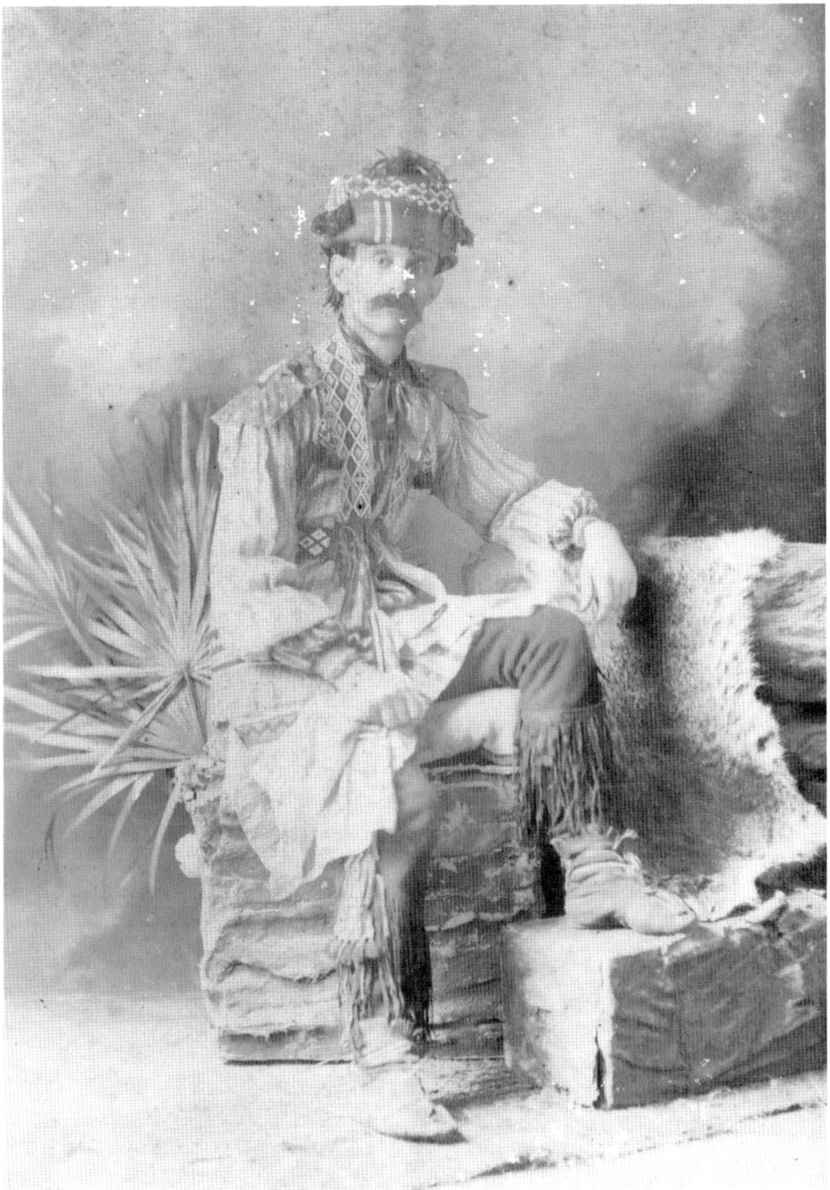

William Stranahan, Seminole Indian Trader

The older brother of Frank Stranahan, William, went west and worked for the railroads. He worked his way up from carpenter and member of a bridge building crew to train conductor. William Stranahan worked for many railroad companies during the 1880s and 1890s and travelled throughout the western territories. He wrote a booklet, *Gold and Silver Mining and Railroad Building in the West, from 1865–1893*. In the late 1890s, Stranahan showed up at Stranahan's Trading Post on the New River. Through his friendly relations with the Seminoles, he obtained ethnographic materials, which he later donated and sold to the United States National Museum (Smithsonian Institution). After working for a couple of years as a bookkeeper at the trading post, Stranahan returned to his vagabond ways and left Florida, perhaps due to issues with creditors. In letters to Frank, he speaks of travelling the West and maybe venturing to Mexico or Panama. However, it appears that he eventually returned to Ohio.

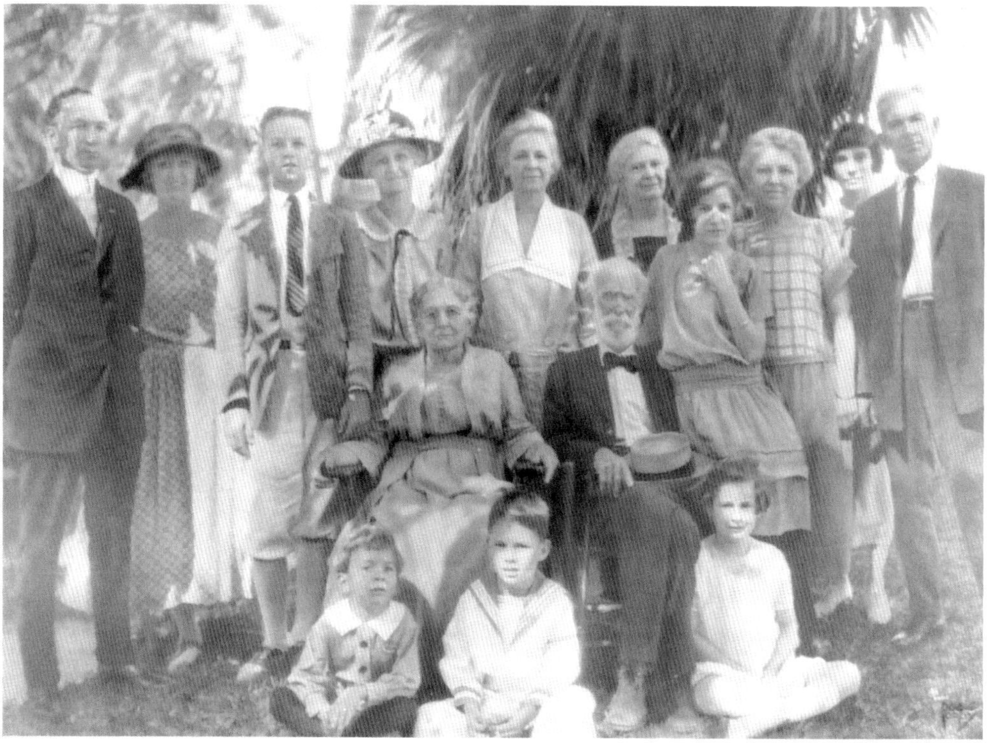

Philemon Bryan (seated right), Railroad Construction Overseer and Owner of New River Inn
In 1887, Philemon Bryan became the first mayor of New Smyrna, Florida, where he eventually owned seven citrus groves and four packinghouses and operated a large general store. Following the Big Freeze of 1895, which destroyed all of his trees, and the destruction of his store by fire in the same year, Bryan was contracted by Henry Flagler to construct a 10-mile section of the Florida East Coast (FEC) Railway. Bryan, with his son Tom, oversaw 400 black laborers on the construction of the roadbed from Pompano to the New River. On February 22, 1896, the first FEC train arrived in Fort Lauderdale. Bryan settled here and went back into farming. He purchased a parcel of land west of the train station and built the New River Inn. It remained in operation until 1955. Today, the New River Inn and the Philemon Bryan home are part of the Fort Lauderdale History Center complex.

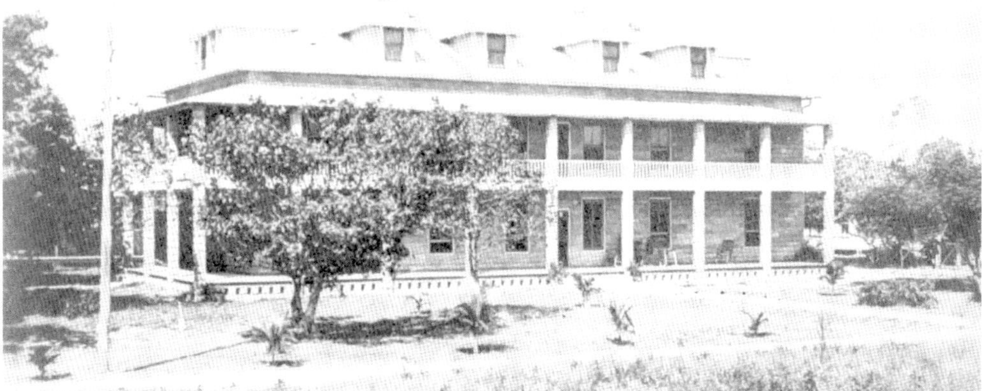

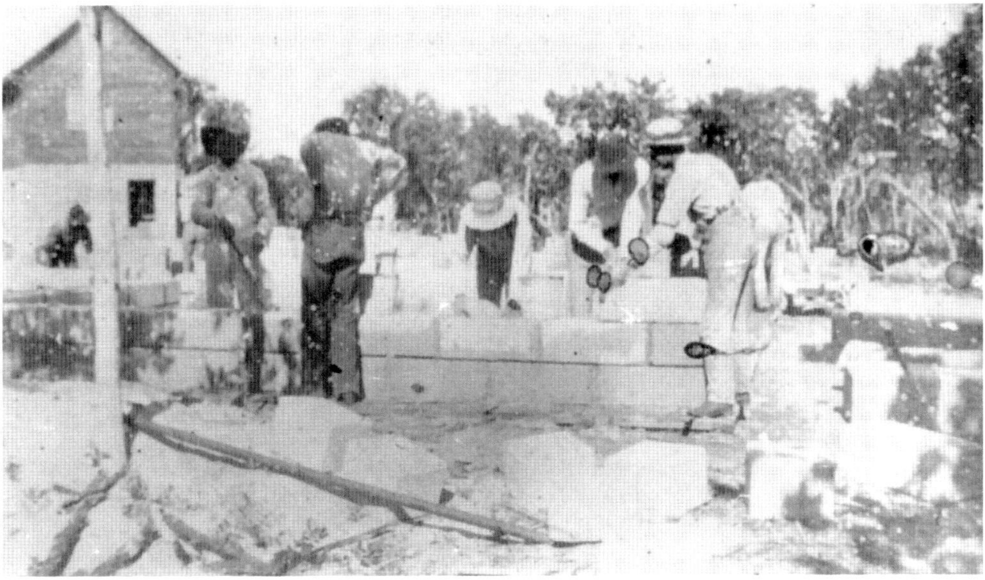

Edwin T. King, City's First Building Contractor

Edwin King arrived in 1895 after hearing that the FEC Railway was building a track to Miami. Anticipating that the area would become a shipping point for fruits and vegetables, he bought 90 acres south of the New River. King's family arrived on the first train in 1896, and his home served as a site for early community dances and meetings. He was a superior carpenter and cabinetmaker and became the first building contractor in town. King built the first two schoolhouses, the New River Inn, the Stranahan House, the Las Olas Inn, and the first Methodist Church. He was also a boat builder and contractor for dredging operations between Lantana and Deerfield Beach. King also made coffins and provided the land for Evergreen Cemetery. In 1911, he was chosen as president of the first city council. By 1918, King had left Fort Lauderdale because it was "getting too big" and moved to Lake Okeechobee.

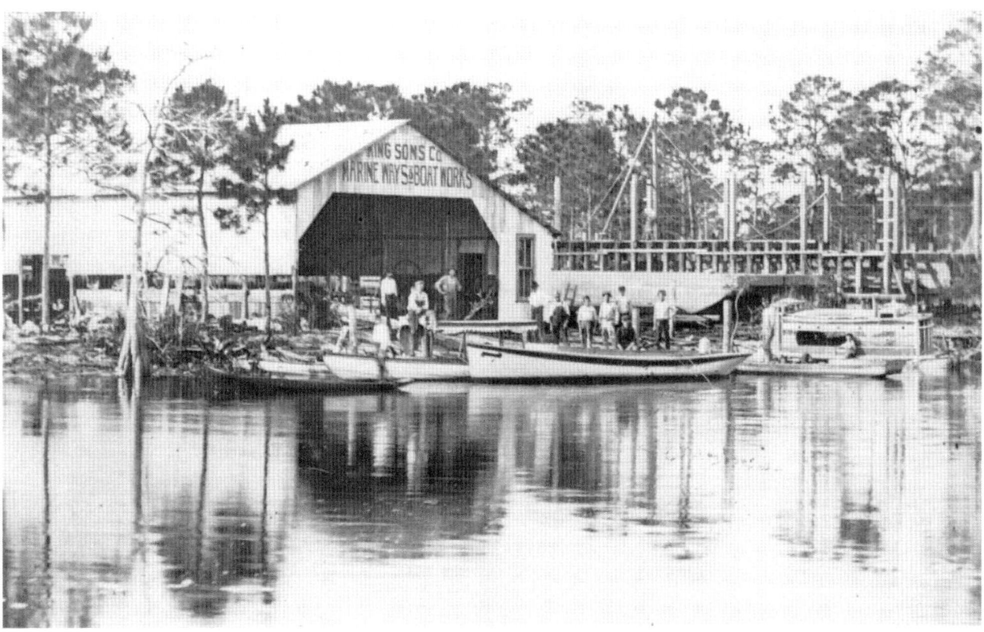

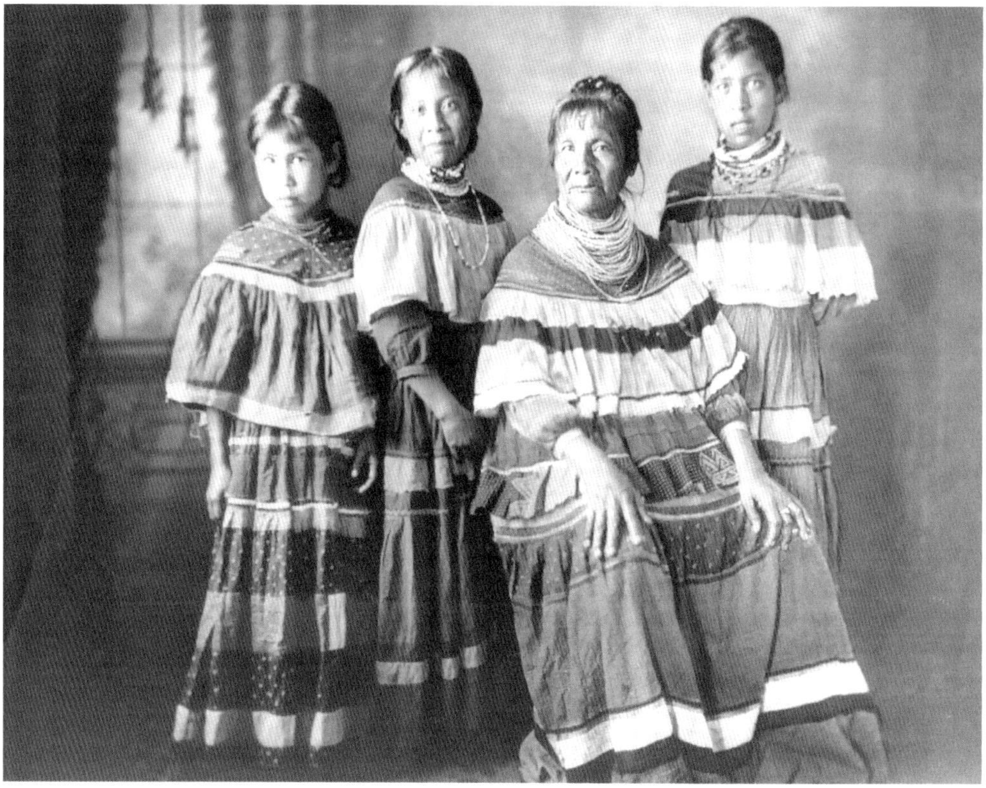

Annie Jumper Tommie (seated), Seminole Indian Medicine Woman
Born in 1856, Annie Jumper Tommie of the Panther Clan established the last permanent Seminole camp in Fort Lauderdale on the north fork of the New River in 1902. Here, the Seminoles interacted with the early settlers, and the camp later became a tourist attraction for early visitors to the area. Tommie became a tribal matriarch in 1924 and was instrumental in relocating the Seminoles to the Dania Reservation in 1926.

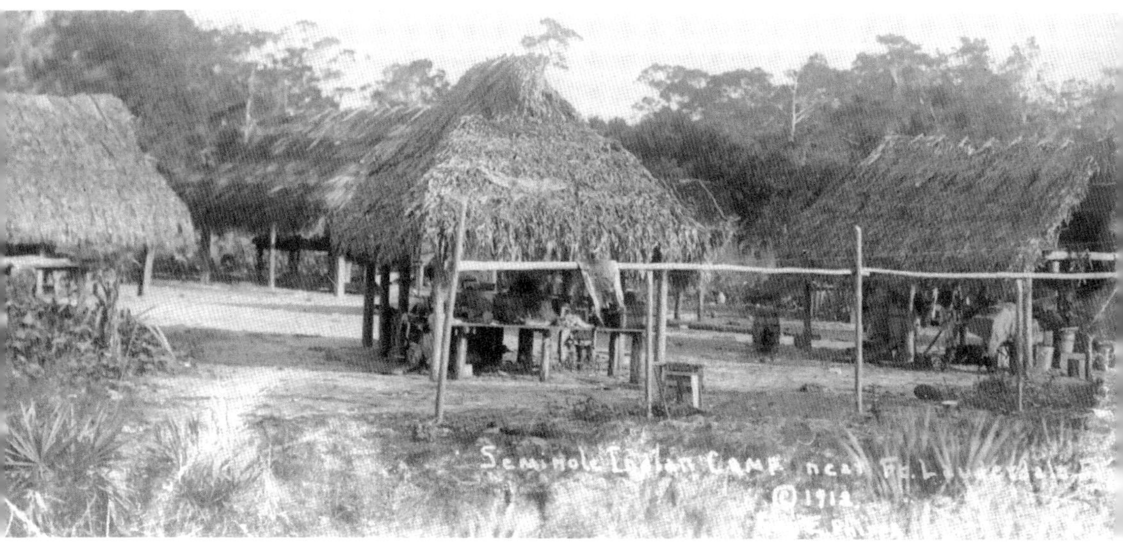

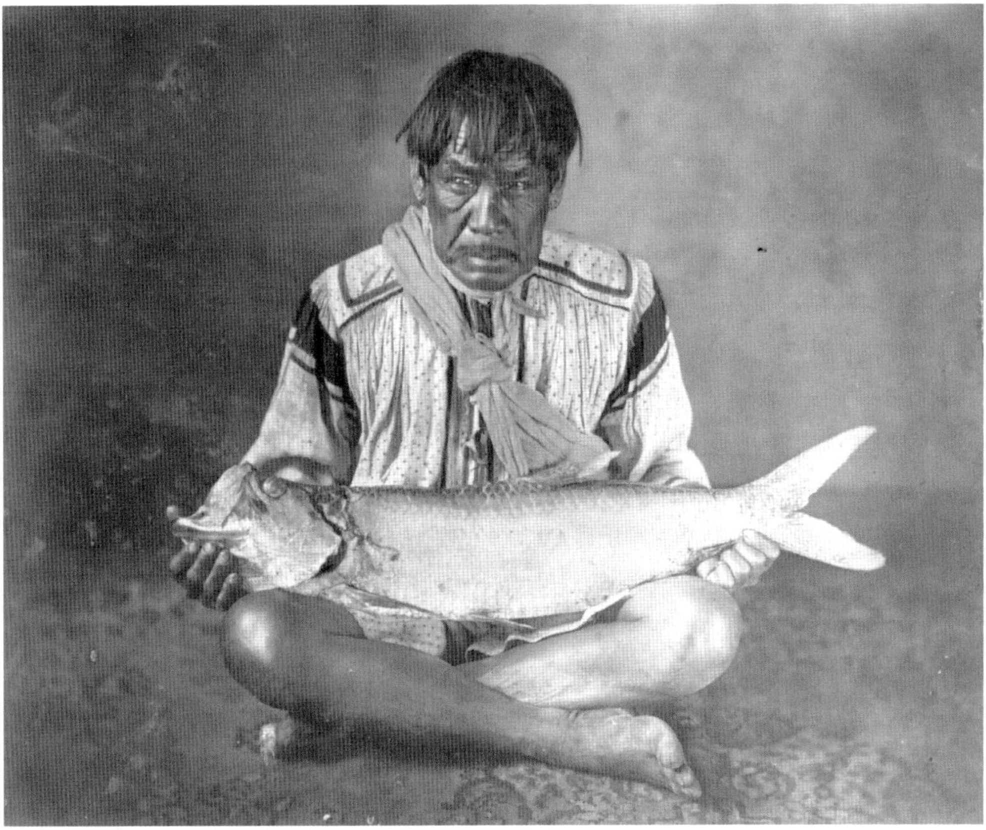

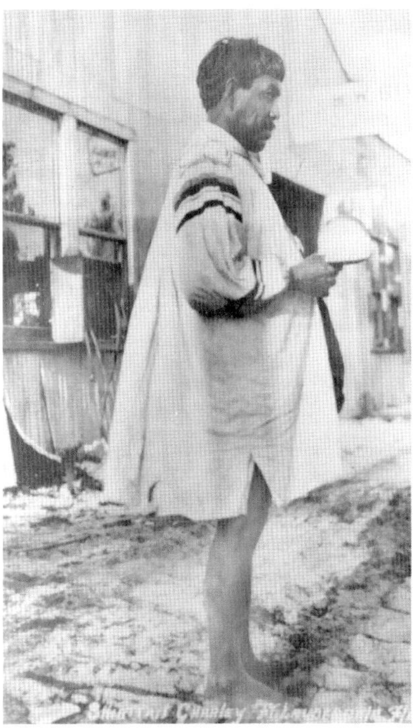

Shirttail Charlie Tommie, Seminole Indian
"Shirttail" Charlie Tommie was seen frequently around Fort Lauderdale in the early 1900s. He was normally seen wearing a long shirt. The local legend of the time was that he had killed his wife and was sentenced by the Seminoles to wear a dress. In reality, Tommie was wearing a traditional Seminole long shirt. He spent his days panhandling and taking photographs with the tourists. In 1925, Tommie passed away and was buried near his family's former camp on Broward Boulevard.

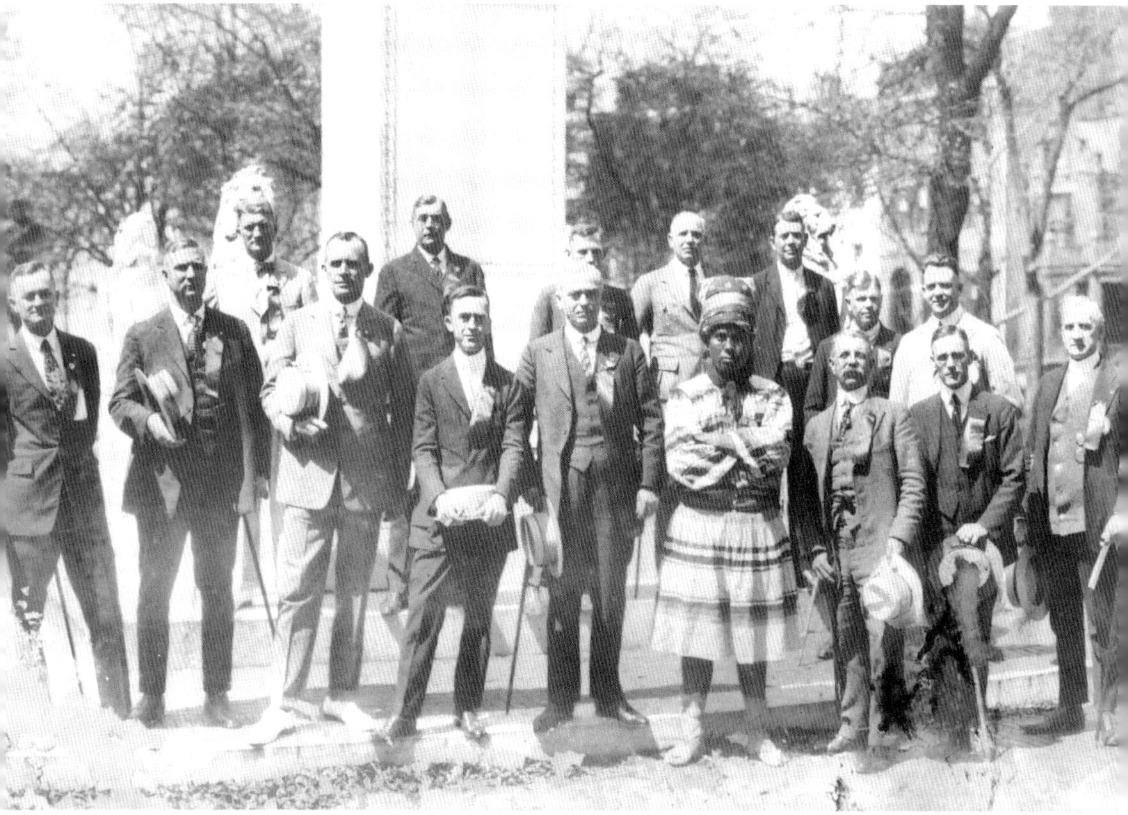

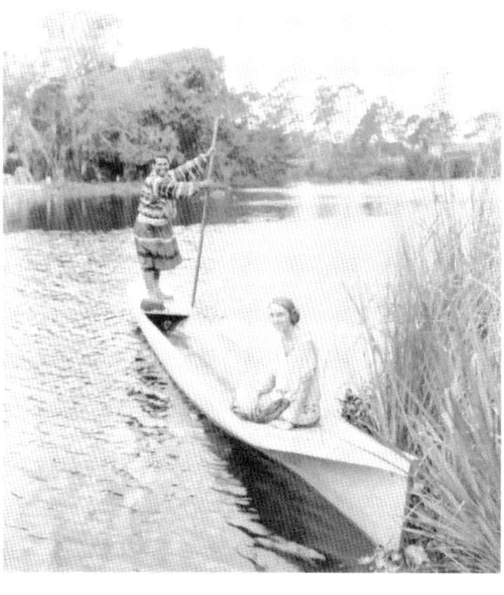

Tony Tommie, First Seminole Indian to Attend Public School

The son of Annie Jumper Tommie, Tony Tommie was the first Seminole to attend public school in Fort Lauderdale. He had previously been enrolled (November 1913–February 1914) at the Carlisle Indian Industrial School in Pennsylvania, sponsored by former mayor William Marshall. In 1914, at the age of 19, Tommie enrolled at the local school. He attended until 1916. At his mother's camp, he taught other children the alphabet, basic reading, and math. In the late 1910s, Tommie was working as a talent scout and casting director of the Native American extras for early films shot in South Florida. In the 1920s, he was the "headman" at the Musa Isle Indian Village in Miami.

CHAPTER TWO

Developing a Town

The early development of Fort Lauderdale began with the arrival of the Florida East Coast (FEC) Railway in 1896. Henry Flagler set about creating the FEC by buying up the existing Florida east coast railroads. He eventually established a rail system from Jacksonville to Key West. The FEC established Fort Lauderdale as a shipping point for produce—especially tomatoes—to northern markets. In 1904, Governor Broward vowed to drain the Everglades and thus provide more fertile land for farming. In anticipation, 3,000 prospective land buyers descended upon the small village in 1911 for the Richard Bolles land lottery.

As the population grew during the teens and early 1920s, new neighborhoods were developed. D.C. Alexander foresaw the potential of the beach and built Las Olas by the Sea in 1914. Charles Rodes and W.F. Morang purchased the mangrove swamps along Las Olas Boulevard and began dredging and constructing finger islands. Tom Stillwell and M.A. Hortt began building up Idlewyld and the Riviera Isles. Frank Croissant laid out a grid of streets and boulevards on the south side of town. Architects Francis Abreu and Courtney Stewart designed many of the now historic buildings in the Mission Revival style. John Peterman designed many of the official buildings, including the city hall, South Side School, and the Dillard School.

Following the devastating 1926 hurricane and the subsequent Great Depression, development slowed considerably. A few bright spots highlighted this time, such as the openings of Port Everglades in 1928, the Fort Lauderdale Airport (Fogg Field) in 1929, and the Lauderdale Beach Hotel in 1936. Alfred Kuhn was developing Victoria Park. Until the influx of US servicemen during and after World War II, population growth had been at a moderate pace. The postwar boom forever changed Fort Lauderdale. In 1940, there were approximately 18,000 residents. By 1950, this number was over 36,000 and approaching 84,000 in 1960.

Gill Construction Company began building new homes for the returning G.I.s before getting into the hotel business. L.C. Judd and Company developed the beach properties of Harbor Beach Islands and Ocean Harbor. Coral Ridge Properties began building single residence homes and oceanfront condominiums on the former Arthur Galt property. Victor Nurmi completed the abandoned Morang islands. The work of architects Charles McKirahan, William Crawford Sr., Paul Bradley, William Bigoney, John Randal McDonald, and Dan Duckham still exist today.

The 1960s and 1970s saw the beginnings of urban renewal that continues to this day. The older neighborhoods have seen the replacement of many of the early residences with "McMansions." The downtown and beach areas have seen the rise of new condominium towers and luxury hotels. Fortunately, the City of Fort Lauderdale passed a historic preservation ordinance in 1976, and to date, there are three historic districts, 54 designated historic sites, and 10 buildings recognized by the National Register of Historic Places.

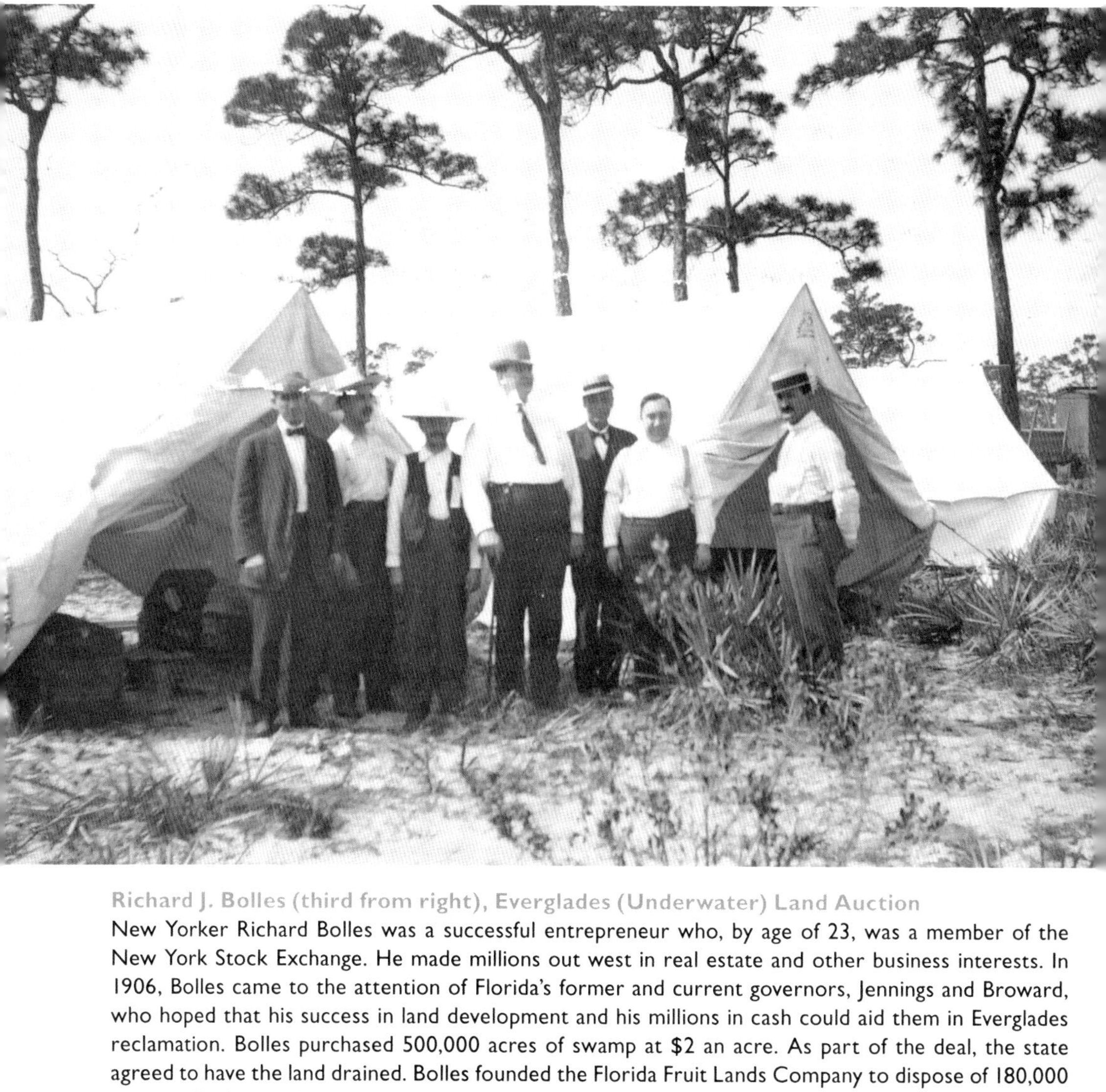

Richard J. Bolles (third from right), Everglades (Underwater) Land Auction

New Yorker Richard Bolles was a successful entrepreneur who, by age of 23, was a member of the New York Stock Exchange. He made millions out west in real estate and other business interests. In 1906, Bolles came to the attention of Florida's former and current governors, Jennings and Broward, who hoped that his success in land development and his millions in cash could aid them in Everglades reclamation. Bolles purchased 500,000 acres of swamp at $2 an acre. As part of the deal, the state agreed to have the land drained. Bolles founded the Florida Fruit Lands Company to dispose of 180,000 acres in Dade and Palm Beach Counties. He sent salesmen all over the country, touting the Florida paradise. For $240, a buyer could purchase a contract to bid on a farm and town lot through a scheduled auction. On March 11, 1911, the Progresso Land Auction occurred, and 3,000 people descended upon the small village (143 residents) of Fort Lauderdale. A large tent city was erected. When the event started, the "drawing" was cancelled and the buyers were told that tracts of land had already been selected for them and they were expected to just sign the deeds. Many did, but many cried foul when they realized they could not pick out their land, and worse yet, it was still very much underwater. Lawsuits were filed against Bolles for his illegal lottery and underwater plots, but he was found not guilty in federal court, as the State of Florida had not completed the drainage project. Bolles's enterprise did have an impact on Fort Lauderdale, as it was forced to incorporate as a city to handle the influx of new residents. It put the city "on the map."

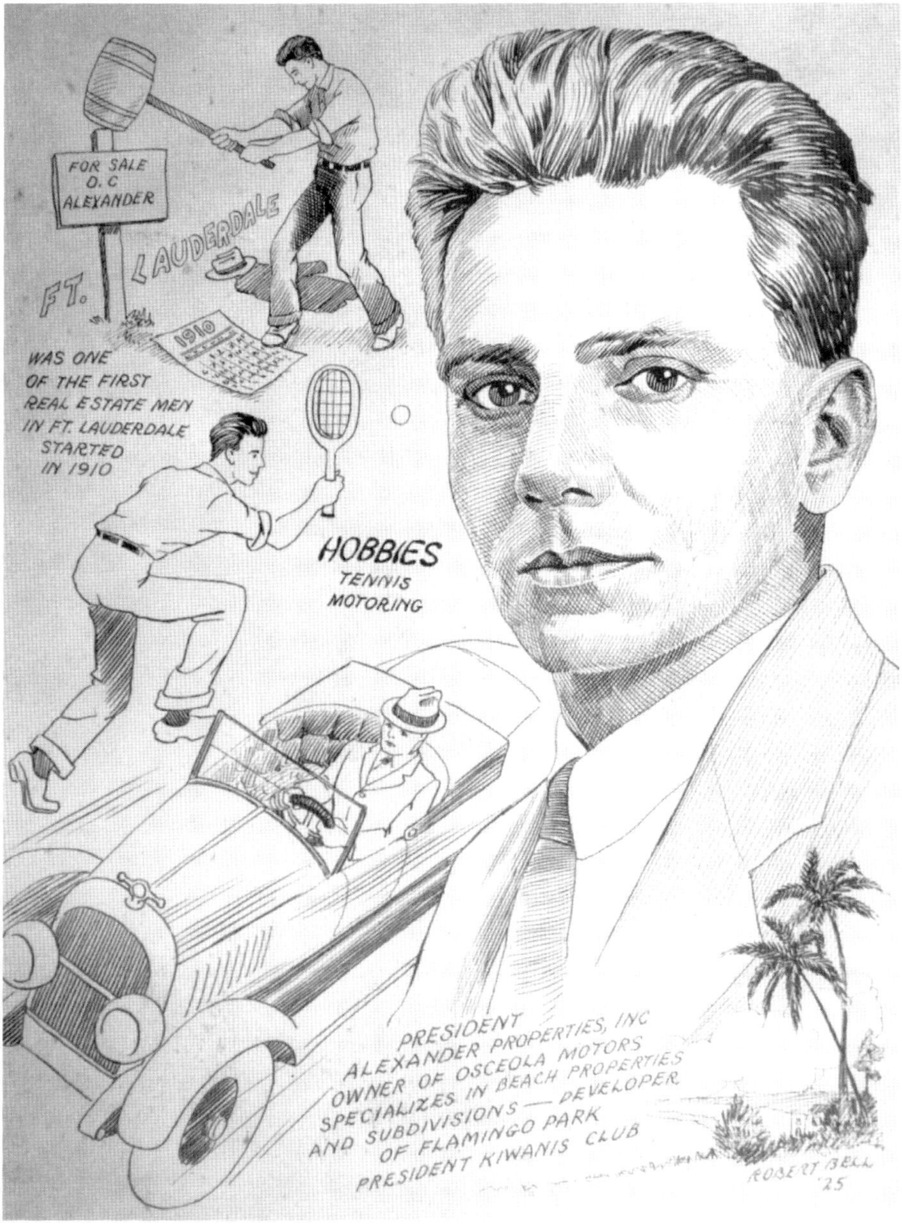

David Clifford Alexander, First Beach Property Developer

Stanford graduate D.C. Alexander visited his parents in Fort Lauderdale in 1909 and returned in 1910. At a time when the city was concentrated downtown at the railroad, he was the first one to see the potential of the beach. In 1914, Alexander purchased 32 acres of oceanfront land and called his development Las Olas by the Sea. He built Atlantic Boulevard and subdivided the property. Part of his purchase included Tom Watson's hunting lodge, which Alexander turned into the Las Olas Inn, the first hotel at the beach. In 1923, he helped to organize the Kiwanis Club. By 1926, Alexander also owned Osceola Motors, a Chrysler dealership which later sold Willys and Austins. He also donated a 100-foot-wide swath of land for a city park at the beach, where a large pavilion was built for picnics and swimming parties.

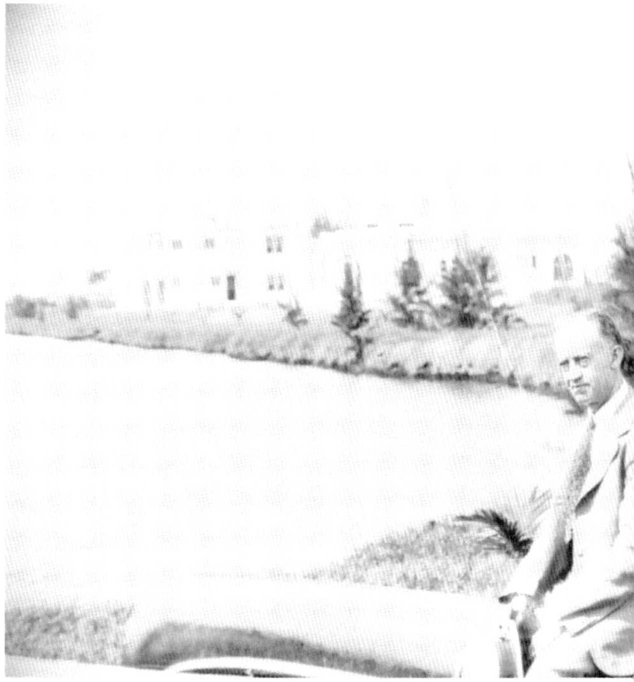

Charles G. Rodes Sr., Finger Island Developer

The son of a Confederate veteran, Charles Rodes arrived in Fort Lauderdale in 1907. He started farming a 50-acre tract and eventually opened a general merchandise store. In 1921, Rodes purchased a one-mile-wide section of mangrove swamps along the south side of Las Olas Boulevard for $400 an acre. He dredged a series of canals creating the Isles of Venice, which he sold for $600,000. In 1925, he took 52 family members on a month-long train trip from Florida to California. Rodes lost his fortune in the bust following the 1926 hurricane. After World War II, he bought a large tract of land on Merritt Island, Florida and began building homes. Rodes later sold some of this land to the U.S. government, and it became part of the Cape Canaveral Space Center.

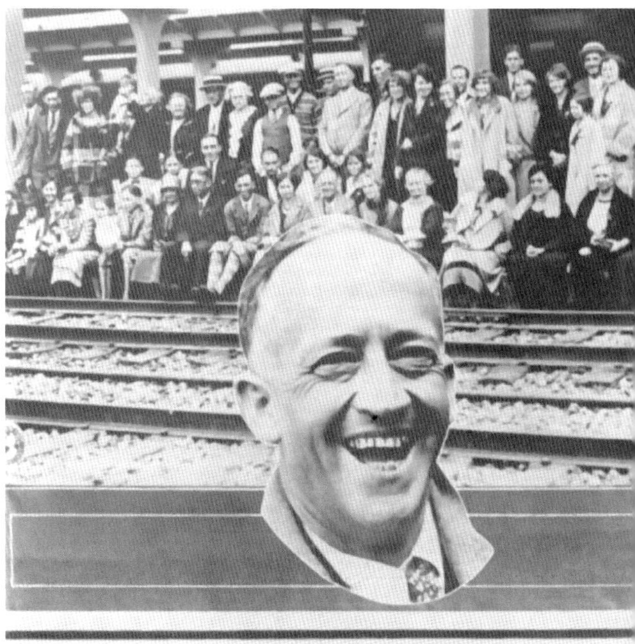

Takes Family of 52 on Touring Trip

C. G. Rodes, inset, a real estate man of Florida, is a real "man" and to show his appreciation of his relatives he is taking "his uncles, his cousins and his aunts" on a trip across the States and paying all expenses.

Francis Abreu, Cuban Boom Time Architect

Francis Abreu, of Cuban and Spanish descent, graduated the Cornell University College of Architecture in 1921. He came to Fort Lauderdale in 1924 and became the second registered architect in the city. Abreu quickly became one of the most sought-after architects in town. He designed many residences and public structures, most in the Mediterranean Revival style. In 1925, it is estimated that Abreu projects represented $3 million and half the construction in Fort Lauderdale. Many of the structures still stand today, including the Riverside Hotel, St. Anthony's School, the Needham House, the Erkins House, and the West Side Fire Station. Abreu remained in Fort Lauderdale until 1928, when he moved to Sea Island, Georgia. There, he designed a home for playwright Eugene O'Neill.

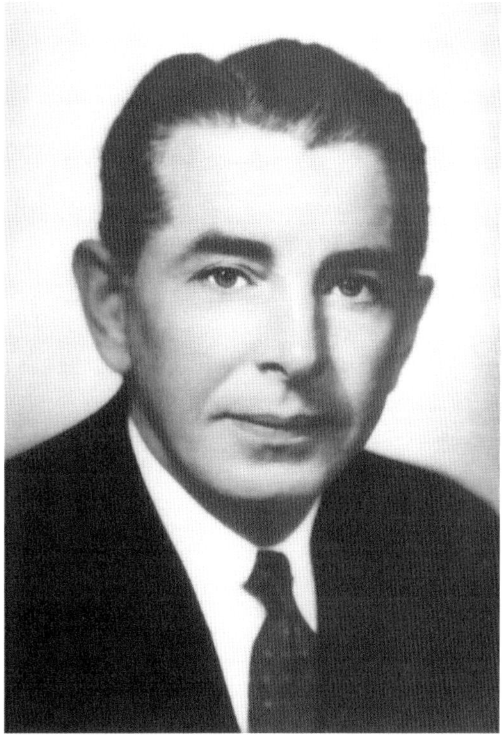

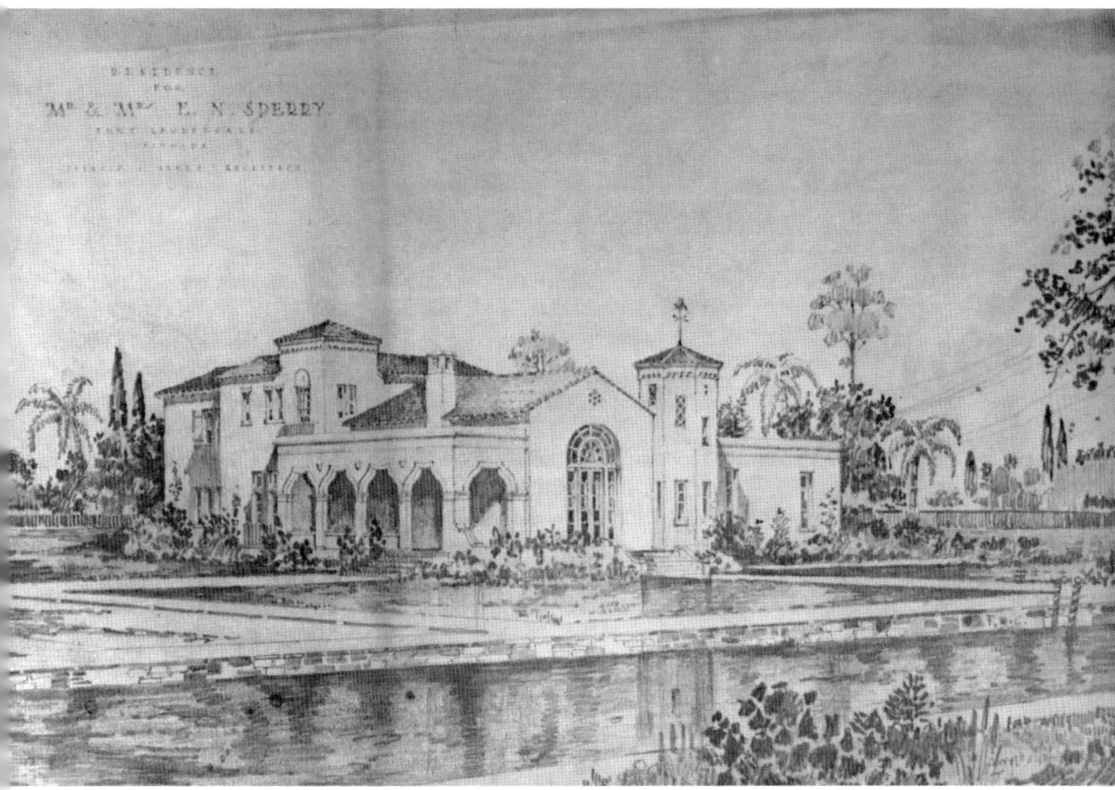

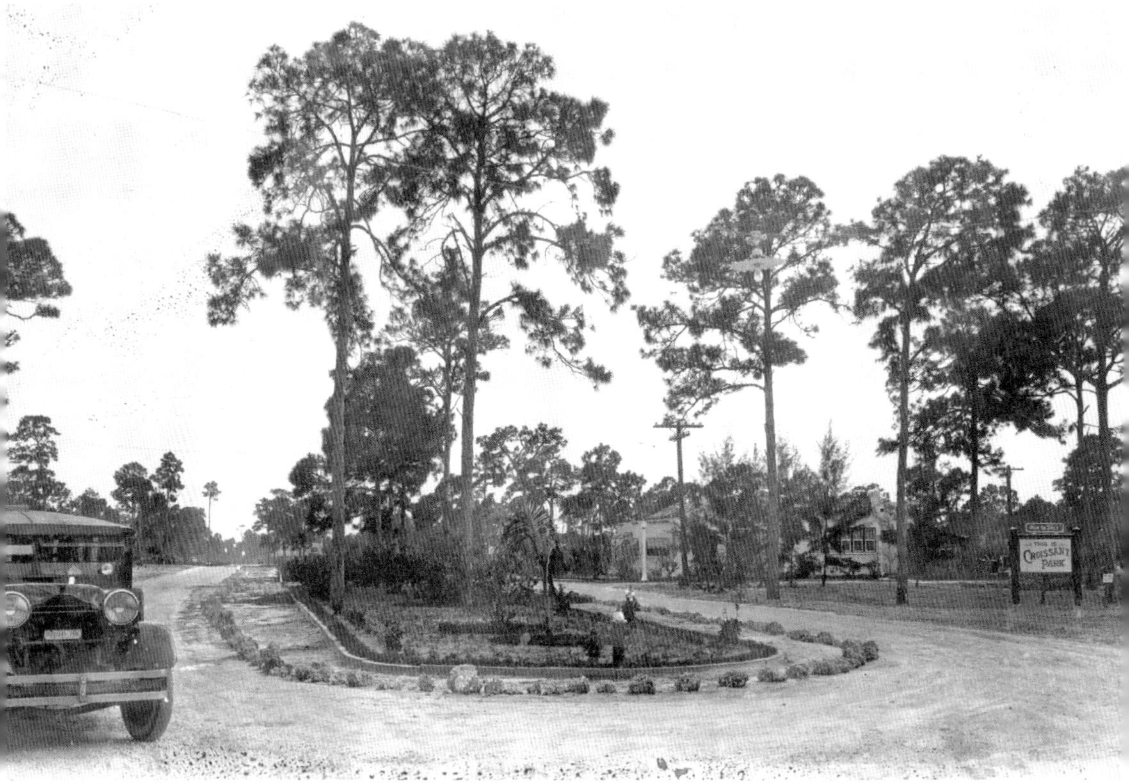

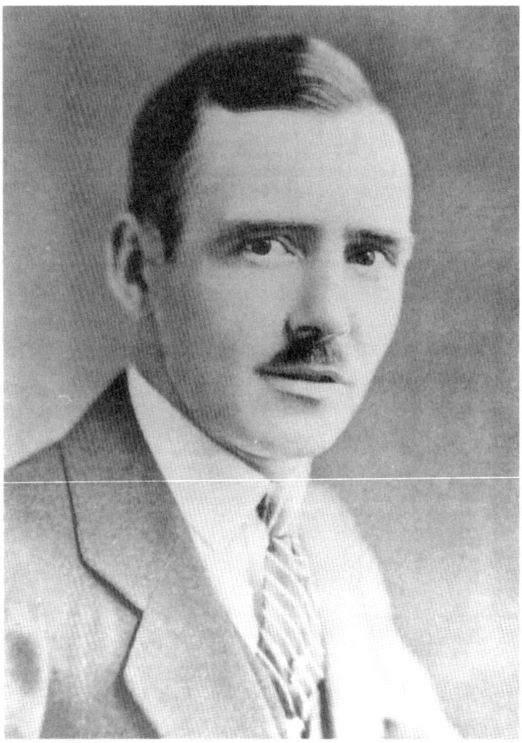

G. Frank Croissant, Southside Developer

Born in Brooklyn, New York, Frank Croissant started his career in real estate in 1908 as a salesman. In 1916, he received the Salesman of the Year medal from the Salesmanship Congress of America. Croissant went into business for himself in Detroit in 1917 before moving to Chicago in 1922. While there, he worked for Henry Ford to build Calumet City, Illinois. In 1924, Croissant arrived in Fort Lauderdale with 96 of his best salesmen to cash in on the land boom. He bought 1,270 acres and built 86 miles of boulevards and 172 miles of sidewalks for Croissant Park in southwest Fort Lauderdale. Croissant advertised his development by staging beauty pageants and maintained a fleet of 11 buses to bring prospective buyers in from Palm Beach and Miami. Following the land bust after the 1926 hurricane, it is estimated that Croissant lost $20 million. He left Fort Lauderdale but retired there in the late 1940s.

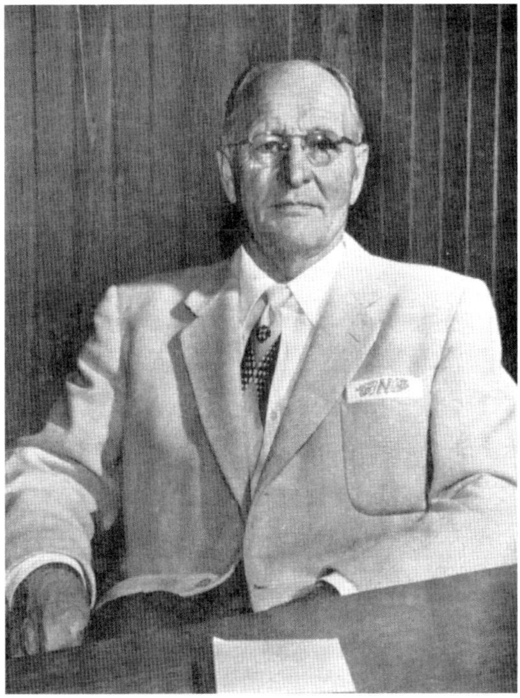

Victor Nurmi, Nurmi Isles Developer
A Finnish immigrant who had immigrated to the United States in 1901, Victor Nurmi became a successful land developer in Saginaw, Michigan. He had been a winter visitor to Fort Lauderdale since 1929, and in 1944 he purchased the four undeveloped finger islands north of Las Olas Boulevard for $250,000. The land had originally been under development by W.F. Morang but had sat dormant since the land boom collapse in the late 1920s. Nurmi spent the next 15 years building 250 homes on the islands. Besides each lot being waterfront property, Nurmi also incorporated underground utilities and subdued street lighting into the design of his subdivision. Today, the Nurmi Isles are considered one of Fort Lauderdale's most beautiful neighborhoods.

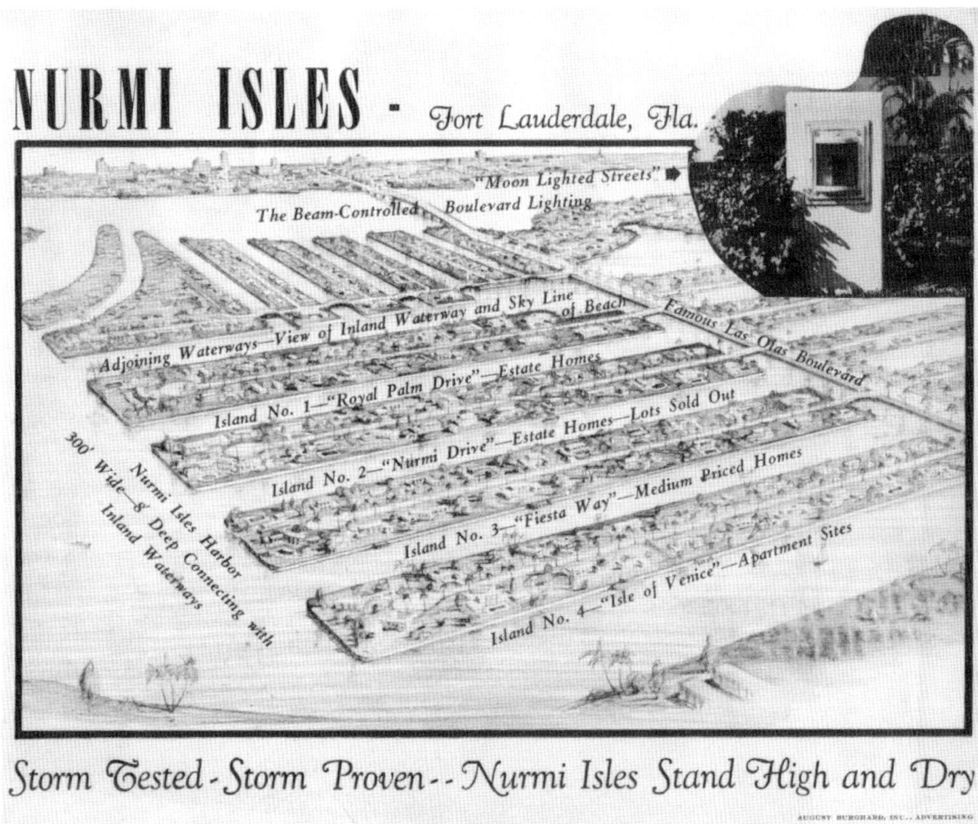

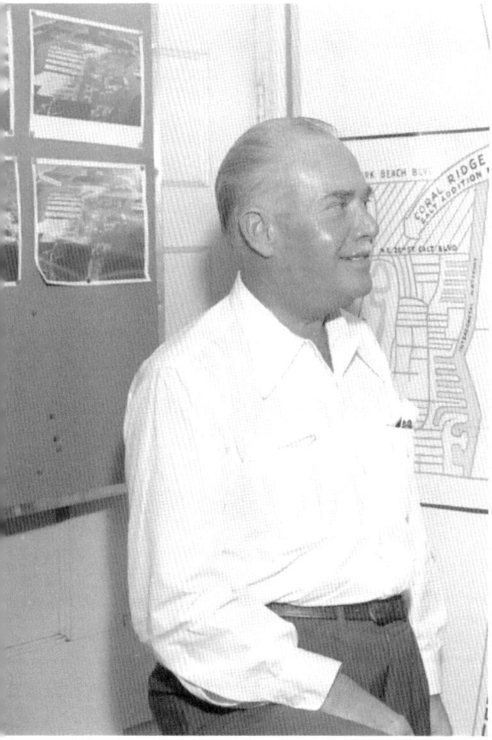

James S. Hunt Sr., Coral Ridge and Galt Ocean Mile Developer

A man of many talents and careers, James Hunt served as a pilot with the Royal Flying Corps during World War I and as a small boats invasion commander with the US Coast Guard during World War II. He retired as a rear admiral, the first in the Coast Guard to retire at that rank. Between the wars, Hunt owned three automobile dealerships in Detroit. In 1923, he originated the Blue Book for used car values. A winter visitor to Fort Lauderdale in the 1930s, Hunt built the Coral Sands Hotel in 1939. He moved to Fort Lauderdale permanently in 1945. During the late 1940s, Hunt teamed with Steve Calder and Joseph Taravella to form Coral Ridge Properties (CRP) and purchased 95 acres on the northern edge of Fort Lauderdale from Arthur Galt. There, they built 7,000 homes. In 1953, CRP purchased Galt Ocean Mile for $19.4 million to build high-rise condos. CRP purchased 10,000 acres of bean fields in northwest Broward County and turned it into the city of Coral Springs in 1963. Westinghouse Electric bought CRP for $67 million in 1966. Hunt is credited by many as being the man who had the most to do with the concept and actual development of the greater Fort Lauderdale area. (Left, courtesy of the Fort Lauderdale Historical Society, Gene Hyde Collection.)

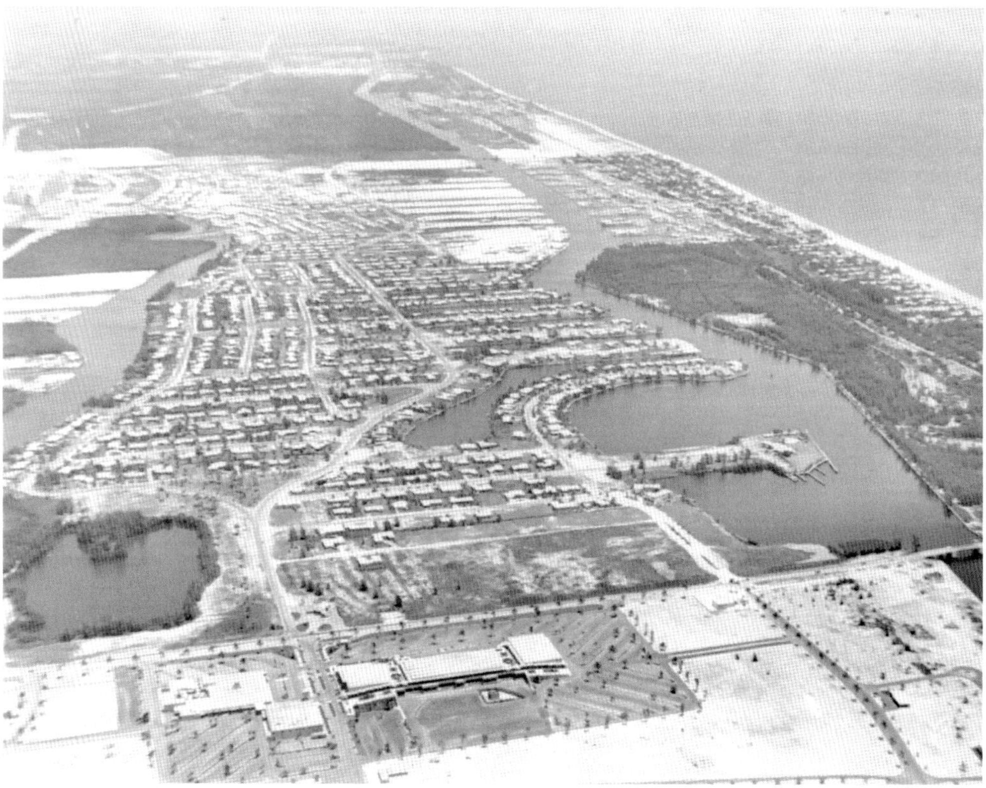

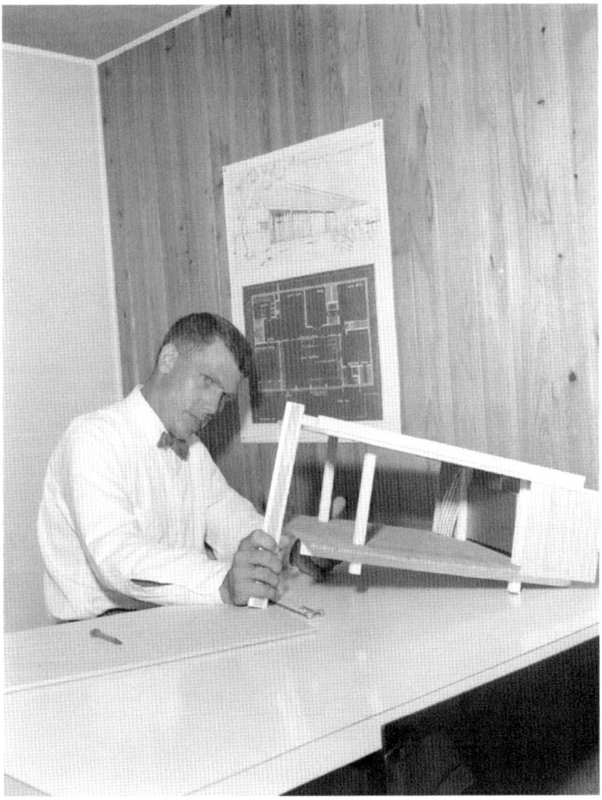

William F. "Bill" Bigoney, Environmentally Sensitive Architect
Bill Bigoney attended New York's Pratt Institute and Harvard University Graduate School of Architecture. He came to Fort Lauderdale in 1949 and designed the police station. A pioneer of environmentally sensitive architecture, Bigoney designed homes without air conditioning to take advantage of natural breezes. He designed 233 waterfront homes in Lauderdale Harbors and Rio Vista. Other projects included the Fifteenth Street Fisheries and Marina Bay. Bigoney was involved with the Sailboat Bend Civic Association and was a key force in getting historic designation for the area. (Courtesy of the Fort Lauderdale Historical Society, Gene Hyde Collection.)

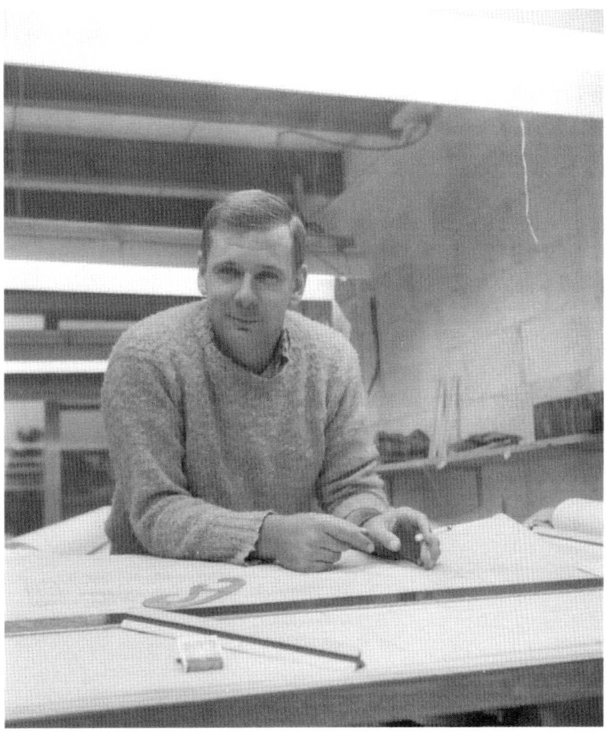

Edward Stone Jr., Preeminent Landscape Architect
Edward Stone Jr. received his master's degree in landscape architecture from Harvard University. In 1960, he founded Edward Durell Stone Jr. and Associates (EDSA), which specializes in recreation-based communities and resorts. EDSA incorporates open space and flora in an environmentally conscious manner. Some of EDSA's projects have included Atlantis in the Bahamas, the Riverwalk in Fort Lauderdale, Downtown Disney's West Side, and the PepsiCo Global Headquarters. EDSA is one of the preeminent planning and landscape architecture firms in the world. In 1994, Stone received the American Society of Landscape Architects Medal, their highest honor. (Courtesy of the Fort Lauderdale Historical Society, Gene Hyde Collection.)

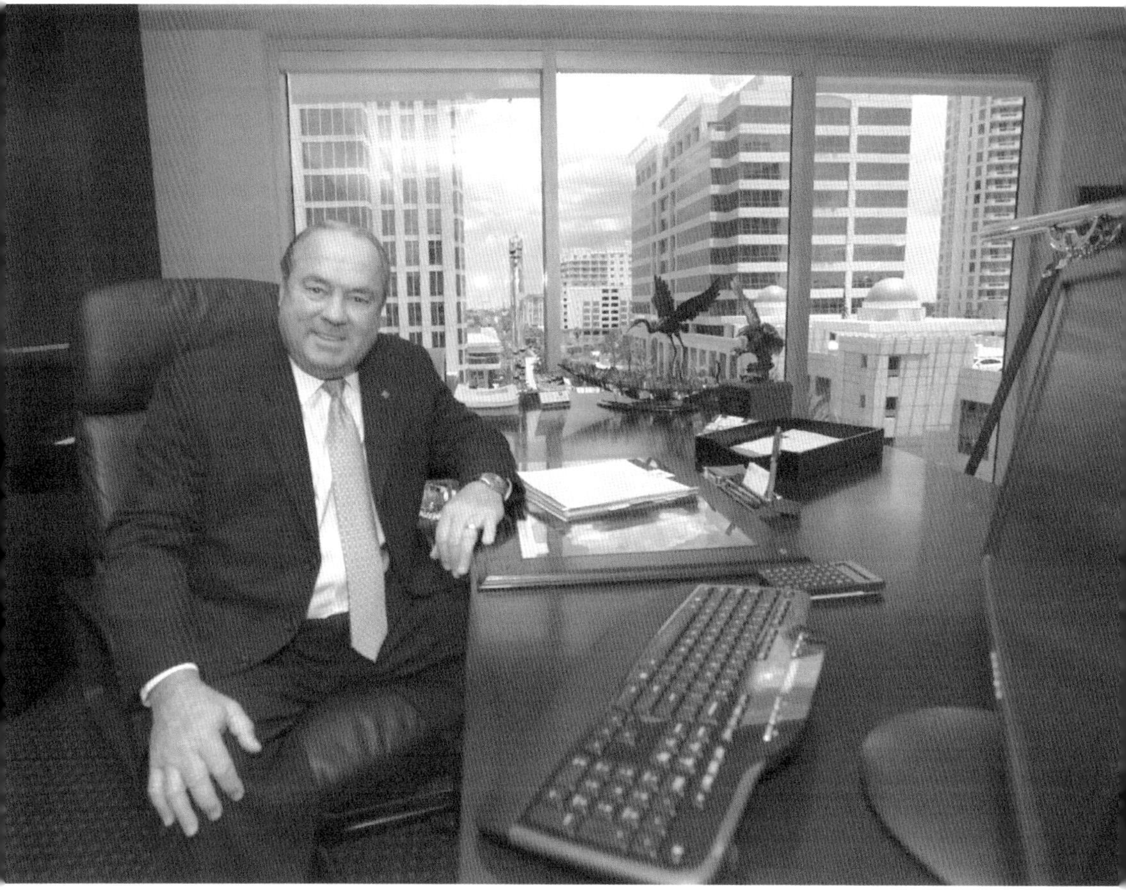

Terry Stiles, Commercial Real Estate Developer
Howard Stiles founded the Stiles Construction Company in 1951 as a small residential general contracting firm. In 1971, after his father's passing, Terry Stiles, age 23 and studying veterinary medicine at the University of Kentucky, became chief executive officer. Since then, he has grown the company into a full-service real estate firm that includes architecture, property, and asset management, leasing, and landscaping. The Stiles Corporation has constructed nearly 40 million square feet of projects and is an industry leader in the Southeast. The company made its mark by building corporate parks and shopping centers and redeveloping downtown Fort Lauderdale. Stiles was named National Developer of the Year in 2000 by the National Association of Industrial and Office Properties (NAIOP) and was the NAIOP South Florida Chapter's Developer of the Year in 1990, 1993, 1997, 1999, and 2003. He has also received the Urban Land Institute Southeast Florida/Caribbean District Council's 2009 Lifetime Achievement Award. Stiles is also a longtime board member of the Jack and Jill Children's Center and the Museum of Discovery and Science. Stiles was named the 1985 Broward County Business Leader of the Year, the 1999 Fort Lauderdale Citizen of the Year, and the 2003 *Sun-Sentinel* Philanthropist of the Year. (Courtesy of the Stiles Corporation.)

CHAPTER THREE

Business Leaders

As a settlement grows in geographic size, the services needed for that expanding town increase as well. Growing and prospering businesses, especially small businesses, are the lifeblood of a developing municipality. Farming was the first industry in the New River region and initially drew people to the area. The first retail establishment was Stranahan's Trading Post, where early settlers and the Seminole Indians could get supplies.

Within a few years of incorporation in 1911, Fort Lauderdale boasted three hotels, three general stores, two banks, a Chinese laundry, a bakery, and a boatyard. Gate City Novelty Works, a millwork company, opened in 1911 and remained open until 1976. Fishing charters became popular, and fish packinghouses sprung up along the riverbanks. Max Lehrman, a Jewish businessman, arrived in 1916 and opened a department store. T.C. Williams, a black man, operated a grocery and general store in the downtown.

Real estate became a booming business as the canals began draining the Everglades and opening up new land. Hodges Real Estate Company started in 1924, and the family still operates it today. T.S. Cobb opened the Bedd-O-Rest Company, a mattress manufacturer, in the northwest section of town in 1925. Archie Robbins and Fred Maxwell established shopping arcades. As more people moved into Fort Lauderdale in the 1920s, new hotels, apartments, restaurants, lawyers, lumber companies, groceries, gas stations, clothing stores, and funeral homes opened. In 1922, a "color line" was established, and by 1927, the city was segregated and African Americans could only own businesses in the northwest quadrant.

In the 1930s, the beach began to become a larger part of the city's economy, and new hotels were built. The main concentration for business was still centered on downtown and the Las Olas Boulevard corridor. The black community of the northwest held its own with entrepreneurs like Sylvia Aldridge, John Hill and Willie Walker.

The tourist industry exploded after World War II, and hotel and nightclub business took off. The large influx of new residents spurred on the construction business. The postwar economy provided tens of thousands of new jobs as the need for construction workers, maids, waitresses, bartenders, and guest services increased. Of course, all of these new residents needed clothes, groceries, appliances, cars, dentists, doctors, and more. Fort Lauderdale is a major manufacturing and maintenance center for yachts and is the home port for 42,000 boats and approximately 100 marinas and boatyards.

Many of Fort Lauderdale's businesses have remained within the founding families, and quite a few can trace their history back 50 years or more.

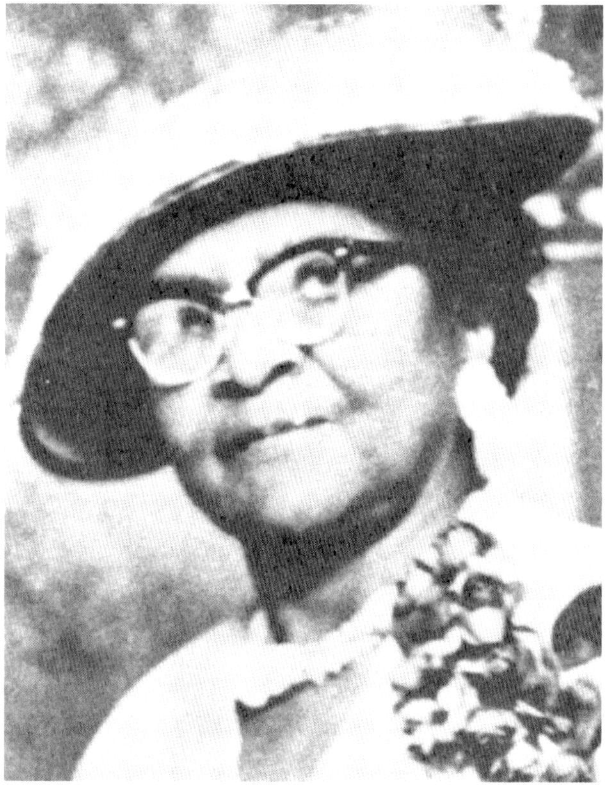

Sylvia Hill Aldridge, Early Black Entrepreneur

Sylvia Aldridge arrived in Fort Lauderdale in 1904. Initially, she was a domestic worker but eventually started Sylvia's Employment Agency to help African Americans find jobs. Aldridge wanted to get black women out of the fields and helped them find jobs as cooks and maids. Later, she started Victory Cabs in order to drive African Americans to work. In 1938, Aldridge led the fundraising effort to make Provident Hospital (the black hospital) a reality. She was also a member of the Northwest Federated Woman's Club. (Courtesy of the African-American Research Library and Cultural Center.)

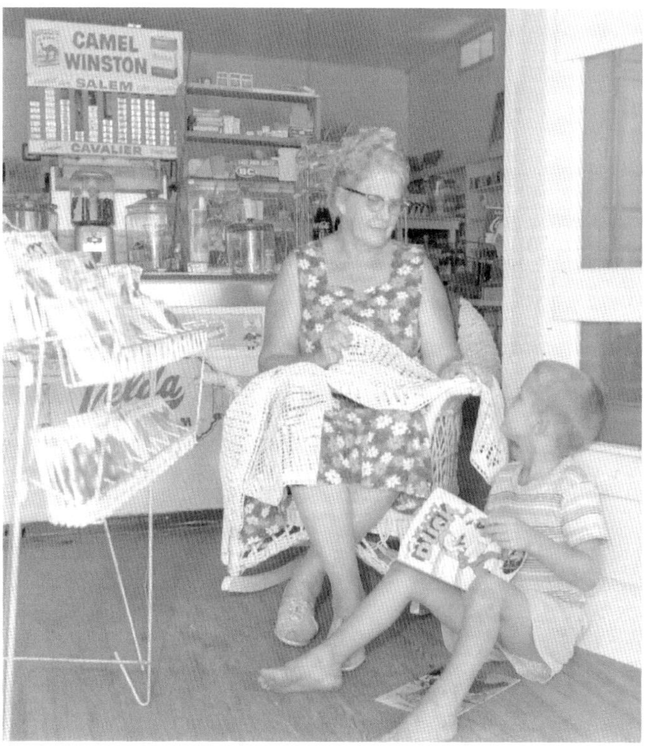

William and Frankie Melton, Longtime Cash Store Owners

William and Frankie Melton came to town in 1921. They started a store in their garage in 1922, which at the time was the only store between downtown Fort Lauderdale and Pompano Beach. It became a stopping place for locals and "tin can" tourists from the north. Melton's Cash Store catered to everyone, whether they were rich or poor, black or white. In 1924, the store was enlarged, adding gas pumps and a meat department. After William's death in 1959, Frankie continued operating the store until 1968. (Courtesy of the Fort Lauderdale Historical Society, Gene Hyde Collection.)

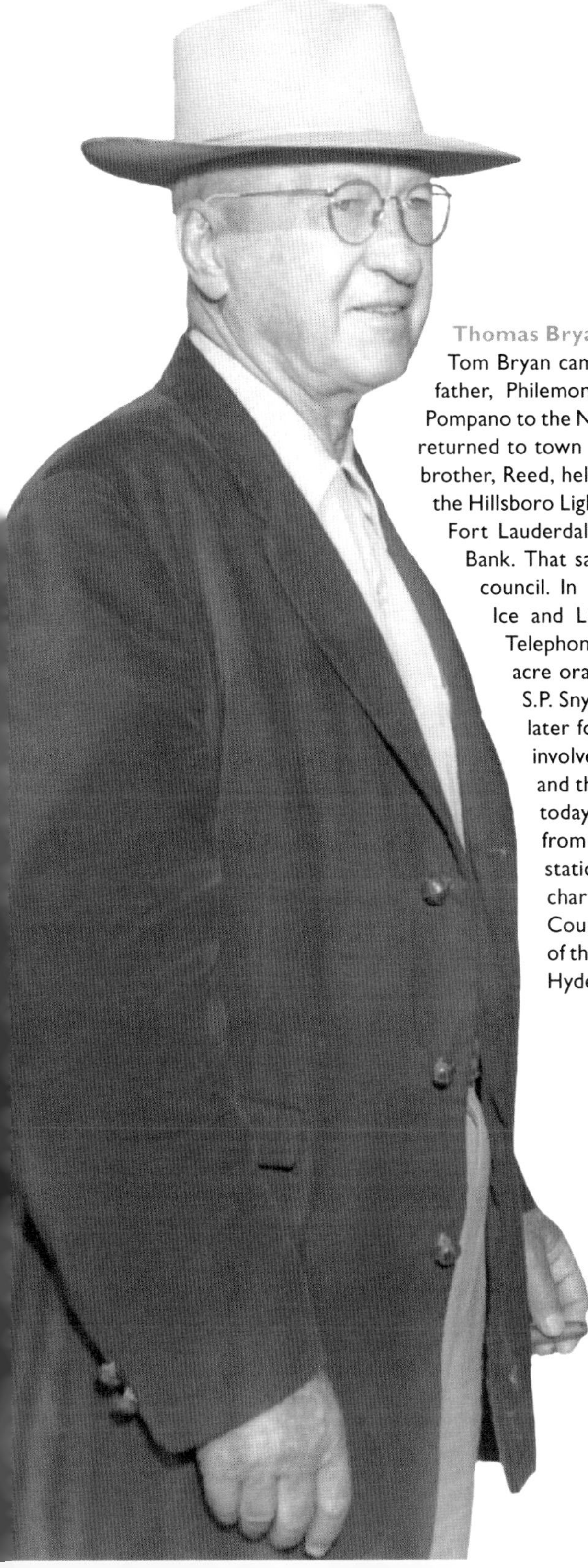

Thomas Bryan, Commercial Property Developer
Tom Bryan came to Fort Lauderdale in 1895 to help his father, Philemon, build the FEC Railway roadbed from Pompano to the New River. A graduate of Emery College, he returned to town to start several businesses. Bryan and his brother, Reed, helped haul the steel for the construction of the Hillsboro Lighthouse. In 1911, Bryan helped to establish Fort Lauderdale's first bank, the Fort Lauderdale State Bank. That same year, he was elected to the first city council. In 1912, Bryan started the Fort Lauderdale Ice and Light Company and the Fort Lauderdale Telephone Corporation. He also owned an 800-acre orange grove. In 1917, Bryan partnered with S.P. Snyder in his road construction company and later formed his own company. He also became involved in real estate and built the Bryan Arcade and the Bryan Building, both of which still stand today. Bryan served as a state representative from 1927 to 1929. He started the first radio station in town, WFTL, in 1939. Bryan was a charter member of the Masonic Lodge, the Country Club, and the Yacht Club. (Courtesy of the Fort Lauderdale Historical Society, Gene Hyde Collection.)

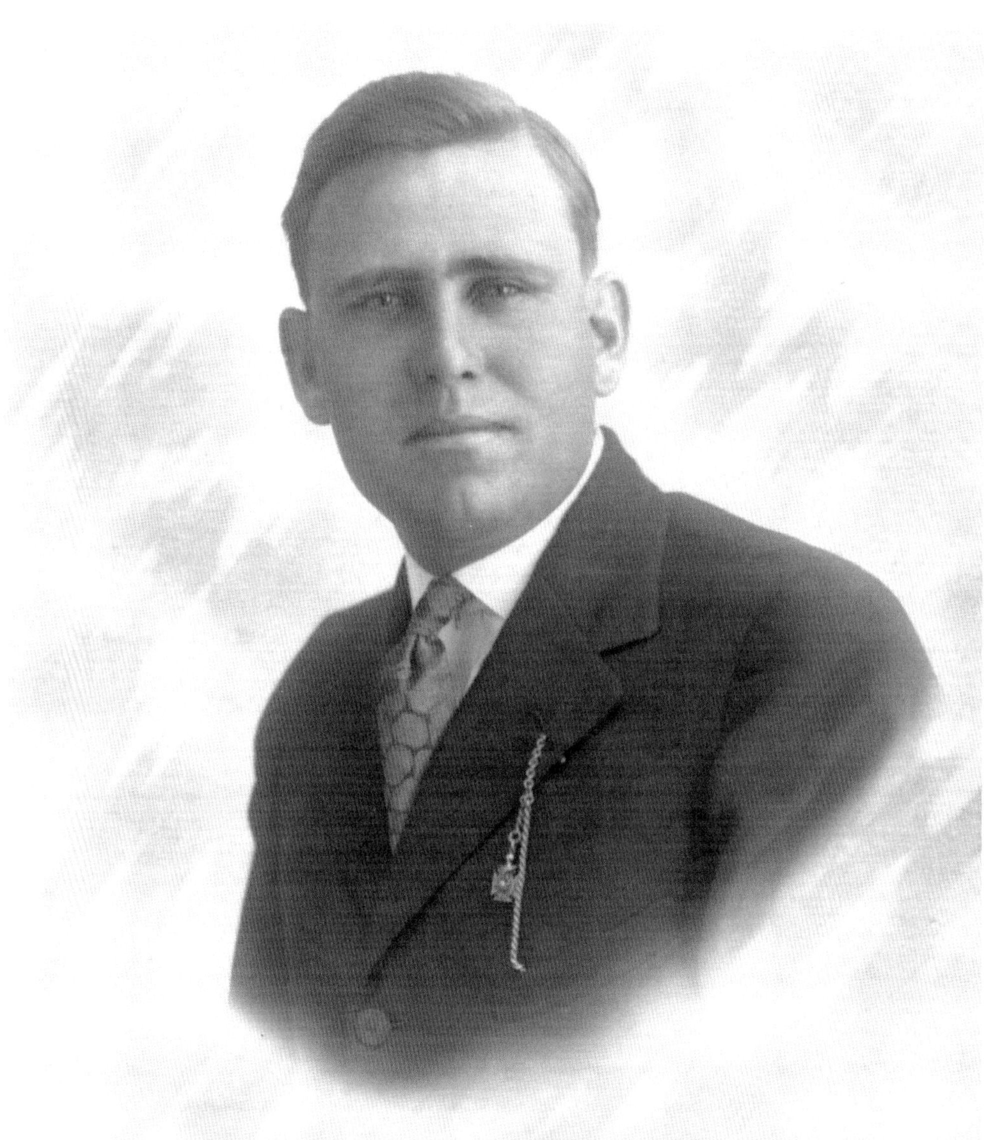

William Cabot Kyle, Entrepreneur

The son of a Confederate army colonel, William Cabot Kyle was born in Alabama in 1885. At the age of 15, he joined the FEC Railway as a telegraph operator in Jupiter, Florida. Kyle transferred to Fort Lauderdale in 1900 and eventually owned and managed the Everglades Grocery, the first modern grocery in the town. In 1911, he was elected to the first city council. Kyle also organized the White Star Bus Line, was the first president of the Fort Lauderdale Bank and Trust Company, and served as the first chairman of the Napoleon B. Broward Drainage District. He formed the Idlewyld Building Company and developed one of the best residential areas in the city. He was a leader in the movement to create Broward County. From 1921 to 1925, he served in the Florida state legislature, representing Broward County, and was the chairman of the canals and drainage committee. Kyle married Lucy Rodes, the sister of Charles Rodes, Sr. Kyle was an enthusiastic hunter and fisherman and was friends with the Seminoles and Chief Billy Bowlegs. Kyle was a millionaire but lost it all during the economic bust following the 1926 hurricane.

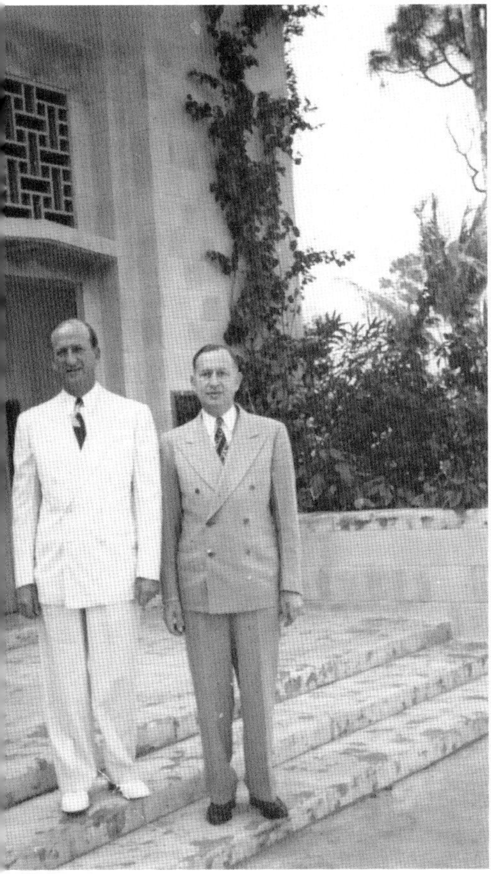

Katz Family, Jewish Merchants and Founders of Temple Emanu-El

Brothers Moe and Mack Katz came to Fort Lauderdale in 1924 from Daytona Beach. Mack and his wife, Sadye, opened the town's first women's clothing store—Mack's Ladies Shop—and ran it until 1952. Mack was one of the founders of the Fort Lauderdale Merchants Association. He also helped to organize the first Jewish Appeal in the late 1920s. Moe was in real estate and also a banker, joining First Federal Savings and Loan Association in 1935. Moe and Mack were the founders of the Fort Lauderdale Hebrew Congregation (later Temple Emanu-El), which had its first services the night before the 1926 hurricane. Sadye started the first Jewish Sunday School in 1931 and, during World War II, helped to establish the Service Men's Center. Later, she was instrumental in raising funds for the War Memorial Auditorium and Holy Cross Hospital. In 1935, Moe and Mack donated land for the construction of a permanent home for Temple Emanu-El. With the assistance of Sam and Charles Lerner (of the Lerner chain of retail stores), Broward County's first synagogue was completed in 1937. Moe served as the first president of the temple. (Left, courtesy of the Jewish Museum of Florida-FIU.)

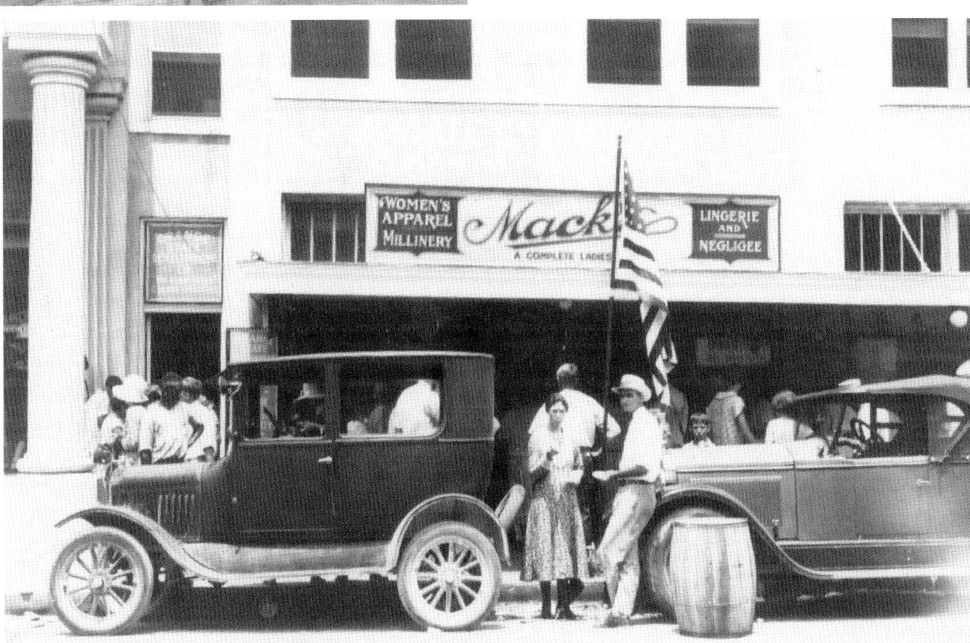

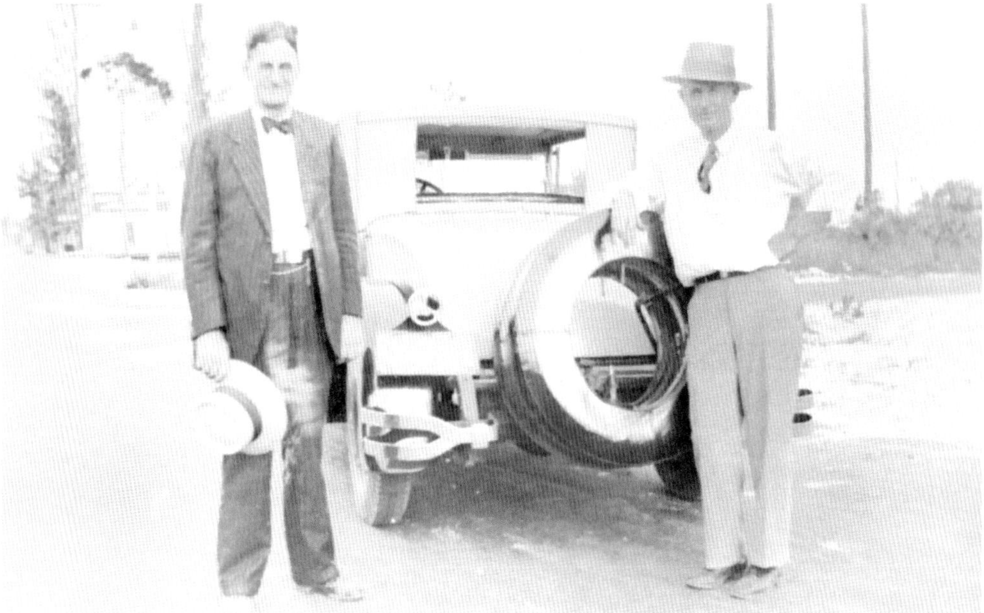

Byron (left) and S.P. Snyder, Road Contractors

At the age of 10, Byron Snyder arrived in Fort Lauderdale. In 1925, he and his father founded S.P. Snyder and Son, Inc., one of the first road construction companies in Fort Lauderdale. They built many of the city's streets, roads, and highways, including Las Olas Boulevard and Federal Highway. Snyder also developed the Lauderdale, Forest Lawn, and Broward Memorial Gardens cemeteries. He was also instrumental in the development of Stillwell Isle and Harbor Beach. Snyder served on the Post War Planning Committee of the Fort Lauderdale Chamber of Commerce and was a founder of the Everglades Bank in 1956. He served for 20 years on the Fort Lauderdale Housing Authority and donated land and provided a housing facility for the northwest branch of the YMCA to meet the needs of the elderly and black community. Snyder also donated 62 acres for S.P. Snyder Park. He was named Fort Lauderdale Citizen of the Year in 1981.

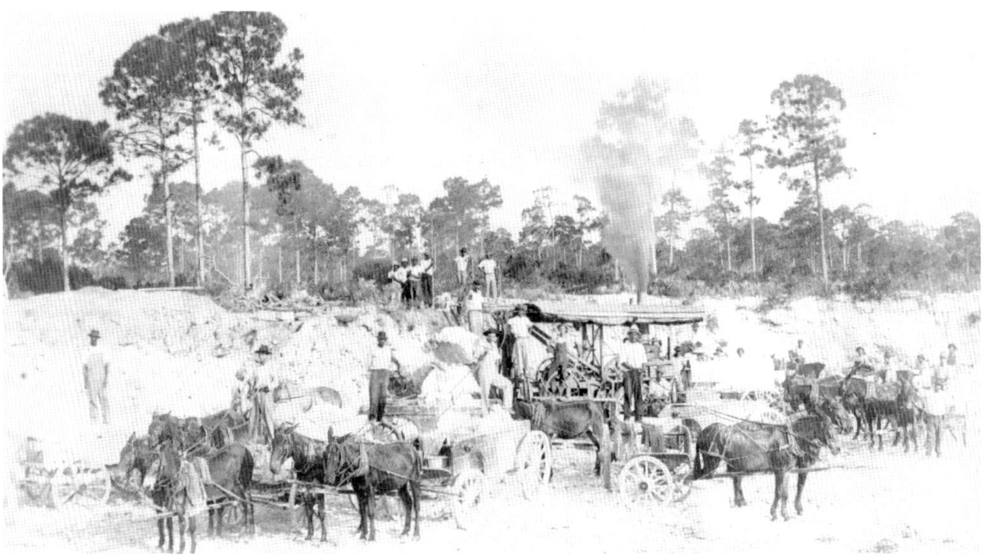

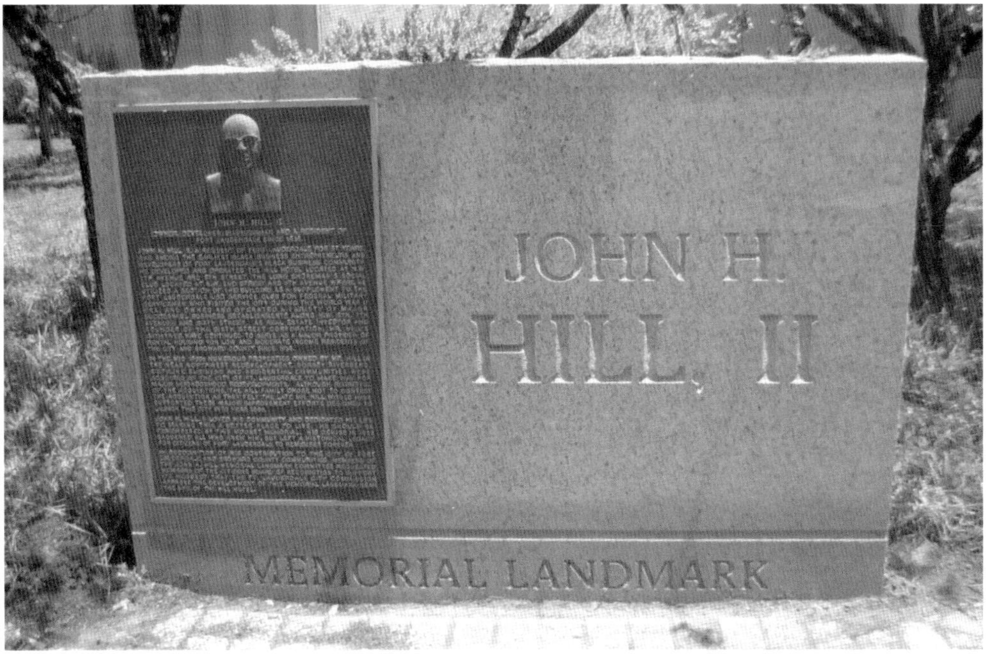

John Henry Hill II, First Black Millionaire
John Hill came to Fort Lauderdale in 1935. Armed with only a fourth grade education and money saved from working as a railroad cook, he opened Hill's Grocery, the first black-owned grocery store in Fort Lauderdale. Hill was one of Broward County's first black developers and eventually owned a number of businesses and became the largest property owner in the black section of town. He owned a liquor store, a chain of funeral homes, the Windsor Club, the Hill Hotel, and several housing developments. During World War II, Hill ran the USO Service Club for black soldiers. In the 1950s and 1960s, the Hill Hotel was the only accommodation where out-of-town African Americans could stay. This included people such as Ella Fitzgerald, Louis Armstrong, Cab Calloway, and black New York Yankees during Spring Training. (Above, photograph by the author.)

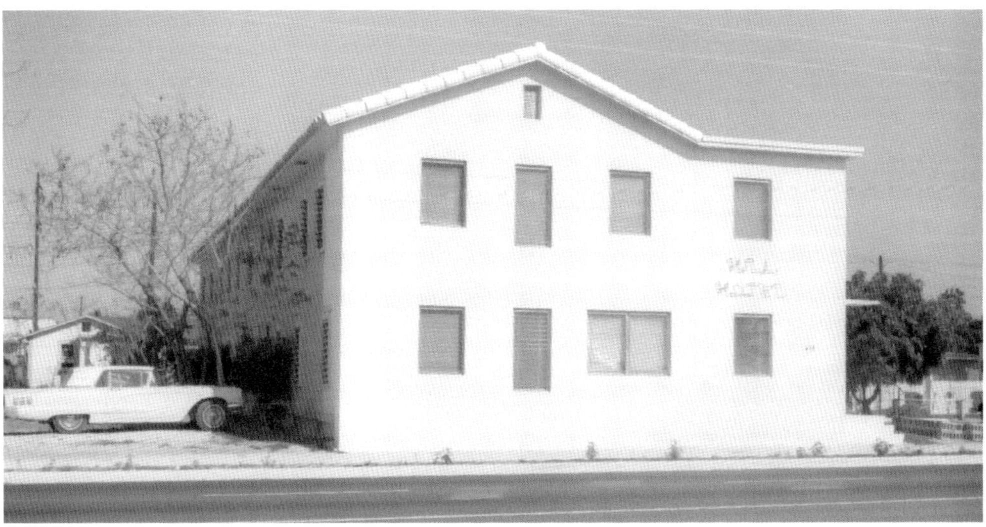

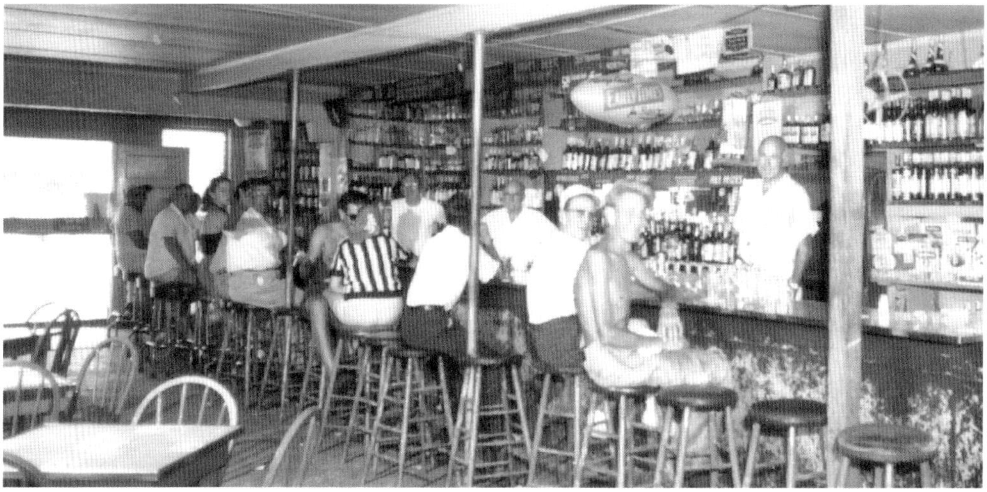

Brownie L. Robertson (center behind bar), Longtime Popular Bar Owner
Brownie Robertson arrived in 1935 and leased the Trianon Ballroom. He bought it in 1938 and changed the name to Club Brownie. Robertson used his background as a booking agent to attract some of the best musicians in the country. At the time, Club Brownie was one of the only white-owned establishments in town that would book black bands. Louis Armstrong, Ella Fitzgerald, and Duke Ellington all played there. Robertson always put his customers first, and he knew everyone by name. After 50 years, he retired in 1985. (Courtesy of the Fort Lauderdale Historical Society, Gene Hyde Collection.)

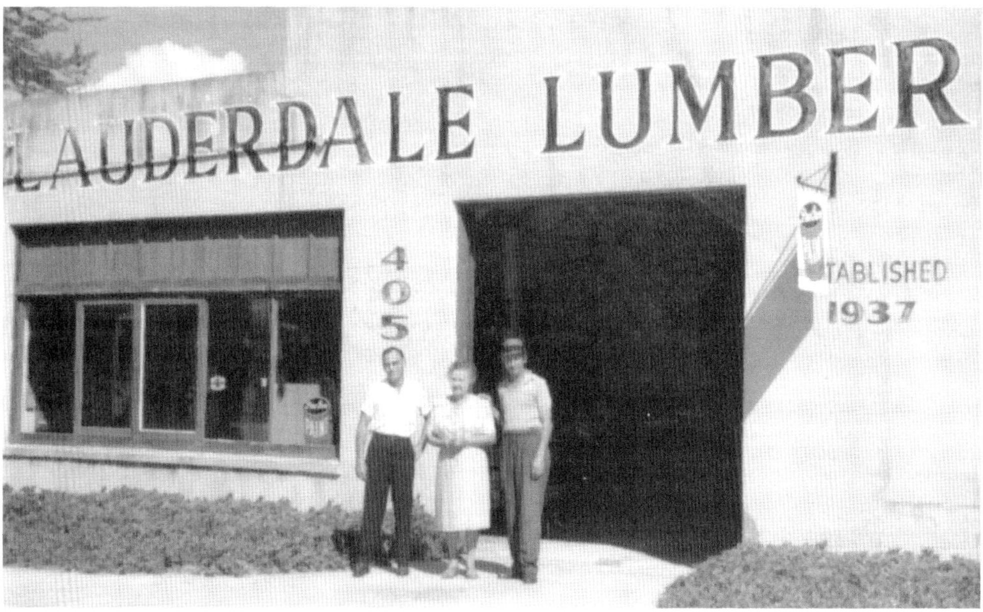

Helen G. Bailey, Founder of Lauderdale Lumber Company
Helen Bailey came to Fort Lauderdale from a ranch in the middle of a South Dakota Indian Reservation in 1918. For 17 years, she worked at the Everglades Lumber Company as a bookkeeper. In 1937, Bailey decided that she could operate one herself and started the Lauderdale Lumber Company. She ran it until her passing in 1967. Bailey was also a charter member of the Fort Lauderdale Business and Professional Women's Club and the Zonta Club.

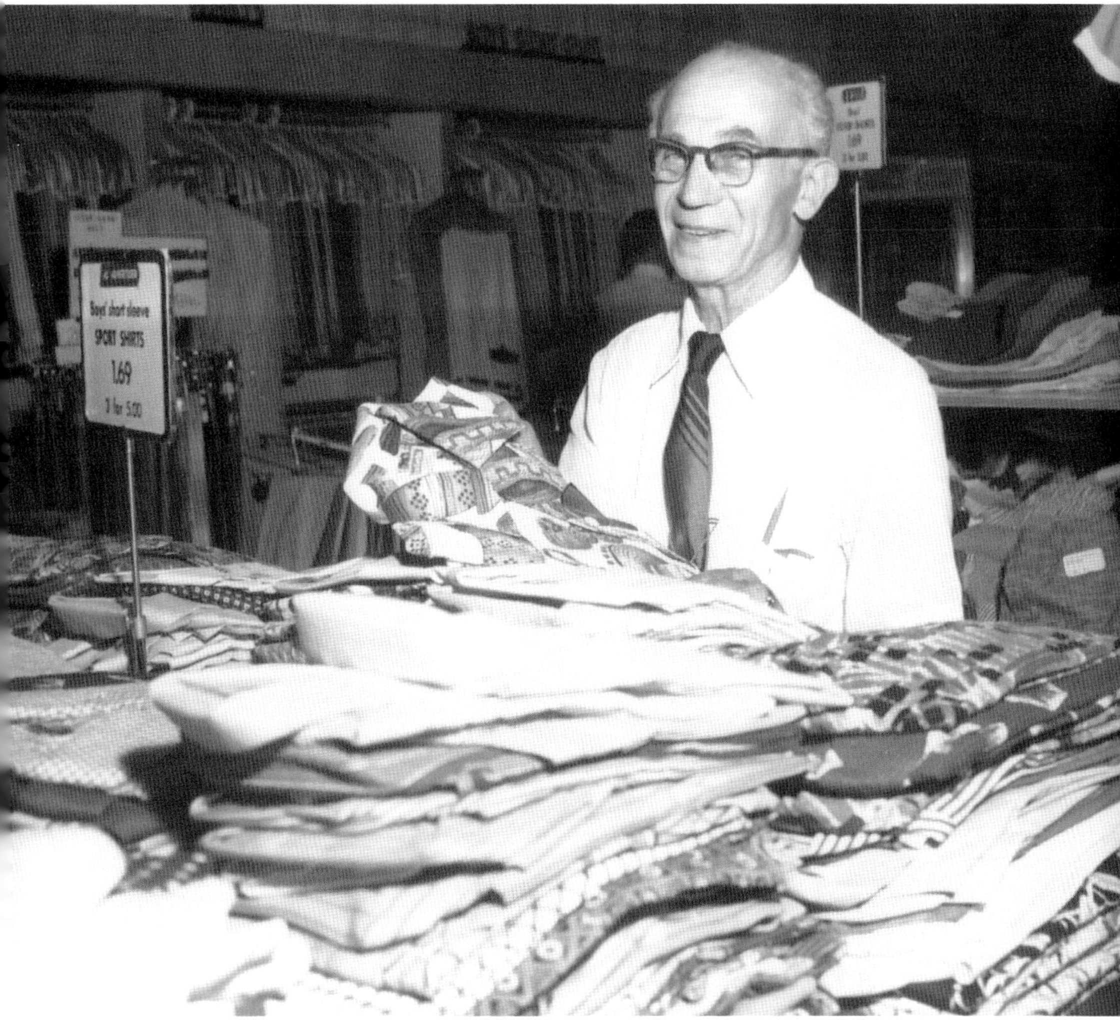

Isadore A. "Pop" Sterling, Santa Claus of Fort Lauderdale
A Jewish Russian immigrant, Isadore Sterling arrived in Fort Lauderdale in 1935 and opened a men's clothing store. Known as the Santa Claus of Fort Lauderdale, Sterling would send a box of clothes and other goods to every Broward County serviceman during the holidays. He also provided clothes for underprivileged children, disaster victims, and indigent defendants in court. Sterling delivered gifts to hospitals and children organizations and donated thousands of books to prisons. In 1951, he founded the Jewish War Veterans' Post No. 730. During the Vietnam War, Sterling was active in Project G.I., the sending of Easter packages. All three of his sons went into the clothing business, and Sterling's remained open until 1999. (Courtesy of the Fort Lauderdale Historical Society, Gene Hyde Collection.)

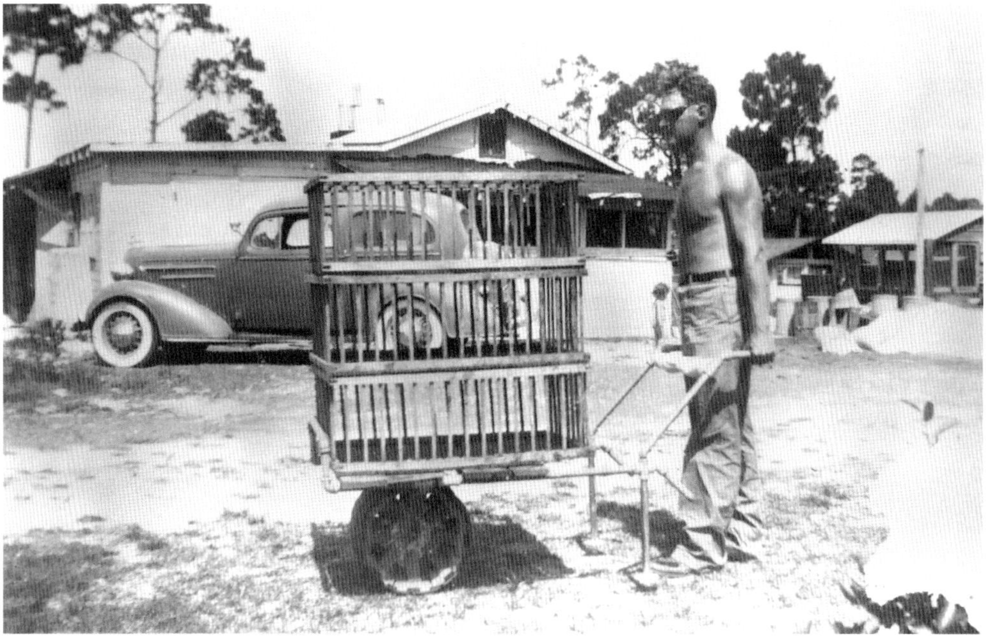

Ralph Gross, Jewish Chicken and Egg Farmer

Ralph Gross moved to town in 1939, purchased 40 acres on west Broward Boulevard, and sold eggs to major grocers such as Pantry Pride. During World War II, Gross sold chickens and eggs to Naval Air Station Fort Lauderdale. In 1955, the city ordered him to close the farm. Gross established an endowment at the University of Miami Louis Calder Memorial Library in 1984. When he first started his poultry farm, Gross had frequented the library to learn more about poultry nutrition and health. (Courtesy of the Jewish Museum of Florida-FIU.)

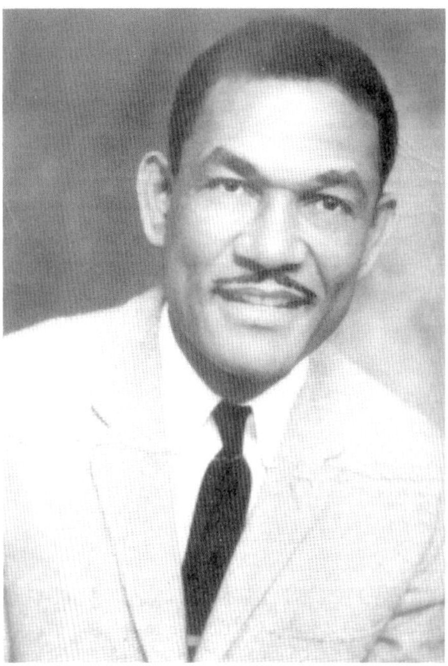

Willie Walker Sr., Grocery Store Owner

Willie Walker's family arrived in Fort Lauderdale in 1924 and became farmers. In 1939, he started Walker's Grocery on Sistrunk Boulevard, one of the first black-owned businesses to open there. Customers could always count on getting fresh produce and fresh meat, as Walker either raised them himself or purchased them from local farmers. He was also among the first business owners to extend credit to his customers.

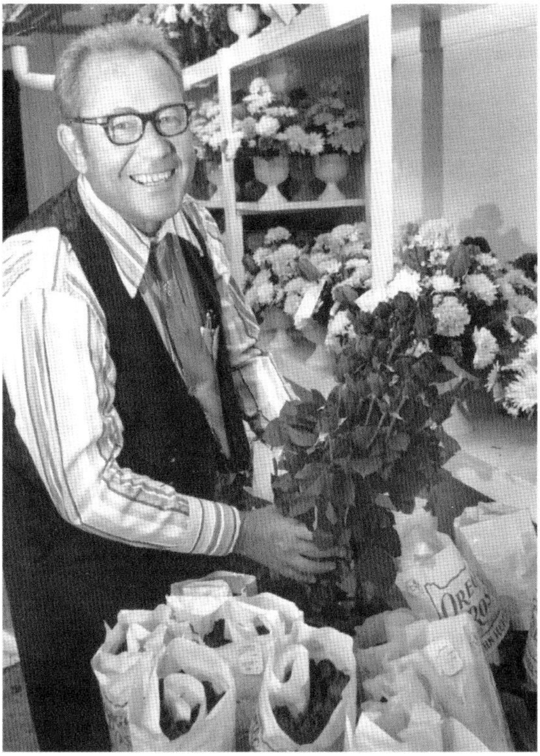

Arthur O. Stone, Florist and Automobile Museum Founder

The son of Polish immigrants, Arthur Stone began his career as a florist by starting as a flower delivery boy in New York City at age 12. Over the next 10 years, he worked for 10 different florists in New York and Florida. Stone came to Miami in 1937 and had just started his own successful shop when he was drafted into the US Army in 1941. After being discharged in 1944, he was living in Fort Lauderdale and decided to buy Buning's Florist Shop for $3,000. John Buning started the shop, located on Las Olas Boulevard, in 1925. Stone built up the business to 34 stores in four states with a $6 million annual revenue. Buning's was the first retail florist in the United States to "go public." In 1999, Stone sold the chain and then founded the Fort Lauderdale Antique Car Museum. The museum is dedicated solely to the Packard automobile. (Courtesy of the Jewish Museum of Florida-FIU.)

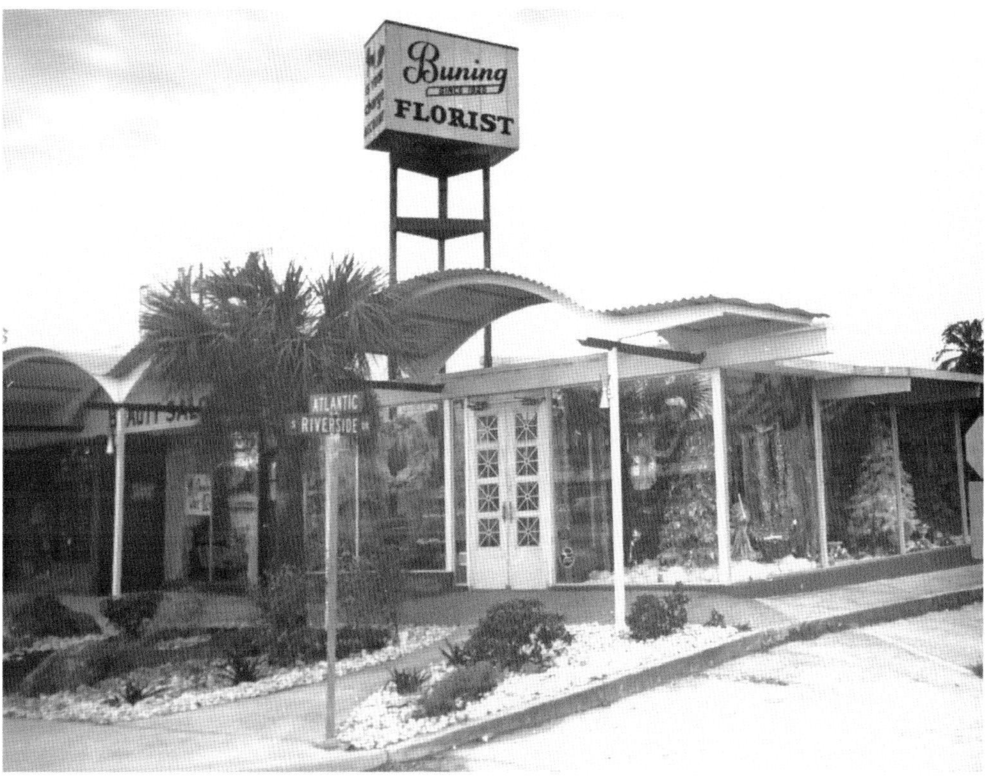

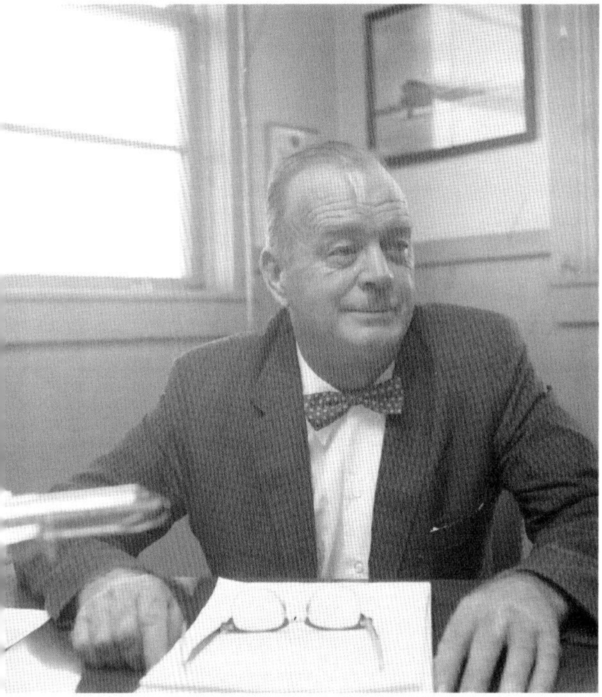

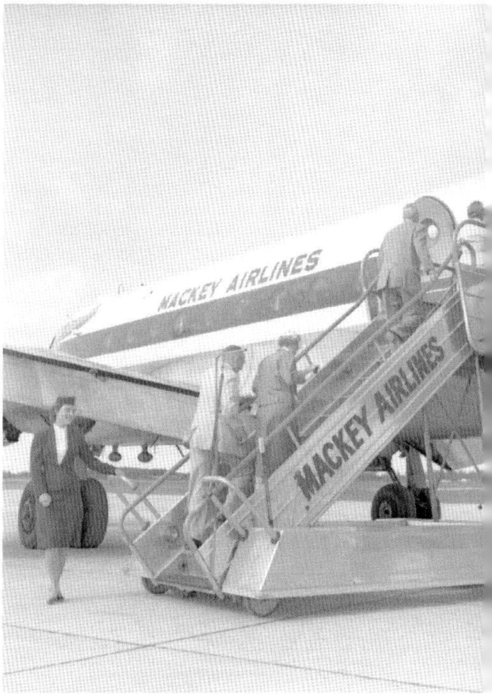

Col. Joseph Mackey, Founder of Mackey Airlines

Joseph Mackey was born in Ohio and began his aviation career in the 1920s as a mechanic's assistant. Part of his salary was flying lessons. In the 1930s, Mackey became a stunt pilot and barnstormed around the Midwest. In 1936, he won the Freddy Lund Trophy for stunt flying. During Prohibition, he flew whiskey from Canada. Mackey moved to Fort Lauderdale in 1936 and opened two filling stations. Early in World War II, he ferried bombers from Canada to England and later was the commander of the Miami Army Air Corps Base, in charge of ferrying parts and supplies to India. In 1946, Mackey founded Mackey Air Transport and began service between South Florida and the Bahamas. However, the government deemed his operations illegal, and it was not until 1953 that Mackey Airlines became an official airline. Mackey Airlines established routes throughout the Caribbean. In 1967, Eastern Airlines acquired it for $19 million. However, Mackey did not remain out of the airline business for long. He established Mackey International Airlines in 1969, flying to the smaller Bahamian islands. In 1981, shortly before his death, Mackey was named to the Aviation Hall of Fame. (Both, courtesy of the Fort Lauderdale Historical Society, Gene Hyde Collection.)

George Burrows, First Black Licensed Master Electrician
A child of Bahamian immigrants, George Burrows served in the Marines during World War II. He used his G.I. Bill to attend Bethune-Cookman College, graduating with an electronics degree in 1948. After Burrows received his state certification as a licensed master electrician, he opened the Burrows Electric Company. His original Fort Lauderdale business license stated he was "to operate in Colored Town only." One of Burrows's first major projects was the installation of lights at the Dillard High School football field. He was also a joint founder of the Black Chamber of Commerce. (Courtesy of the *Sun-Sentinel.*)

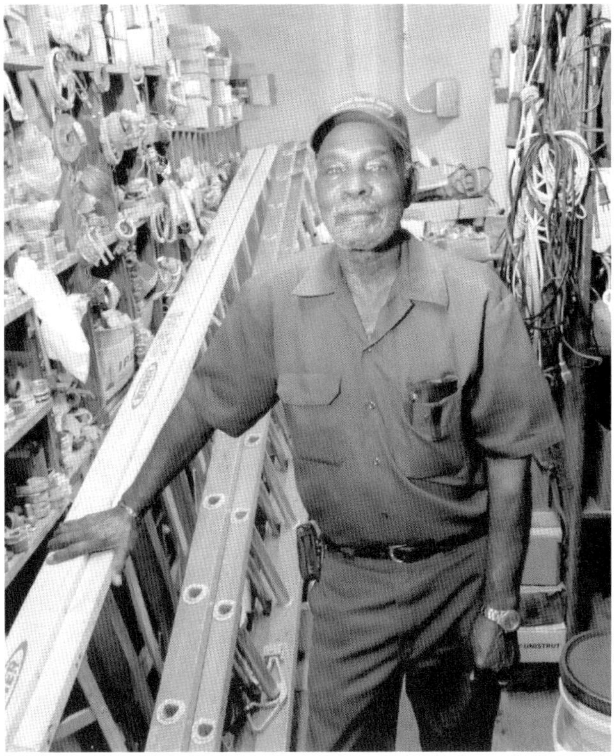

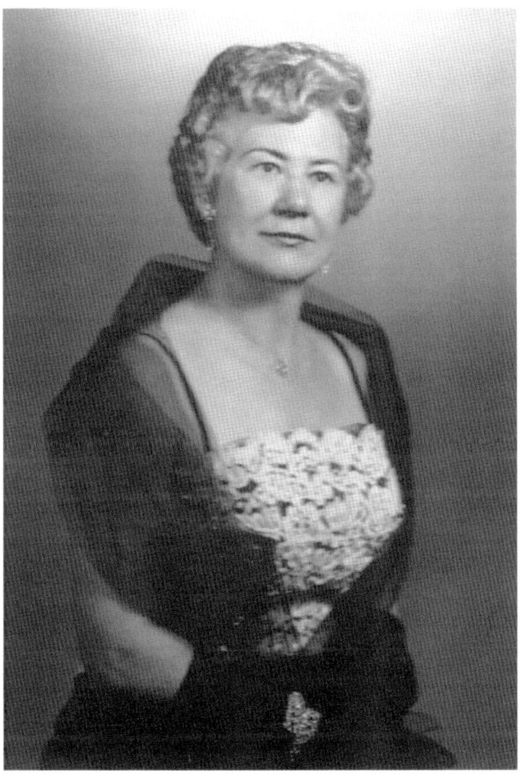

Ila Buntrock, First Woman Owner of Midas Muffler Shop
A widow with three sons, Ila Buntrock came to Fort Lauderdale in 1954. She was a close friend with Midas founder Nate Sherman, and she was awarded exclusive rights to Broward and Palm Beach Counties. In 1956, Buntrock opened her first Midas Automotive Shop on South Andrews Avenue. When she retired in 1983, the family owned 11 shops. (Courtesy of Betsy Buntrock.)

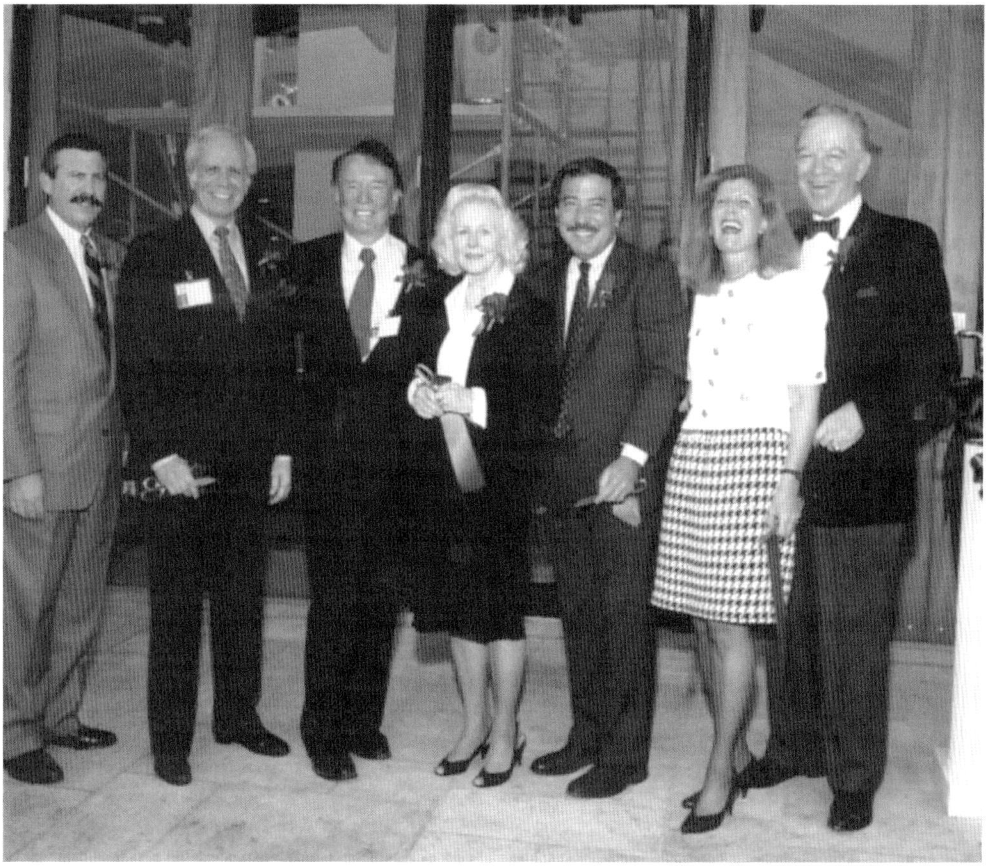

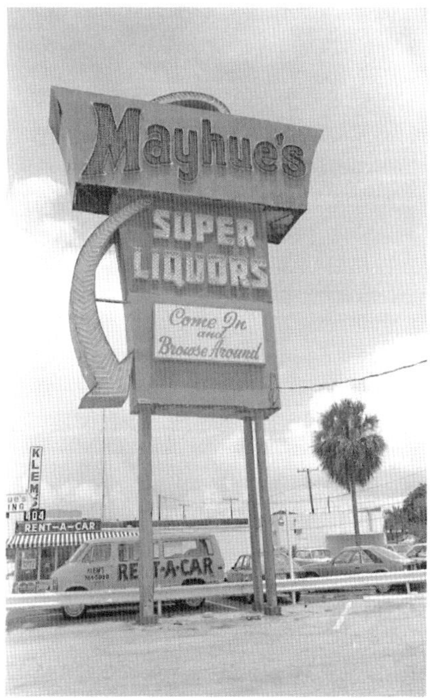

Carl L. Mayhue (third from left), Liquor Store Magnate

At the age of 19, Carl Mayhue got a $1,500 loan from a bank and opened a grocery store at 400 Northeast Sixth Avenue. Upon his return from service in World War II, Mayhue added a liquor store to the grocery. In 1949, he eliminated the grocery to concentrate on the liquor business. He eventually had 10 Mayhue's Super Liquors stores. Not bad for someone who didn't drink. Mayhue was also involved in many civic and arts projects. He was on the board that recommended the construction of Lockhart Stadium, and in the 1950s and 1960s, he helped to fund and organize such projects as the city's first bus benches and beach showers. In the early 1980s, Mayhue spent nearly a decade pushing for the construction of the Broward Center for the Performing Arts. (Above, courtesy of the Broward Center for the Performing Arts.)

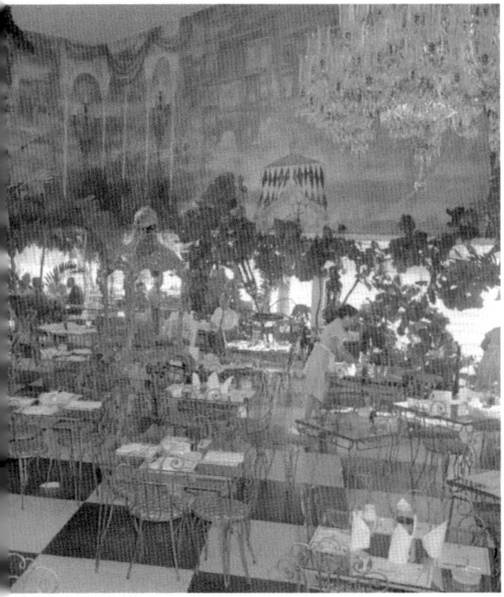

Charles W. Creighton, Restaurateur and Sunrise Shopping Center Owner
Charles Creighton arrived in the early 1950s. He opened the Sunrise Shopping Center in 1954 and Creighton's Restaurant the following year. The restaurant was famous for its "World's Best Apple Pie." Creighton furnished it with $2.5 million worth of antiques, including Russian paintings, French chandeliers, and tables from Napoleon's palace. He sold the restaurant and the shopping center in the late 1970s for $13 million. He was a founder of Holy Cross Hospital and established what became the Fort Lauderdale Mayor's Prayer Breakfast in 1962. (Courtesy of the Fort Lauderdale Historical Society, Gene Hyde Collection.)

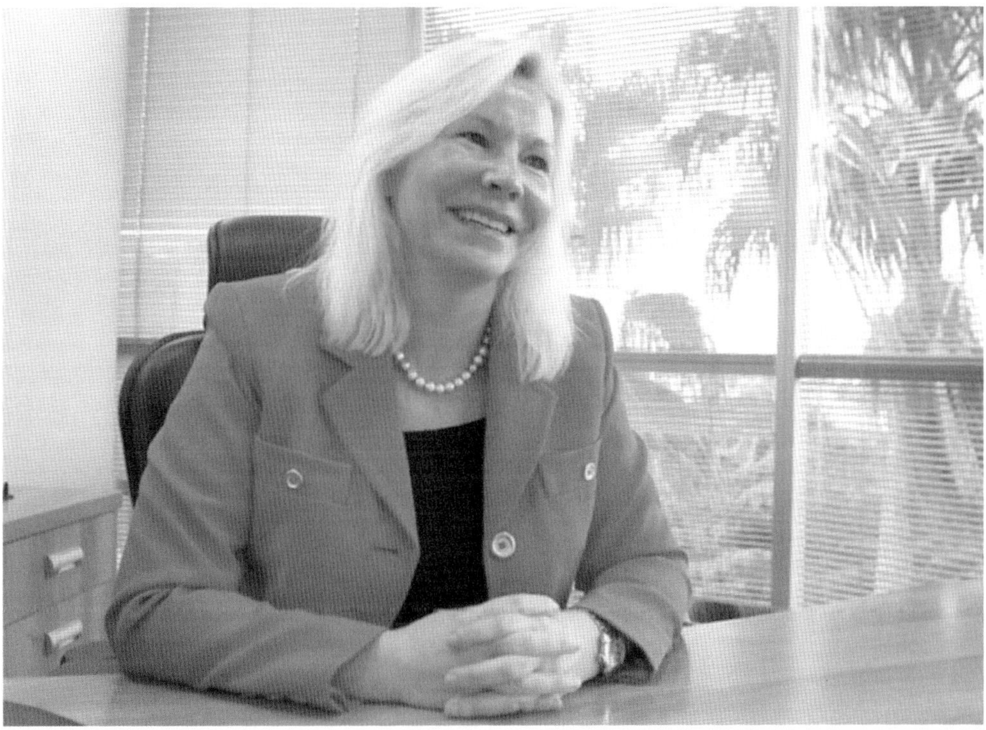

Carmen Castillo, CEO of Largest Latina-owned Business in the Country
Spanish immigrant Carmen Castillo came to the United States in 1987, and while helping a friend in New York, she connected with an entrepreneur in the technology services field. In 1992, Castillo founded Superior Design International (SDI), which recruits IT programmers for large corporations and provides managed services programs. Major customers include IBM, Motorola, and Merrill Lynch. Today, the company has over 2,000 employees worldwide and yields over $1.3 billion. In 2013, hispanicbusiness.com named Castillo Woman of the Year. (Courtesy of *Sun-Sentinel*.)

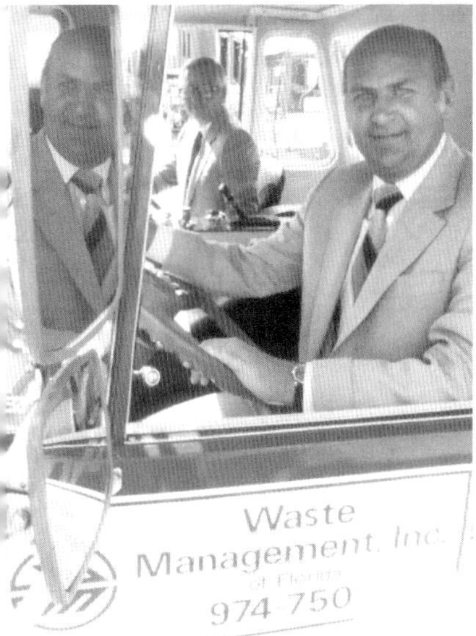

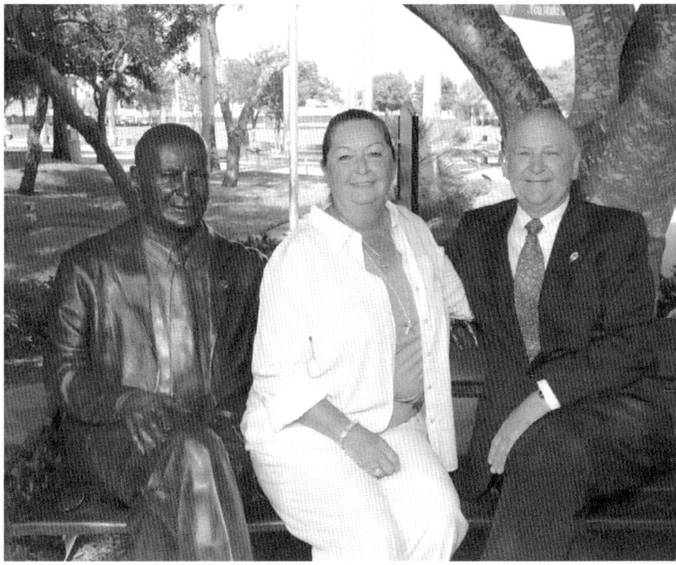

H. Wayne Huizenga, Fortune 500 Entrepreneur
Wayne Huizenga's family moved to Fort Lauderdale from Chicago in 1954, and Huizenga graduated from Pine Crest Preparatory School. In the late 1950s, he worked as a part-time garbage truck driver. In 1962, he bought his own truck and operated as Southern Sanitation Service. By the late 1960s, Huizenga had 20 trucks with routes in Miami, Fort Lauderdale, Tampa, and Key West. In 1971, he cofounded Waste Management and built it into the world's largest collector of waste. Huizenga was able to grow the business by buying out smaller chains and companies. In 1987, he bought a small chain of video stores in Dallas and turned Blockbuster into the world's largest video rental business. At one point, the company was opening a new store every 24 hours. Huizenga sold the company in 1994. He then started building and buying auto dealerships and, in 1996, cofounded AutoNation, which became the nation's largest automobile retailer. Huizenga was also successful in sports team ownership. At one time, he owned the Miami Dolphins, the Florida Marlins, and the Florida Panthers. In 1990, Huizenga purchased 15 percent of the Miami Dolphins, and by 1993, he was the full owner of the team and its stadium. By 2009, he had sold 95 percent of the team to Stephen Ross for $1.1 billion. Huizenga was awarded a Major League Baseball franchise in 1991, and the Florida Marlins won the World Series in 1997. The following year, he sold the team for $150 million. In 1992, Huizenga was awarded a National Hockey League franchise. The Florida Panthers reached the Stanley Cup Finals in 1996, and Huizenga sold the team in 2001 for $101 million. A large donor to Nova Southeastern University, the H. Wayne Huizenga School of Business and Entrepreneurship is named in his honor. Huizenga, a founder of three Fortune 500 companies, was named the 2005 World Entrepreneur of the Year by Ernst & Young and was a 2006 inductee into the Junior Achievement's US Business Hall of Fame.

CHAPTER FOUR

Tourism

Tourism has been an important part of Fort Lauderdale's economy since the 1890s. Visitors traveling to Miami from northern Florida aboard the overland stage stayed at Frank Stranahan's overnight camp before being ferried across the New River. Sportfishing and hunting brought people to the area. Philemon Bryan and Frank Oliver built the first two hotels, and a former packinghouse was converted into the Osceola Hotel. D.C. Alexander opened the first hotel at the beach in 1914, and the first tourist hotel, the Broward Hotel, opened downtown in 1919. The Dixie Highway arrived from the north in 1915 and brought tin can tourists to the area. People could now get to Fort Lauderdale by boat, by train, or by car.

From the 1920s onward, Fort Lauderdale has always seen an influx of winter visitors. Northerners, or as they are called today, "snowbirds," escape the cold and snow and visit tropical Florida. The late 1930s saw the construction of the Lauderdale Beach and Trade Winds hotels at the beach. Following World War II, new hotel construction by Bob Gill, Wynne Casteel, and the Banks family helped turn the town into a true resort destination.

The annual Collegiate Aquatic Forum, which started in 1935, brought coaches and athletes to town for training and competition. The "Spring Break" phenomenon grew directly from the Forum. Following the release of *Where the Boys Are* in 1960, the number of college students jumped from 20,000 to over 50,000. By 1985, when the city imposed its "ban," 350,000 students made the annual trip. Since then, Fort Lauderdale has remade itself into a resort catering to families and wealthier clients.

Nautical recreation is a driving force in Fort Lauderdale's tourism. Sportfishing has been around since the early days, and tourists and locals alike can still partake in daily fishing trips. River cruises provide a nice historical perspective. Everglades airboat rides are a short drive away and provide opportunities to see birds and wildlife, especially alligators. And of course, there is always the beach.

Port Everglades is a major disembarkation point for cruise ships and is also the site of the convention center. Approximately 4 million cruise visitors and 3 million conventioneers make use of Fort Lauderdale's attractions. The annual International Boat Show brings over 125,000 people to the city each year.

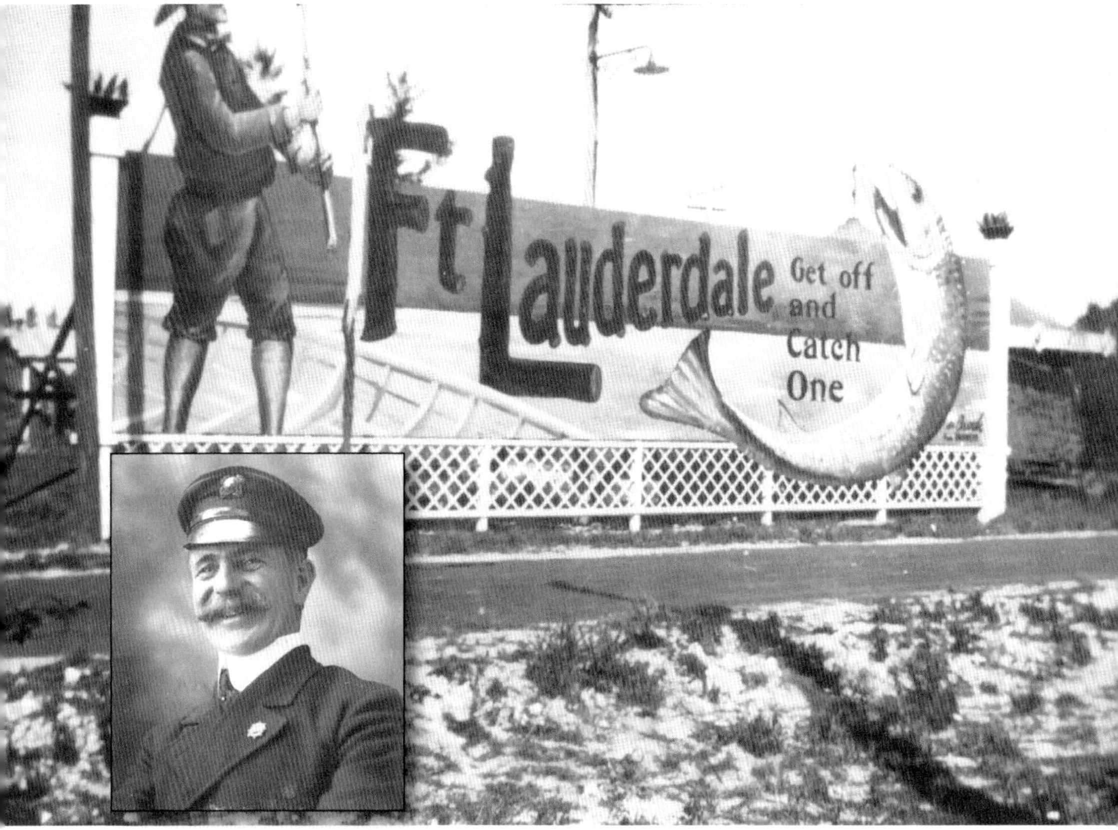

Commodore A.H. Brook, Pioneer Publicist

Born in England, A.H. Brook came to New York in 1869 at age three. He became a signboard advertisement painter for the O.J. Gude Company and rose to the position of general manager. Brook eventually opened his own advertising company, later selling it to the Cusack Advertising Agency. In 1919, he moved to Fort Lauderdale. Once there, Brook began the first real advertising campaign to promote Fort Lauderdale's beach, fishing, and tropical environment. At the railroad station, he painted a large billboard with a fish hooked by a fisherman and the phrase "Get off and catch one." Brook procured signboard advertising for Fort Lauderdale in Miami, Detroit, and New York and coined the term "Venice of America." In 1920, he purchased the Wyldwood Tropical Nursery that housed a large banyan dubbed the "Two Million Dollar Tree." Brook was the first Commodore of the Lauderdale Yacht Club and, in 1921, "rescued" President-elect Harding when his yacht was blocked at the Las Olas Bridge. Brook invited Harding to visit the town and play a round of golf. Commodore Brook was also an organizing member of the Fort Lauderdale Rotary, chairman of the Florida Inland Navigation District (FIND), started South Florida's first big game fishing contest, headed the committee to build the municipal pool, and helped to develop the Annual Collegiate Aquatic Forum. In 1953, the Seventeenth Street Causeway was renamed in his honor.

James B. Vreeland Jr. (left), Sportfishing Boat Captain

Born in 1899 in New York, James Vreeland Jr. came to Fort Lauderdale in 1906 when his father, James Sr., was appointed the seventh keeper of the House of Refuge No. 4. In his early days, Vreeland would go fishing in the morning and then sell the fish from the handlebars of his bicycle on his way to school. He took out his first fishing charter in 1913. During the teens and early 1920s, Vreeland would transport movie stars from location to location along the New River. In the early 1930s, he took out a group of Italian gentlemen to go shark fishing. These men, led by Jack "Machine Gun" McGurn, preferred to "fish" with .45 pistols. Captain Vreeland was a game-fishing boat captain all of his life and would regale his guests with stories and the history of Fort Lauderdale. In addition to his fishing boats, Vreeland also operated glass-bottom sightseeing boats.

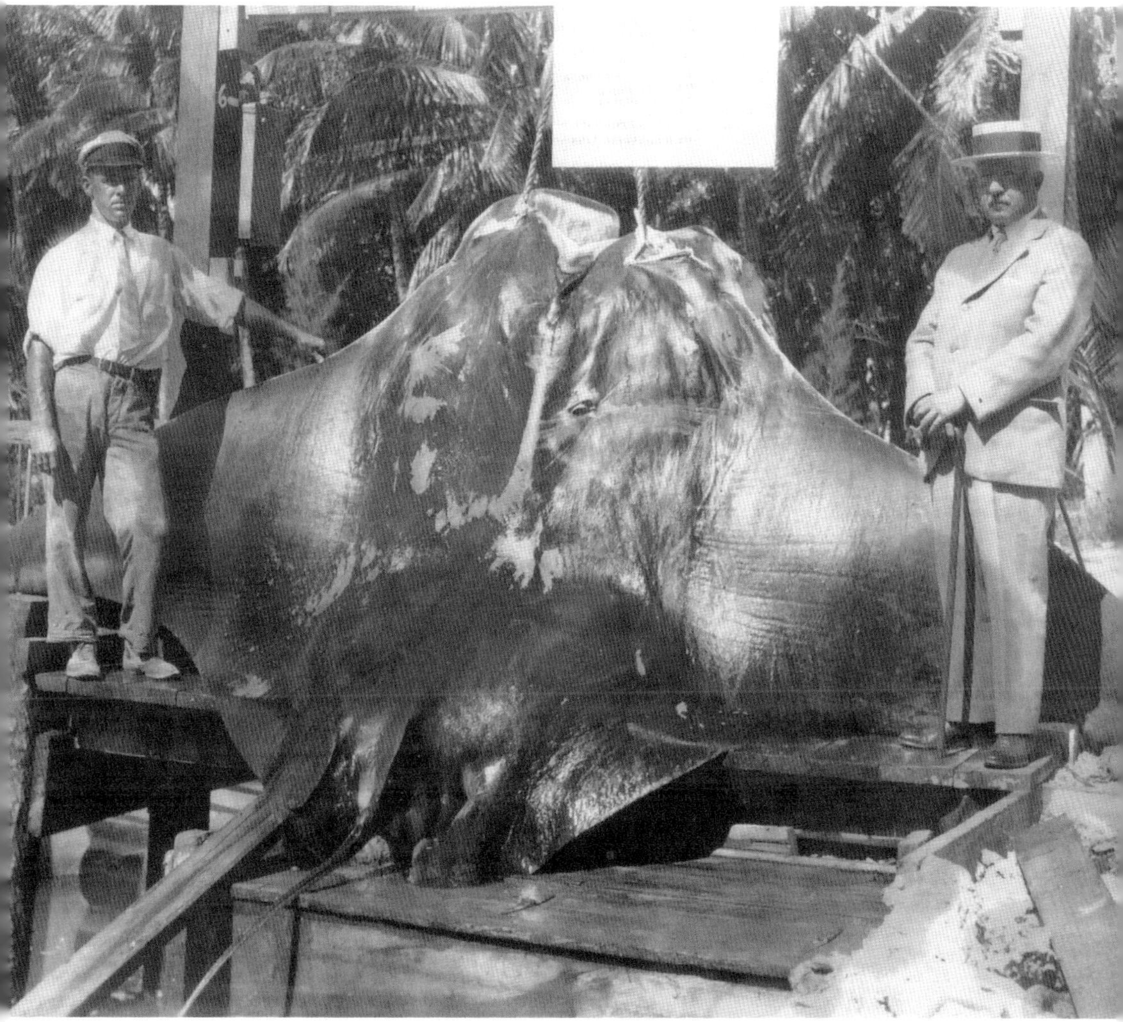

Roy Merritt, Charter Boat Captain

Roy Merritt came to Florida in 1924 from Norfolk, Virginia, where he had worked in the Navy Yard. The family arrived in Fort Lauderdale in 1926, shortly before the hurricane. Merritt bought a big, fat, squat boat, and someone suggested that he get some fishing tackle and take out fishing parties. He charged $25 a day. Merritt gained a reputation for his prodigious catches. In 1947, he bought land in Pompano Beach and built a boatyard. Merritt's Boat & Engine Works is still a family-owned business.

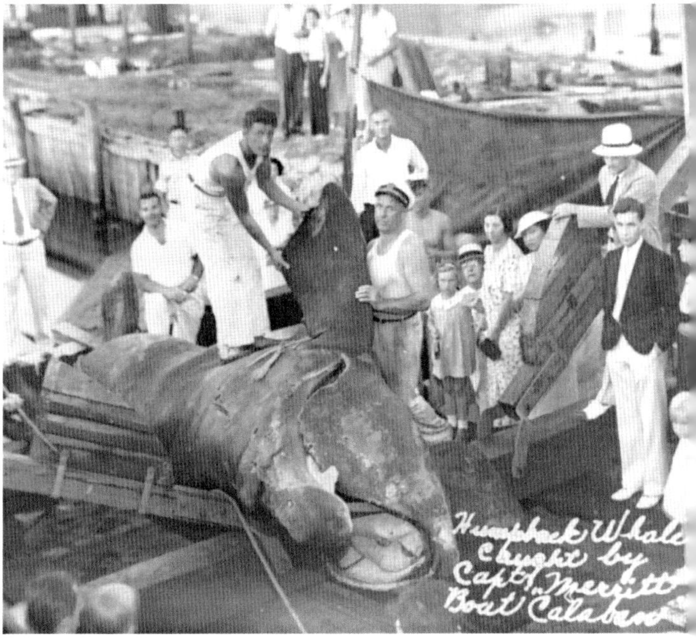

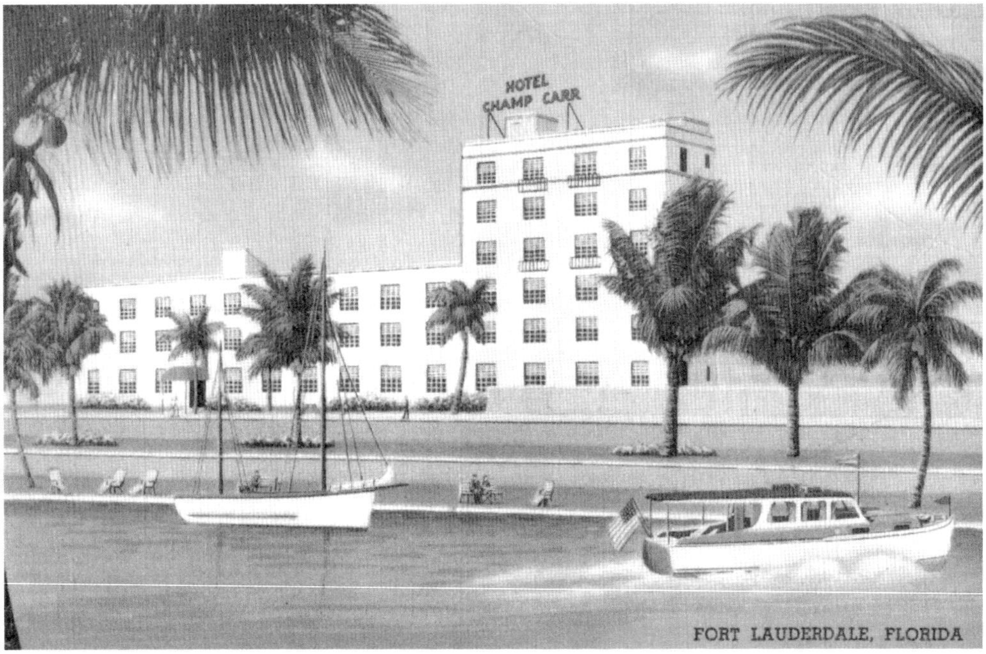

Champ Carr, Fishing Guide and Hotel Manager

Champ Carr served as a fishing boat mate on the *Caliban*. In the 1930s, two wealthy Chicago brothers, Preston and John Wells, would come to town to fish. They met Carr on a charter, and the three men became fast friends. In 1936, the Wells brothers opened a hotel on Las Olas Boulevard, made Carr the general manager, and named it for him. In 1947, Carr stepped down as manager, and the Hotel Champ Carr was renamed the Riverside Hotel, which is still open today.

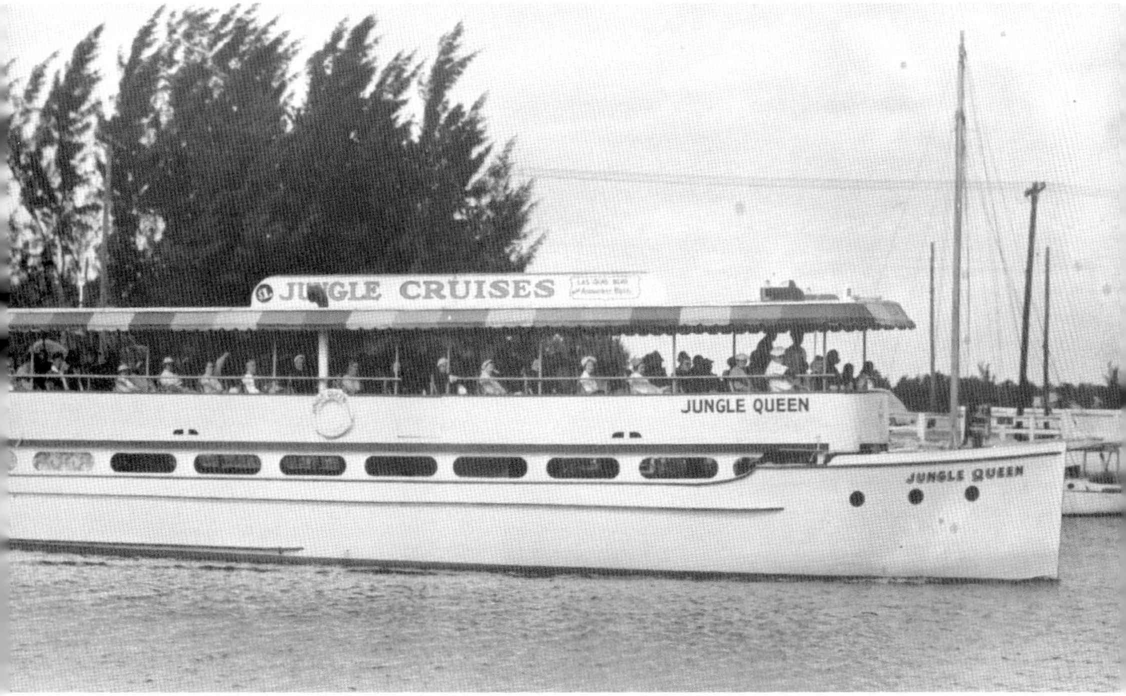

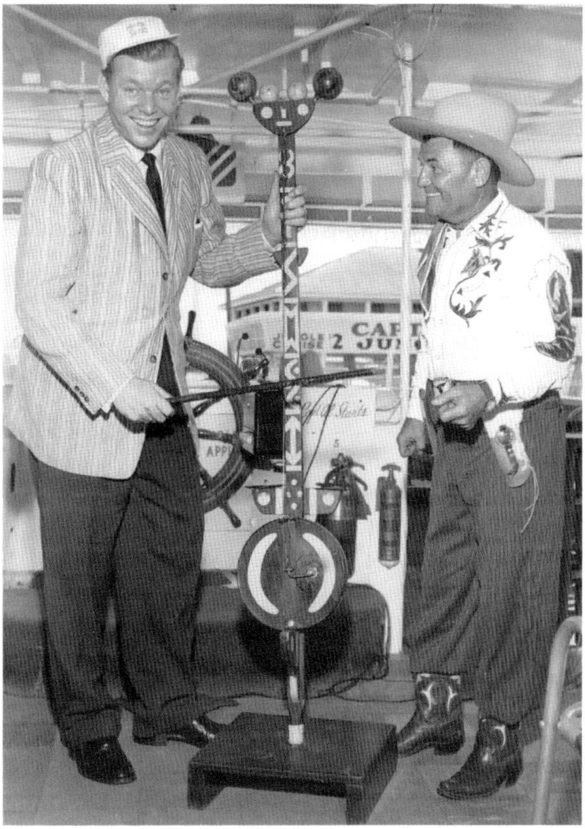

Capt. Al Starts (right), Jungle Queen River Cruises

Al Starts started his career in Akron, Ohio, where he had a shop repairing airplanes. From 1927 to 1929, he operated an 11-plane air circus throughout the Midwest. In 1934, he honeymooned in Fort Lauderdale and never left. The following year, Captain Starts began operation of the *Jungle Queen*, a sightseeing boat that plied the waters of the New River. Over time, he added dinner and a show at a replica Seminole village. In 1953, Starts added a paddle wheel, the *New River Queen*, to his fleet. Starts also invented over 100 patented engines and modifications and was creator of the Pogo Banjo Bongo (pictured at right). In 1958, he sold the *Jungle Queen* to Earl Farber, whose family still operates it today. From 1958 to 1964, Starts built and sold three-fourths of the replicas of the 1901 Rollsmobile. In the 1960s, he got back into the cruise business with the *Southern Belle*. Starts operated that until 1971.

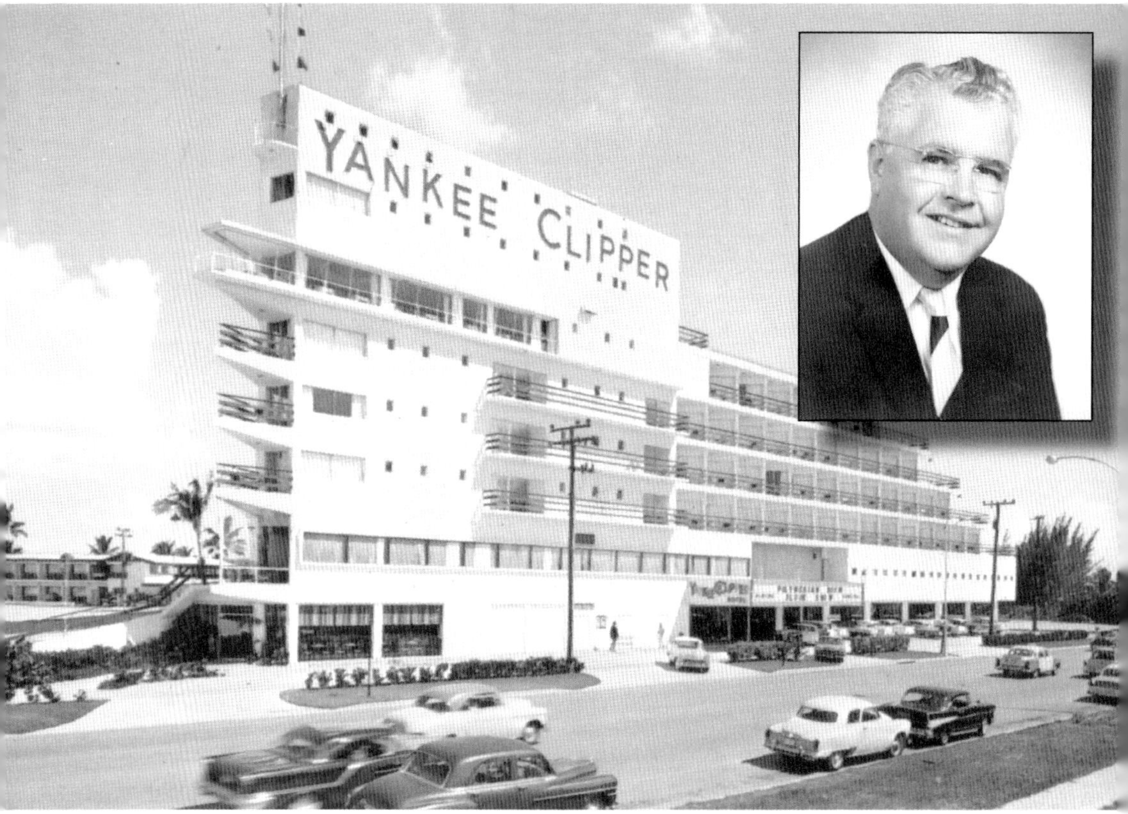

George W. "Bob" Gill Jr., Father of Broward County Hospitality

Following World War II, Chicago-born US Navy veteran George Gill Jr. moved to Fort Lauderdale to get into the year-round construction industry. He and his father founded Gill Construction Company and began building houses, which they sold to returning G.I.s. By 1950, it was estimated that the company was annually building 75 percent of the homes in the city. They built approximately 3,000 houses. In 1948, Gill decided to go into the hotel business, and on New Year's Eve 1949, he opened the 50-room Escape. It was the first hotel on the beach to offer a swimming pool and to stay open year-round. Gill developed three additional properties on the beach: the Jolly Roger (1952), the Yankee Clipper (1956), and the Yankee Trader (1964). The Jolly Roger was the first to offer in-room air-conditioning. The Yankee Clipper was the first to offer a floor show venue. Gill is considered a marketing genius. He would bring northern travel agents to Fort Lauderdale and introduce the foreign market to the city. He was instrumental in bringing the New York Yankees spring training camp to town in the 1960s. Gill helped to promote college Spring Break, and when it was "banned" after 1985, he facilitated the change to a family-friendly resort destination. Gill was a long-standing member of the Broward County Tourist Development Council and also served on the Florida Commission on Tourism. (Inset, courtesy of the Fort Lauderdale Historical Society, Gene Hyde Collection.)

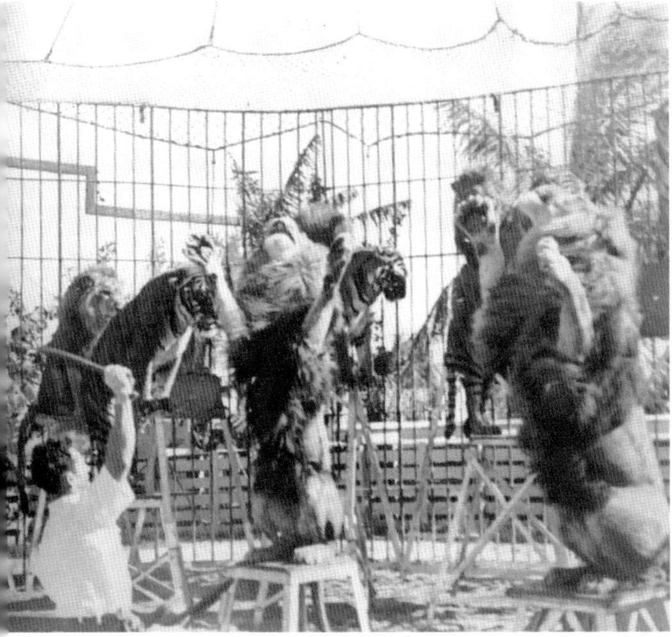

Clyde Beatty, Lion Tamer and Zoo Owner

In 1927, Clyde Beatty was billed as "America's Youngest and Most Fearless Wild Animal Trainer." Armed with a whip, chair, and pistol, he became a celebrated man-eating jungle cat tamer. In 1939, he bought out the McKillop-Hutton Lion Farm on Northeast Tenth Street and turned it into a winter home for his circus and a tourist attraction. Clyde Beatty's Jungle Zoo was open from December 1939 until 1945. Neighbor complaints of lion roars and escaped monkeys along with encroaching city development closed down the site.

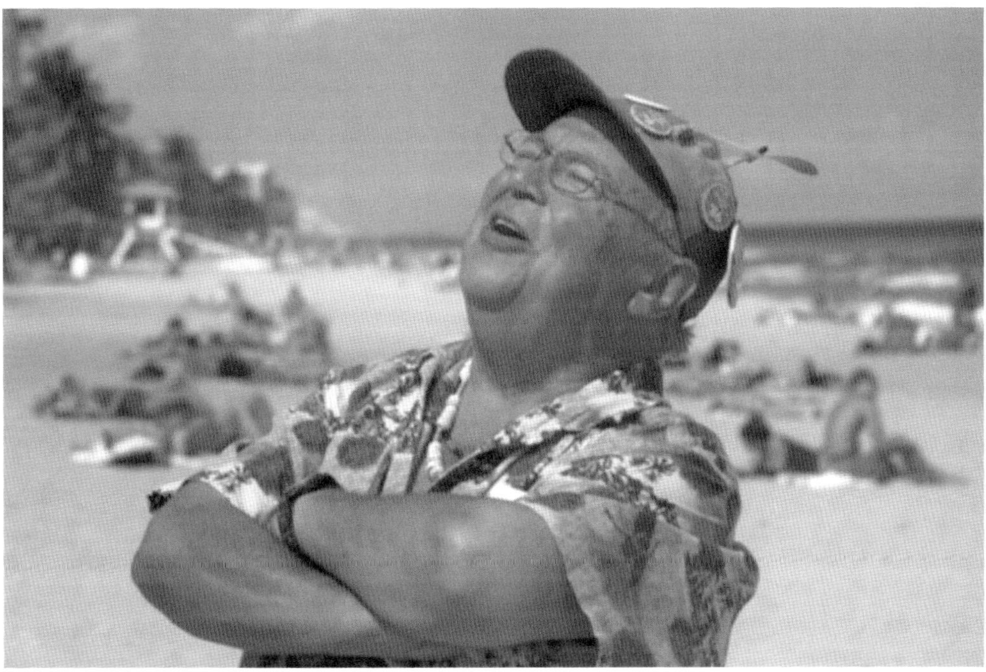

Robert "Crazy Gregg" Newell, Father of Spring Break

The "Father of Spring Break," Robert Newell, discovered Fort Lauderdale in 1953 as a visiting Purdue University undergraduate. He moved to the town in 1957 and began working in the bar business. Newell earned the nickname "Crazy Gregg" after a cheap beer promotion at the Elbo Room. In 1970, he opened the Button on the corner of A1A and Las Olas Boulevard, luring crowds with wild promotions and wet T-shirt, beer-chugging, and banana-eating contests. Newell's efforts helped build Fort Lauderdale into the Spring Break Capital of the World. (Courtesy of *Sun-Sentinel.*)

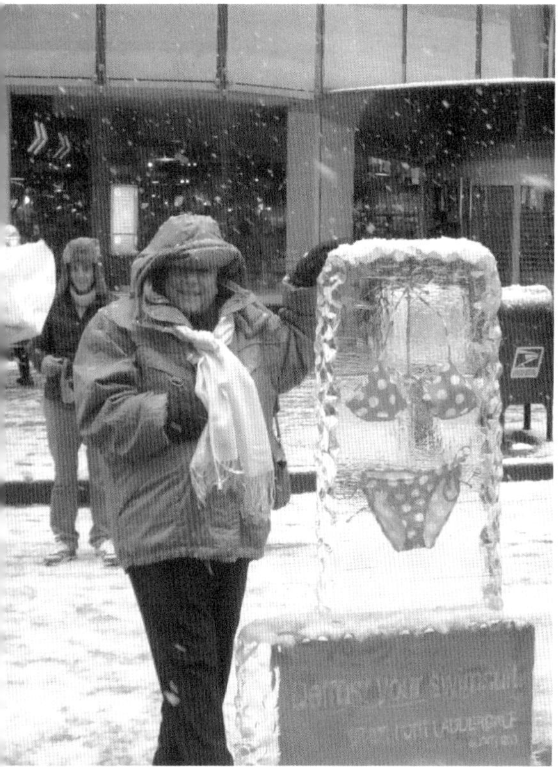

Nicki Grossman, Greater Fort Lauderdale Convention and Visitors Bureau CEO
Nicki Grossman was named president of the Greater Fort Lauderdale Convention and Visitors Bureau (GFLCVB) in 1995. She is responsible for the marketing and promotion of Broward County's convention and tourism efforts. In 2014, these efforts accounted for 14.3 million visitors and $11.4 billion into the local economy. Grossman serves on the Florida Commission on Tourism, and in 2007, she was inducted into the VISIT FLORIDA Tourism Hall of Fame. She has also been named one of the 100 Most Powerful Women in Tourism by Travel Agent. (Courtesy of the Greater Fort Lauderdale Convention and Visitors Bureau.)

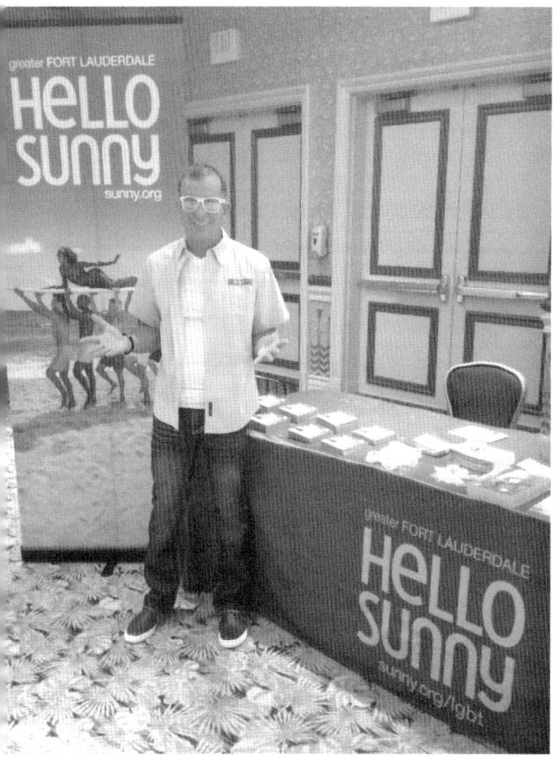

Richard Gray, LGBT Hospitality Marketer
Richard Gray moved to Fort Lauderdale in 1991 and operated the Royal Palms hotel. He set a new standard for gay accommodations, and the hotel became the first gay guest house to achieve a five-star rating. In 1996, Gray approached the Greater Fort Lauderdale Convention and Visitors Bureau (GFLCVB) about promoting Fort Lauderdale as a LGBT vacation destination. The campaign started with $35,000, and by 2014, 1.2 million LGBT visitors were spending $1.4 billion annually. In 2008, Gray sold The Royal Palms, and in 2011, the GFLCVB appointed him the managing director of LGBT marketing. (Courtesy of the Greater Fort Lauderdale Convention & Visitors Bureau.)

CHAPTER FIVE

Government Officials

The first government official in the New River/Fort Lauderdale area was William Cooley, who was appointed justice of the peace in 1831. He had good relations with the Seminole Indians until two white men were acquitted of killing a Seminole chief. They blamed Cooley and attacked his family in retribution. John "Pig" Brown was elected to the state legislature in 1876, becoming the area's first representative. William "Cap" Valentine was appointed justice of the peace in the 1890s.

In 1911, when the city of Fort Lauderdale was incorporated, there were 143 residents. The influx of 3,000 people from the Bolles Land Auction meant that the residents needed to organize the infrastructure and governance of the quickly expanding town. The first city council of William Marshall (mayor), William Kyle, William Berryhill, Ed King, Tom Bryan, and Willie Covington was elected. Frank Bryan and Kossie Goodbread were hired as city clerk and city marshal, respectively. One of the first orders of business was addressing sanitation. The devastating downtown fire of 1912 instigated the emphasis on purchasing fire equipment and forming a volunteer fire department.

A building to hold the city hall, police station, and fire station was constructed in 1914. A new city hall, designed by John Peterman, was opened in 1926. Two subsequent city halls (1948 and 1969) have been built. By 1920, the population had increased by 1,444 percent to 2,065. Shortly before the destructive 1926 hurricane, the population was over 15,000. In 1917, the city hired the first paid fire chief for $25 per month. G.D. TenBrook was appointed marshal in 1920 and was the first to have the title of police chief.

Fort Lauderdale currently has a commission-manager form of government. From 1912 to 1925, there was a city council, with the mayor appointed from the council. In 1925, it was changed to a city commission with an appointed mayor. Since 1982, the mayor has been an elected position, and since 1988, the commissioners are elected by district rather than citywide. Governmental firsts include Genevieve Pynchon elected as the first woman commissioner in 1937, Andrew DeGraffenreidt elected as the first black commissioner in 1973, Virginia Young appointed the first woman mayor in 1973, and Dean Trantalis elected as the first gay commissioner in 2003.

As the county seat of Broward County, Fort Lauderdale also elects commissioners to the county commission. It also serves as the home of the 17th Judicial Circuit Court of Florida and the United States District Court–Southern District of Florida.

On the state and federal levels, Fort Lauderdale is represented by one state senate district, two state representative districts, and two congressional representative districts. In 1944, Dwight Rogers Sr. was the first resident of Fort Lauderdale elected to the US Congress.

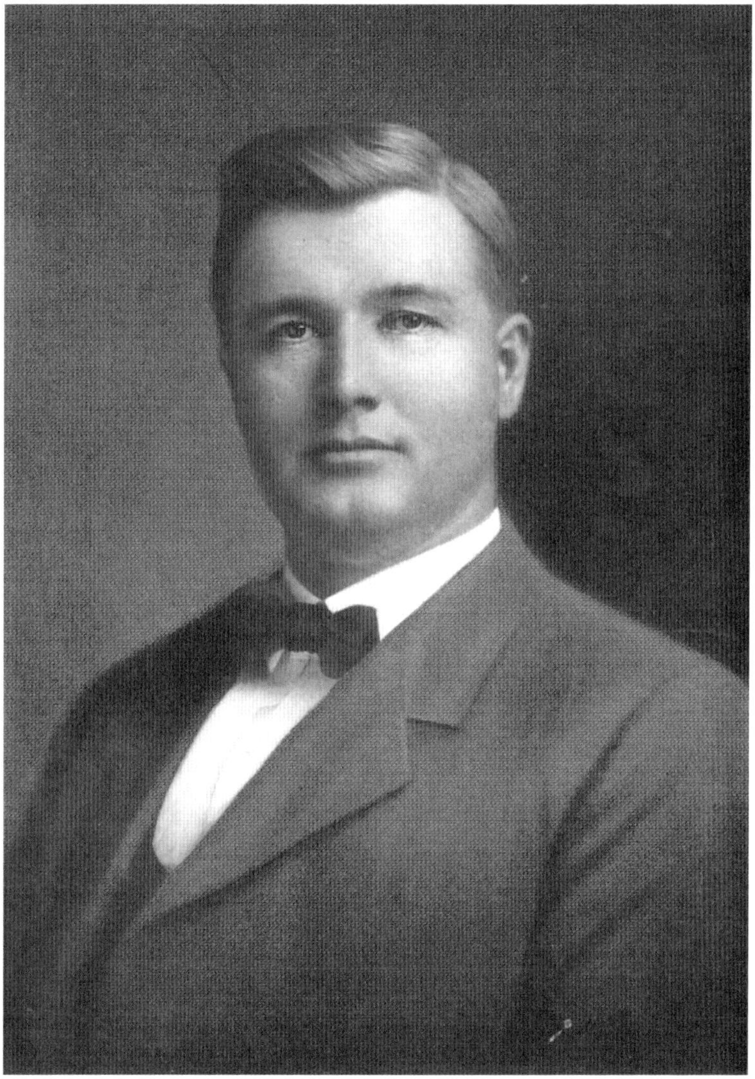

William H. Marshall, First Mayor
A native of Georgia and a Spanish-American War veteran who had fought in Cuba, William Marshall visited an uncle and brother at New River in 1898 on his way back to Georgia. He returned in 1899, bought some land, and began growing vegetables. Marshall became one of the largest vegetable farmers in the area and established an extensive brokerage and shipping firm, the Marshall Produce Company. He pioneered the mail-order business of selling crops directly to retailers. Marshall was a leading proponent for a booming produce trade, land drainage, port facilities, and tariffs. In 1911, he aided in the incorporation of Fort Lauderdale and was appointed the first mayor. He won reelection in 1912. When Broward County was formed in 1915, Marshall was elected the first representative to the legislature and served two terms. He chaired the committee on canals and drainage. In 1925, Marshall began construction on the Wil-Mar Hotel but was unable to complete it due to the economic depression that occurred following the 1926 hurricane. It stood as a girder skeleton for many years. Marshall considered one of his greatest successes the passage of the Tariff Act of 1930 to protect Florida growers from cheaper Cuban and Mexican vegetables. In 1964, the Southwest Fourth/Seventh Avenue Bridge across the New River was dedicated in his memory.

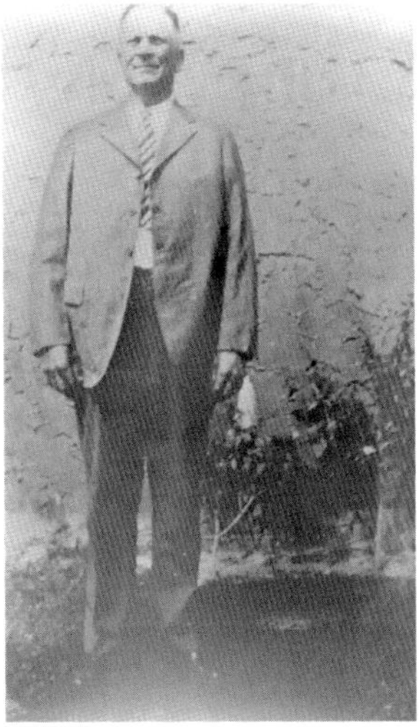

Kossie A. Goodbread, First Town Marshal

Kossie Goodbread arrived in 1908 and was initially a tomato farmer but was appointed a Dade County deputy sheriff in 1909. When the town incorporated in 1911, he was appointed the city marshal. Goodbread was paid $40 a month plus $1 per arrest. He was also the tax assessor and tax collector. As the only town employee, Goodbread was also responsible for trash and privy cleaning. He usually had one prisoner who would go around with a wagon and the "sanitary" mule. Goodbread served until 1913 before going into road construction.

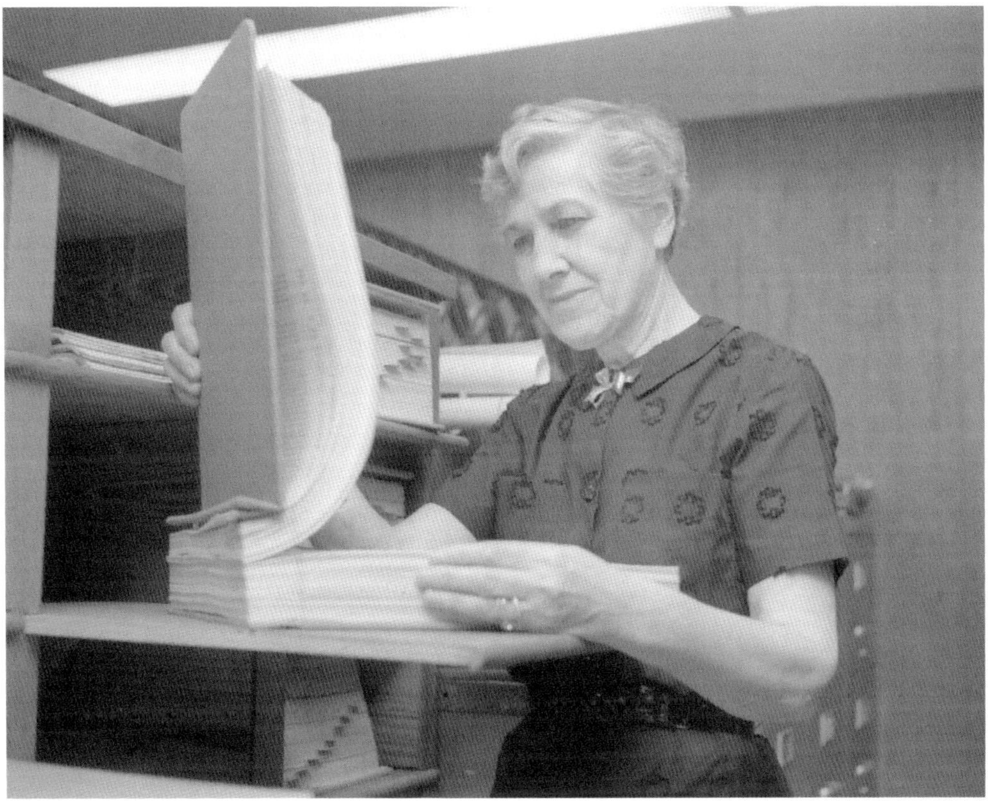

Florence Hardy, Longtime City Clerk

Florence and William Hardy arrived in 1924 and ran a drugstore. In 1928, Florence became the secretary to the city manager. She was appointed auditor and clerk of the city in 1937 and became the assistant city manager in 1941. From 1946 to 1952, she was the acting secretary of the Fort Lauderdale Civil Service Board, and in January 1954, she was appointed acting city manager—the first woman to hold the position. After she retired in 1963, Florence became the director of the Fort Lauderdale Historical Society. (Courtesy of the Fort Lauderdale Historical Society, Gene Hyde Collection.)

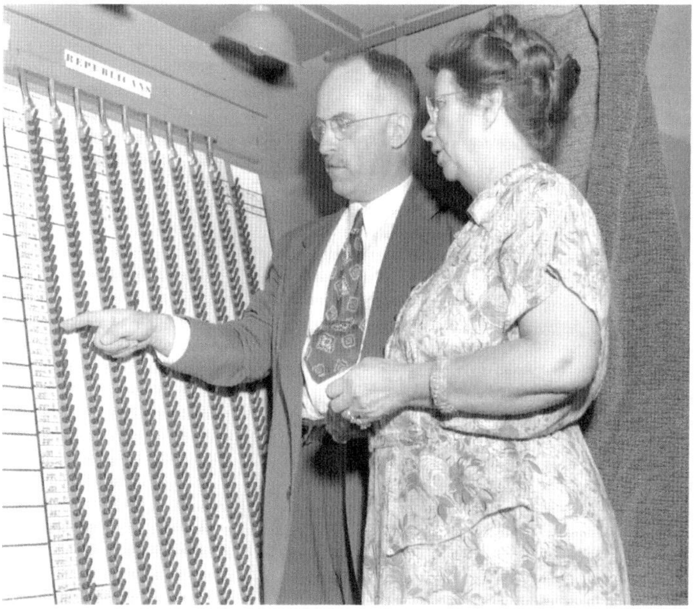

Easter Lily Gates, First Woman Elected as a Broward County Official

Easter Lily Gates was born on Easter Sunday in 1889 and was a milliner and designer of hats before she married. In 1918, she moved to Fort Lauderdale, where she and her husband operated an orange grove and turkey farm. They sold breeding stock and eggs all over the southern United States and Cuba. Her husband passed in 1926, and to support her two sons, Gates took a job as a school bus driver—the first woman to do so in Fort Lauderdale. In 1928, she ran for Broward County supervisor of registration and became the first woman elected as a Broward County official. Gates held the position until she retired in 1968. She was instrumental in creating permanent registration records, acquiring voting machines, and registering African Americans and Indians. In 1956, Gates became the first woman president of the Florida State Association of Supervisors of Registration. (Below, courtesy of the Fort Lauderdale Historical Society, Gene Hyde Collection.)

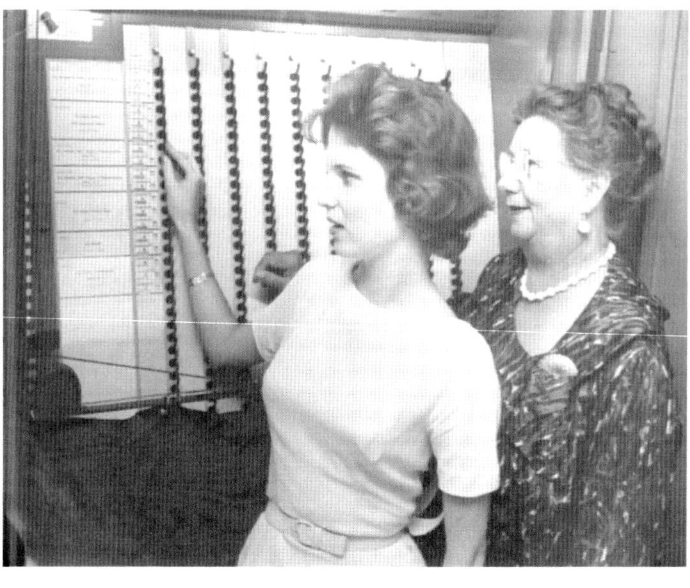

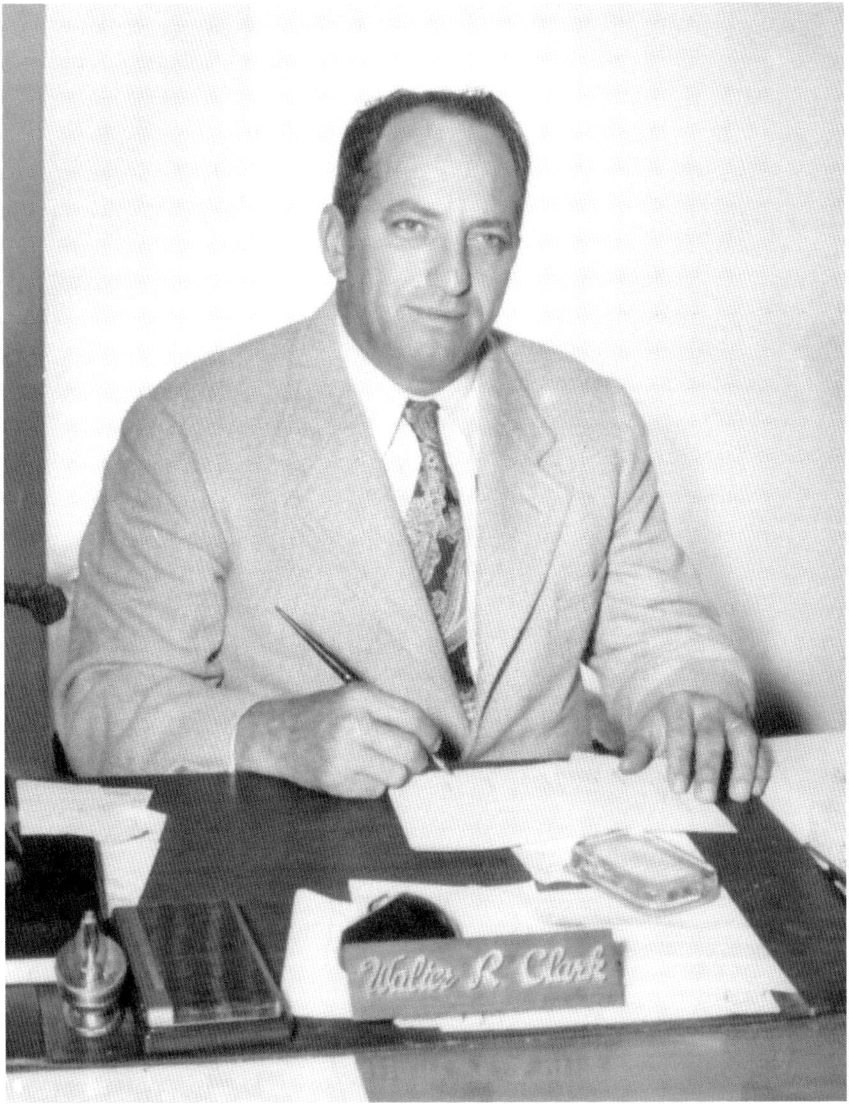

Walter R. Clark, "Corrupt" Broward County Sheriff
The longest tenured Broward County sheriff, Walter Clark, was elected to the position in 1932. He was reelected four times, serving until 1950. The Clark family came to Fort Lauderdale in 1902 and made a living as farmers. Clark operated a small butcher shop and grocery store before running for sheriff. As sheriff, he became one of the county's most popular and powerful Depression-era politicians. He was able to weave together a powerful alliance of political and business interests. During his tenure, Sheriff Clark turned a blind eye to illegal gambling in the county. He had an "understanding" with the Mob-run operations and was even a part-owner of Broward Novelty Company, a slot machine and bolita business. He was suspended by Governor Holland in 1942 for not enforcing the gambling laws but was reinstated (with back pay) by the Florida Senate in 1943. Called before Senator Kefauver's crime committee in 1950, Sheriff Clark responded to his lack of gambling enforcement by saying, "I let them have what they want for the tourists down here." Governor Warren suspended Clark, and he was indicted on gambling and tax evasion charges. He won acquittal on all charges. Clark passed away in 1951, and 500 people attended his funeral.

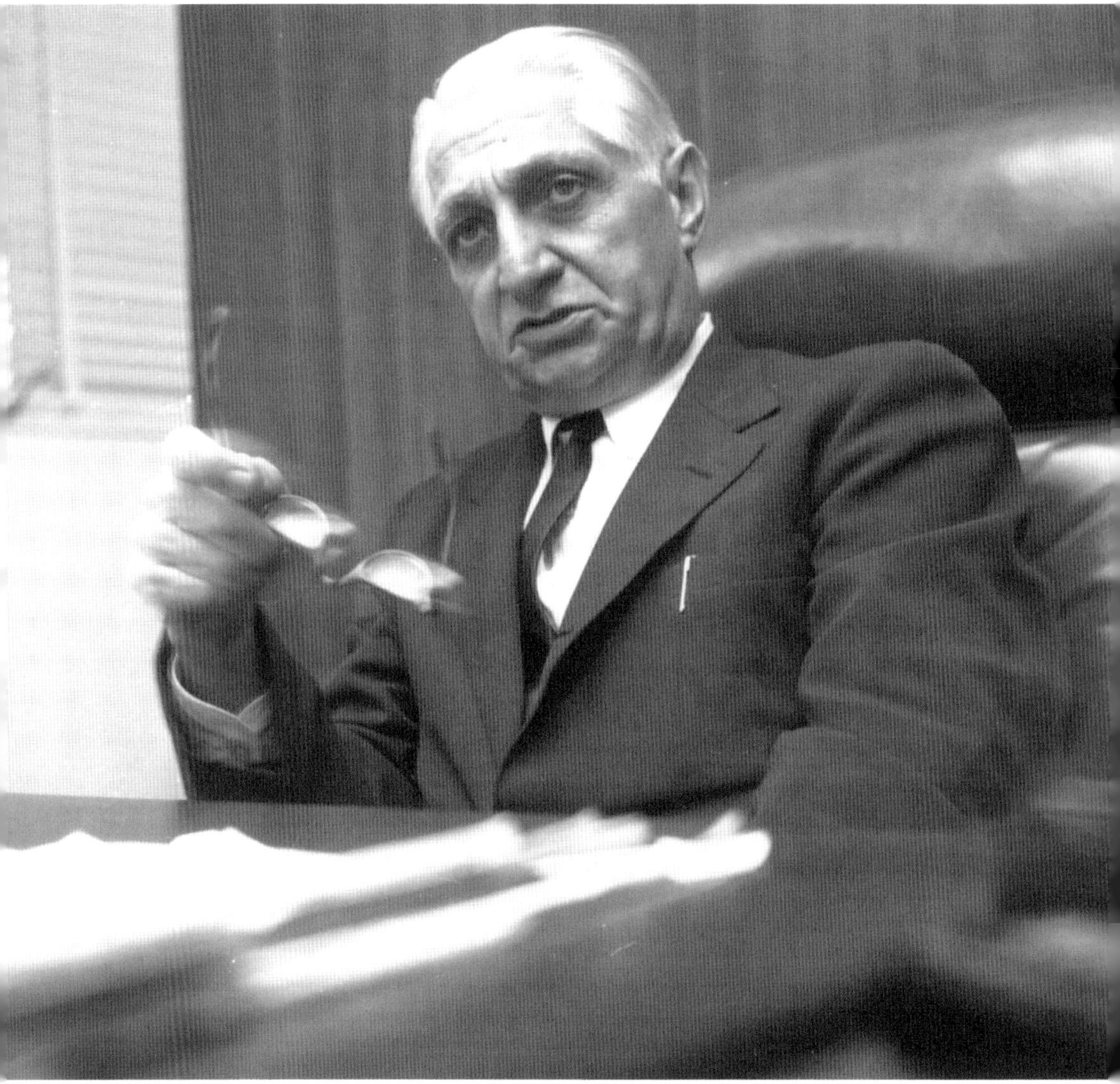

Judge Boyd H. Anderson Sr., "Public Servant No. 1"

In 1917, Judge Boyd Anderson's family moved to a small farm on the outskirts of Fort Lauderdale. He attended Fort Lauderdale High School, was active in athletics, and graduated in 1920. Boyd became a clerk for county judge Fred Shippey in 1928. He "read law" during the evenings and on the weekends with local lawyers. In 1933, Judge Shippey became seriously ill, and Gov. David Sholtz appointed Boyd as judge. After his appointment, Boyd took law classes at the University of Miami. He passed the Florida Bar in 1949. Judge Anderson won nine consecutive elections, running unopposed except in 1936. He championed the cause of simplified government with close ties to the people and was also concerned with the care of the elderly, especially those with mental illnesses. As the county grew, Judge Anderson led the efforts to reorganize the court system into the probate, juvenile, criminal, and civil divisions. He also served as the chief air raid warden for Broward County during World War II, chairman of the Boy Scouts South Florida Council, and deacon at the First Presbyterian Church. Judge Anderson served as a judge for 35 years until his passing in 1968. The high school in Lauderdale Lakes was named in his honor in 1972. (Courtesy of the Fort Lauderdale Historical Society, Gene Hyde Collection.)

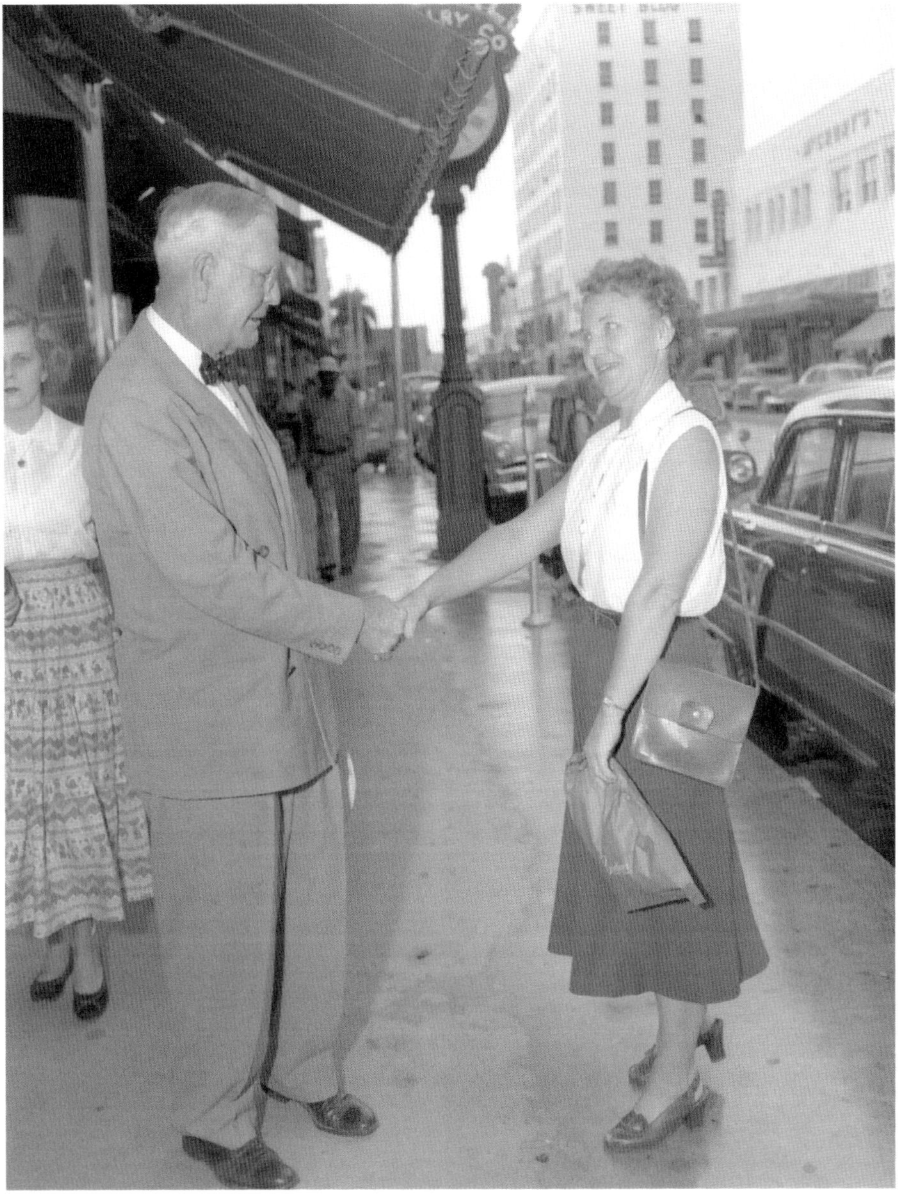

Dwight L. Rogers Sr., US House of Representatives

A University of Georgia and Mercer University graduate, Dwight Rogers Sr. arrived in Fort Lauderdale in 1925 and opened a law firm with John Morris Sr. Today, Rogers, Morris & Ziegler is Broward County's oldest law firm. Rogers served in the Florida legislature from 1930 to 1938 and was Speaker pro tempore in 1933. During his time in Tallahassee, Rogers sponsored the Homestead Exemption Act. In 1944, he was elected as the Florida Sixth District US representative. Rogers was the first Fort Lauderdale resident to be elected to Congress. He was reelected five times. In 1947, Rogers helped the city acquire the former US Coast Guard base at the beach (today Bahia Mar) and also helped Broward County gain control of Naval Air Station Fort Lauderdale as a regional airport. Upon his death in 1954, his son Paul was elected to his seat. Rogers Junior High School is named in his honor. (Courtesy of the Fort Lauderdale Historical Society, Gene Hyde Collection.)

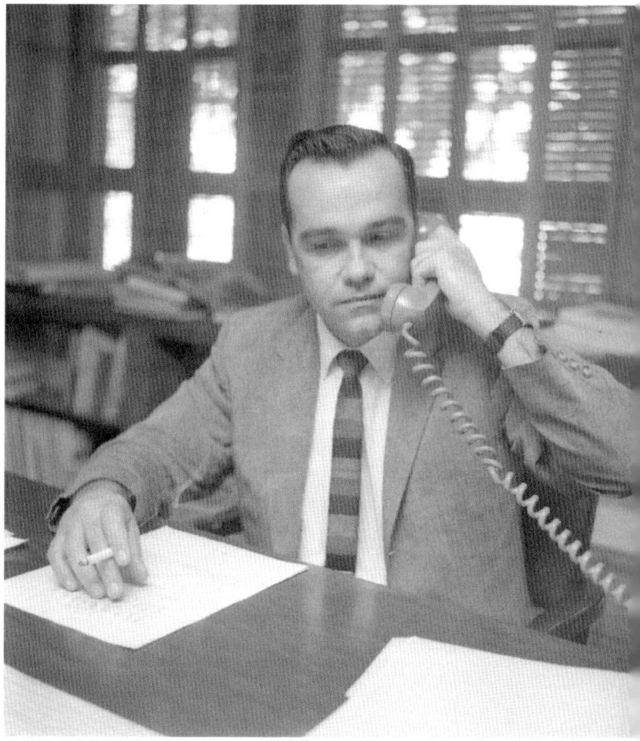

Robert H. Bubier, Longest Serving City Manager

The Bubiers arrived in 1941, and Robert dropped out of high school to join the Navy. After World War II, he worked for the *Fort Lauderdale News* and the *Hollywood Sun-Tattler* from 1953 to 1956 before working in city and federal personnel departments. Bubier was hired as an assistant city manager in 1962 and appointed acting city manager in December 1962. He remained the city manager for the next 12 and a half years, the longest tenure in city history. After his passing in 1974, the city dedicated a park in his honor. (Courtesy of the Fort Lauderdale Historical Society, Gene Hyde Collection.)

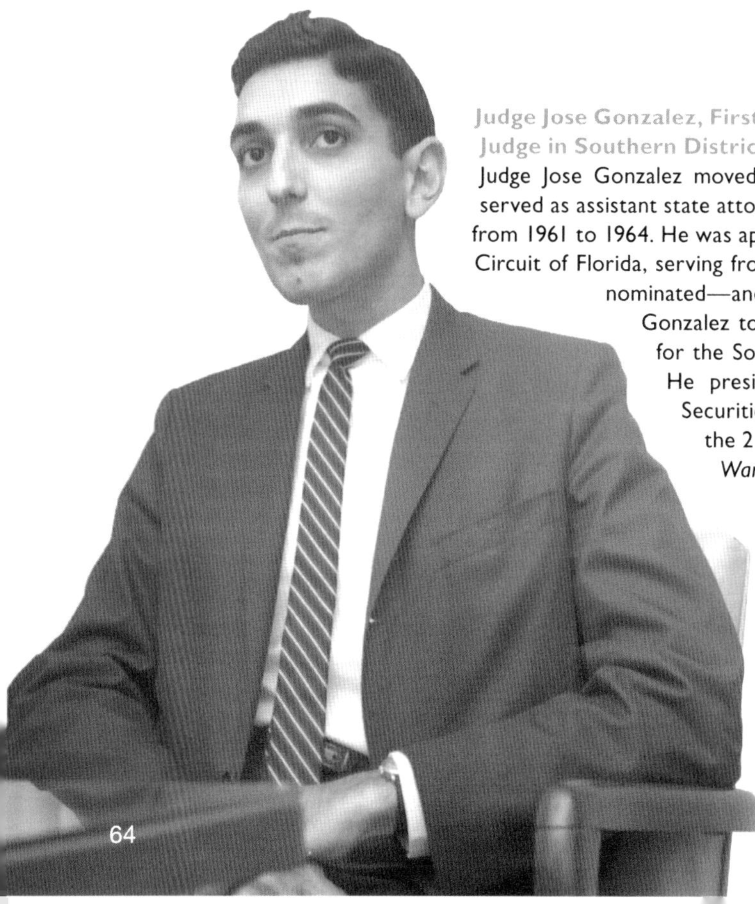

Judge Jose Gonzalez, First and Longest Serving Hispanic Judge in Southern District of Florida

Judge Jose Gonzalez moved to Fort Lauderdale in 1958 and served as assistant state attorney for the 15th Circuit of Florida from 1961 to 1964. He was appointed a circuit judge on the 17th Circuit of Florida, serving from 1964 to 1978. President Carter nominated—and the US Senate confirmed—Gonzalez to the United States District Court for the Southern District of Florida in 1978. He presided over the ESM Government Securities fraud case and also ruled that the 2 Live Crew album, *As Nasty As They Wanna Be*, was obscene. (Courtesy of the Fort Lauderdale Historical Society, Gene Hyde Collection.)

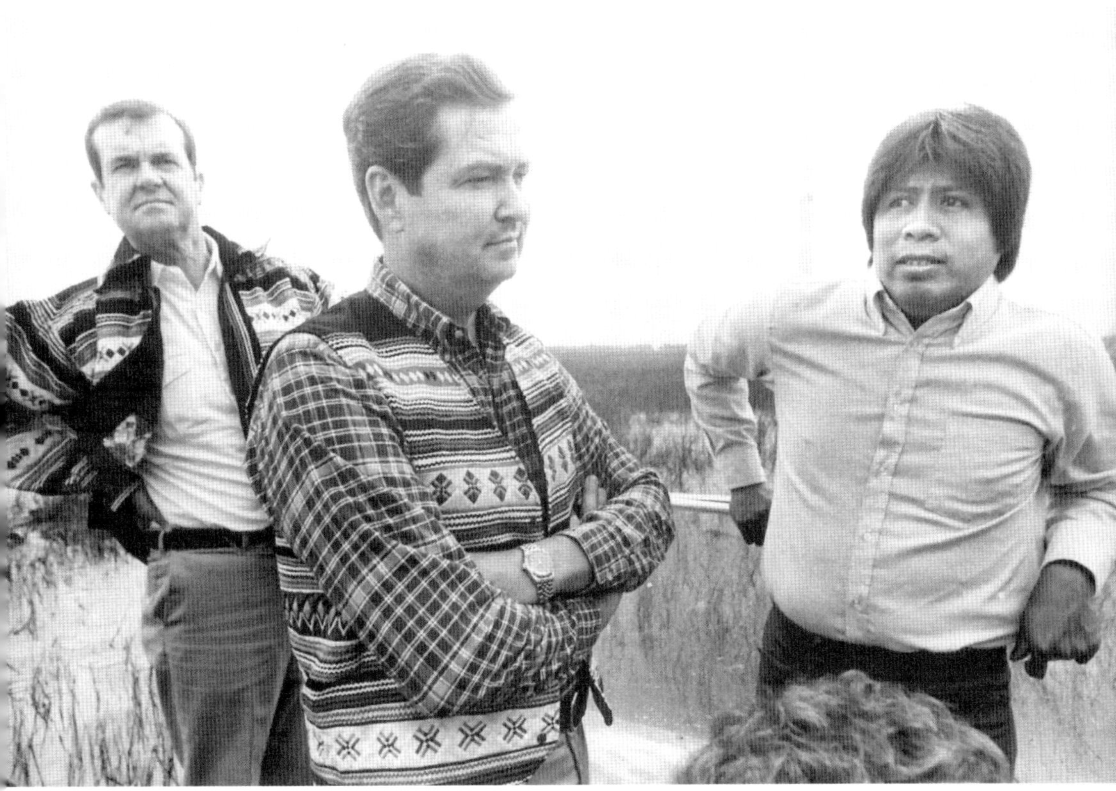

E. Clay Shaw Jr. (center), Mayor and US House of Representatives

Born in Miami, Clay Shaw Jr. graduated from Stetson University with a bachelor's degree in business and a law degree. He also received an MBA in accounting from the University of Alabama. In 1968, Shaw was hired as an assistant city attorney for Fort Lauderdale. He became the city's chief prosecutor and an associate municipal judge (1969–1971). Elected to the city commission in 1971, Shaw served as vice mayor (1973–1975) and mayor (1975–1981). While Shaw was mayor, President Ford named him Special US Ambassador to Papua New Guinea. In 1980, Shaw ran for the Florida 15th District and won the US House seat with 55 percent of the vote. He was reelected 12 times, three times unopposed and winning with an average of 60.67 percent. Shaw was narrowly defeated (48 percent) in 2006 and retired from politics. While he served in Congress, Shaw introduced the Missing Child Act of 1982 in response to the Adam Walsh killing, aggressively supported legislation to fight the War on Drugs, drafted the landmark welfare reform law in 1996, and pushed through legislation to restore the Everglades. He had a reputation for working cordially across party lines. In 2002, the Seventeenth Street Causeway Bridge was renamed for him. In 2008, Shaw was named a Great Floridian by the Florida Department of State, an honor extended to individuals who made major contributions to the progress and welfare of the state of Florida. (Courtesy of *Sun-Sentinel*.)

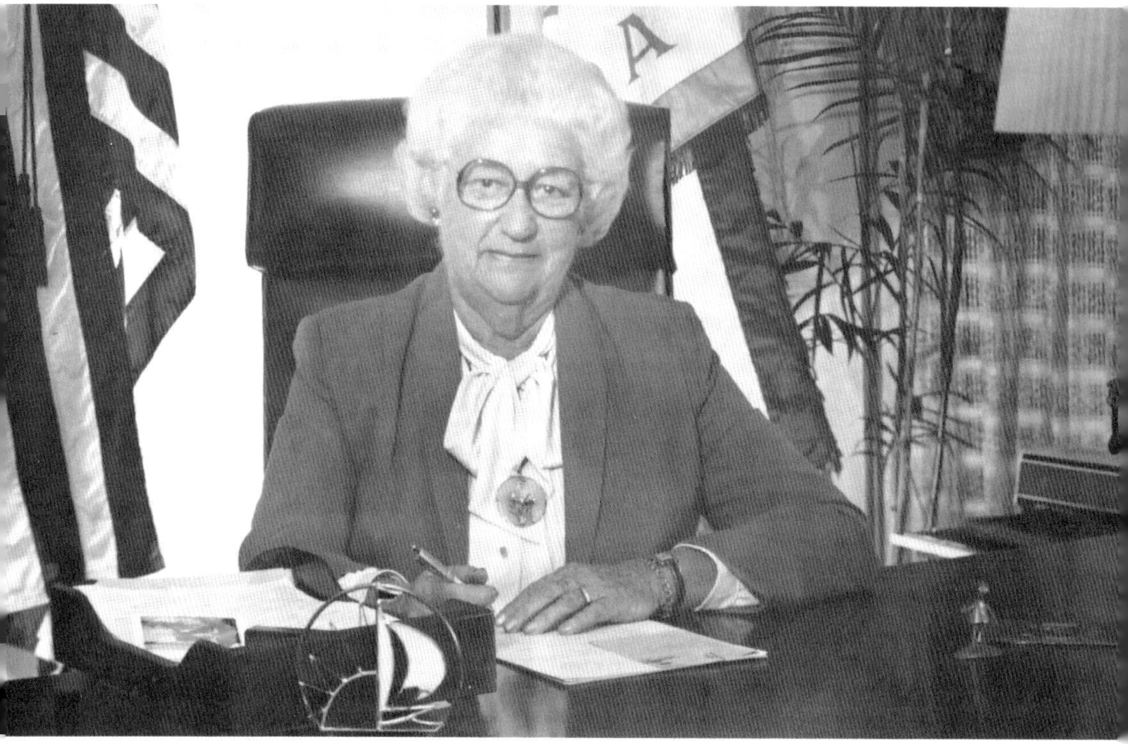

Virginia Shuman Young, First Woman Mayor

The daughter of the pioneer Fort Lauderdale families Shuman and TenBrook, Virginia Young attended Southside Elementary and Fort Lauderdale Central High School. Her first job was as the Fort Lauderdale correspondent for the *Miami Daily News*. In 1953, while a school bus driver, Young was elected to the Broward County Board of Public Instruction. She was instrumental in merging the board with the Broward County School Board in 1957 and served as the first woman chairman in 1961. Her husband, George, was in the construction business, and Virginia was a co-owner until 1977. Young was elected to the city commission in 1971 and was appointed as the first (and only) woman mayor in 1973. She continued to serve on the city commission until 1985, appointed mayor again in 1981. While on the city commission, Young recruited women to serve on city advisory board. In 1975, she wrote the history book *Mangrove Roots of Fort Lauderdale*. Young became the first woman director of the Fort Lauderdale Landmark Bank in 1974, was the first woman elected president of the Florida League of Cities in 1977, and was the first woman to serve on the Downtown Development Authority in 1986. She received the Distinguished Citizen Award in 1985 and was further honored with a city park and elementary school named after her.

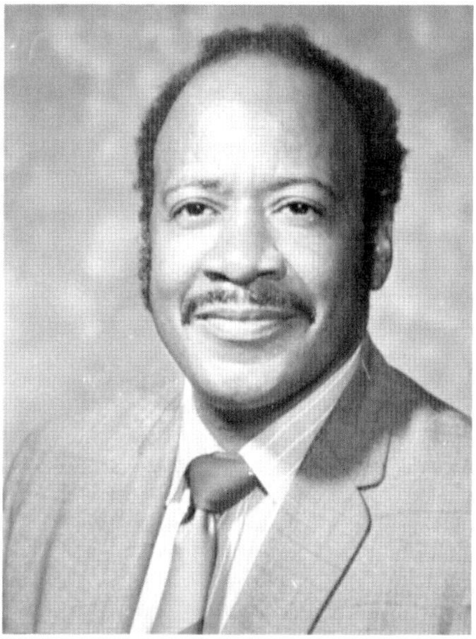

Andrew DeGraffenreidt II, First Black City Commissioner

In 1973, the same year that it got its first female mayor, Fort Lauderdale also got its first black commissioner, Andrew DeGraffenreidt. Although he was not the first black man to run for the city commission (that distinction belongs to Nathaniel Wilkerson Jr. in 1957), DeGraffenreidt was the first to win. Elected at a time when elections were citywide and not by district, DeGraffenreidt tackled the issues of crime reduction, increasing the number of minority police officers, and the redevelopment of depressed areas and the downtown area. DeGraffenreidt was reelected in 1975 and 1977.

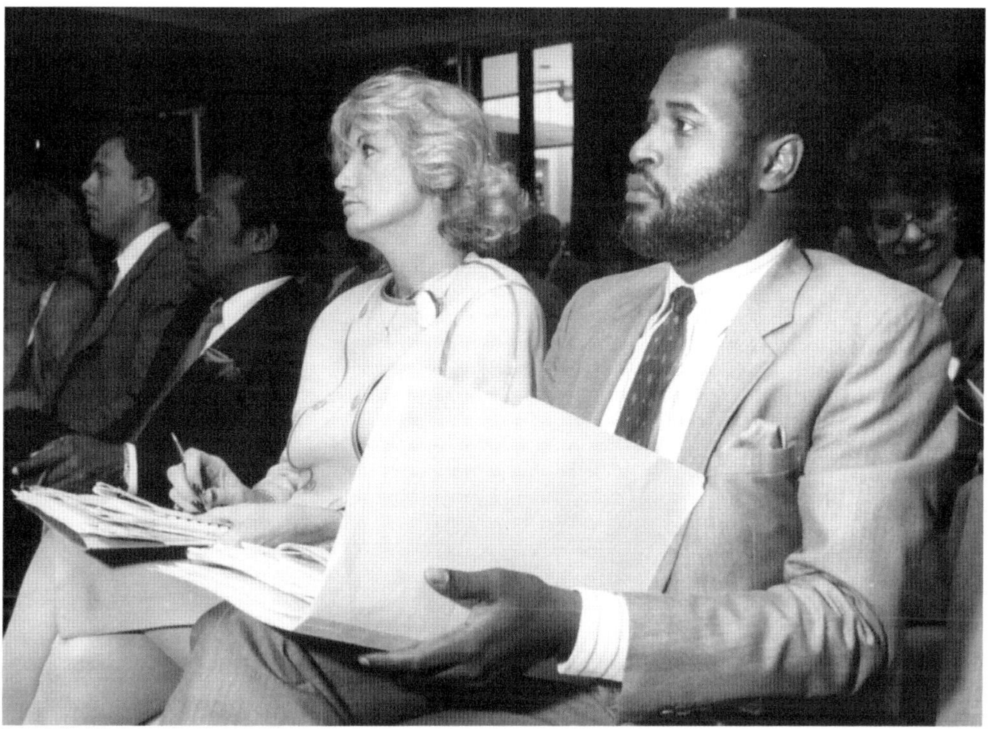

Carlton Moore, Longtime Black City Commissioner

Carlton Moore was the former president of the local branch of the NAACP and pushed for the creation of a citizen oversight board for police officers and the Fort Lauderdale Community Redevelopment Agency. Elected to the city commission in 1988, Moore represented the Third District (predominately black) for 20 years. He fought hard for the economic development of his historically impoverished district. He was also the first black vice mayor in 1989. Moore resigned his seat in 2008 in an attempt to be elected to the Broward County Commission. (Courtesy of *Sun-Sentinel*.)

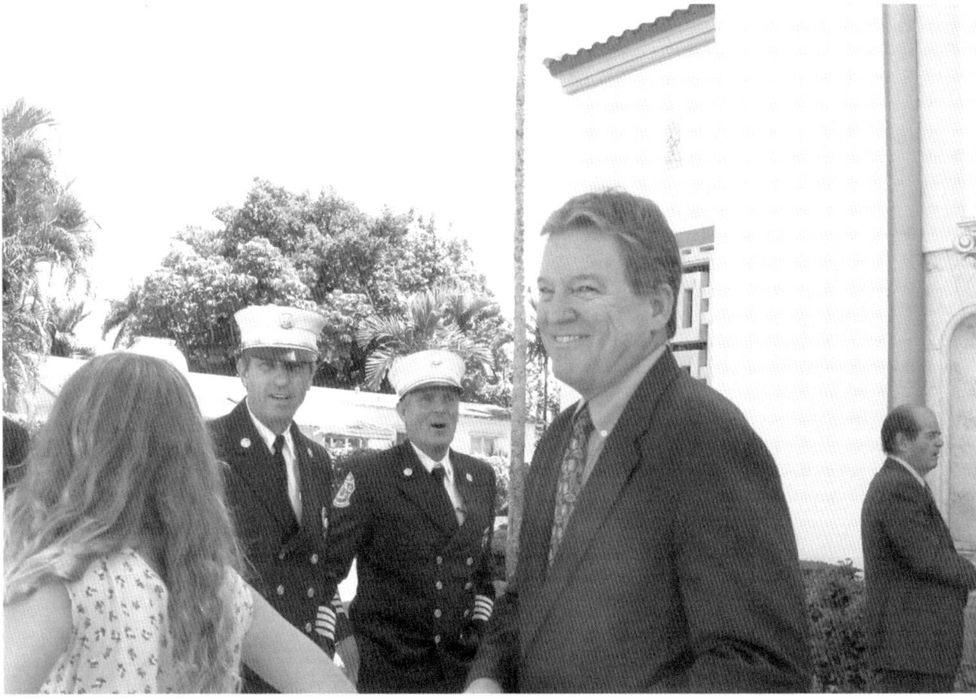

James T. Naugle, Longest Tenured Mayor

A Fort Lauderdale native, James Naugle was elected to the city commission in 1985. He was elected mayor in 1991 and was elected for six consecutive three-year terms. Naugle was a plain-speaking, shoot-from-the-hip, fiscal conservative who was a friend of the residential neighborhoods. Though not always politically correct, Naugle served the city with distinction. During his tenure as a mayor, the revitalization of the beach area and Las Olas Boulevard occurred, Riverwalk was created, the Museum of Discovery and Science was opened, and the Broward Center for the Performing Arts was introduced. (Courtesy of *Sun-Sentinel*.)

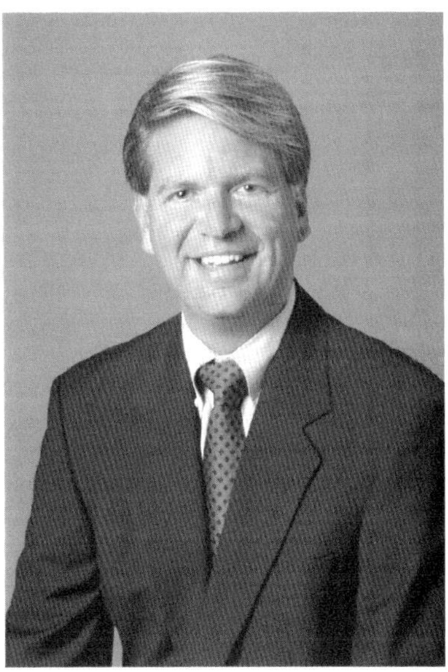

Ken Keechl, First Openly Gay Broward County Mayor

Ken Keechl's family moved to South Florida in the late 1970s. He received his Juris Doctor from Florida State University and settled in Fort Lauderdale, working as an attorney for Brinkley Morgan. He helped build up the firm's commercial litigation and land use litigation practices. Keechl served two terms as president of the Dolphin Democrats (the local LGBT Democratic group). In 2006, he was elected to the Broward County Commission. Keechl was appointed vice mayor of Broward County in 2008 and mayor in 2010. He lost reelection in 2010.

CHAPTER SIX

Arts and Culture

Although Fort Lauderdale had a long-standing reputation as a cultural wasteland, that myth is simply false. The Stranahans and the Kings hosted town dances at their homes, and the House of Refuge was the scene of holiday picnics and fish fries. Prior to the downtown fire of 1912, the Lyric Theatre was open for several years. The town abounded with musicians, and around 1920, Glenn Bates organized and was the bandleader of the first City of Fort Lauderdale band. Llewellyn Marshall, the wife of former mayor William Marshall, was a professionally trained opera singer who staged many performances.

1950 saw the opening of the War Memorial Auditorium, which allowed the symphony and the opera to find a permanent home. It also hosted wrestling and boxing events, graduations, and musical performances by Jerry Lee Lewis and Buddy Holly. Today, it is home to roller derby, MMA fights, and knife and gun shows. The Museum of Art was founded in 1958 in a small storefront. It has expanded to a world-class facility that has hosted exhibitions of Picasso, Kahlo, and Glackens along with the Tutankhamun and the Golden Age of the Pharaohs exhibit. Las Olas Boulevard is home to many art galleries and the Las Olas Art Festival.

In 1966, Louis Parker donated the Parker Playhouse to the city. Musical performances and plays continue to this day. ArtServe opened in 1989 and provides space for a dance studio, artist workspaces, exhibition space, and offices for artists and nonprofits. The Broward Center for the Performing Arts opened in 1991 and hosts musicals, plays, and music events. Other cultural organizations in town include Cinema Paradiso (host of the Fort Lauderdale International Film Festival), Florida's Singing Sons Boychoir, the Fort Lauderdale Children's Theatre, and the Gold Coast Jazz Society.

Both the Stonewall National Museum and Archives and the African-American Research Library and Cultural Center are located in Fort Lauderdale. The city is known for its festivals celebrating ethnic heritage, which include the Sistrunk Historical Festival, Highland Games, Greek Festival, and the Unifest Caribbean Celebration.

The Fort Lauderdale Historical Society was founded in 1962 and today operates the Museum of History, the King-Cromartie House, and the Hoch Heritage Center. The Stranahan House was opened as a historic house museum in 1984, and the Museum of Discovery and Science was founded in 1977.

Moviemaking in Fort Lauderdale dates back to 1917, and through the years, many movies and television shows have been filmed there. This has brought stars to town, with some like Lucille Ball and Desi Arnaz, Sonny and Cher, Lee Majors, Johnny Weissmuller, Herb Shriner and David Cassidy all purchasing homes here. Homegrown talents such as Billy Crudup, Chris Conrad, Bailee Madison, Bob Clark and Jason Kennedy have also made their mark in Hollywood.

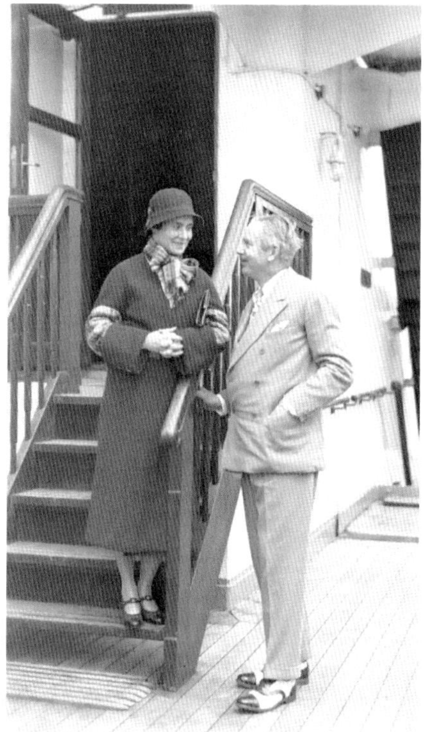

Frederic Clay and Evelyn Fortune Bartlett, Owners of the Bonnet House

A trained muralist and an art collector, Frederic Bartlett painted and decorated his beach estate, the Bonnet House. In 1925, Bartlett donated a collection of Post-Impressionist paintings to The Art Institute of Chicago in memory of his first wife, Helen Birch. In 1931, Bartlett married Evelyn Fortune Lilly. They continued to collect art, and Evelyn became a painter in her own right. After Frederic's death, to preserve the 35-acre estate, Evelyn deeded it to the Florida Trust for Historic Preservation in 1983. Since then, it has been open as a historic house museum.

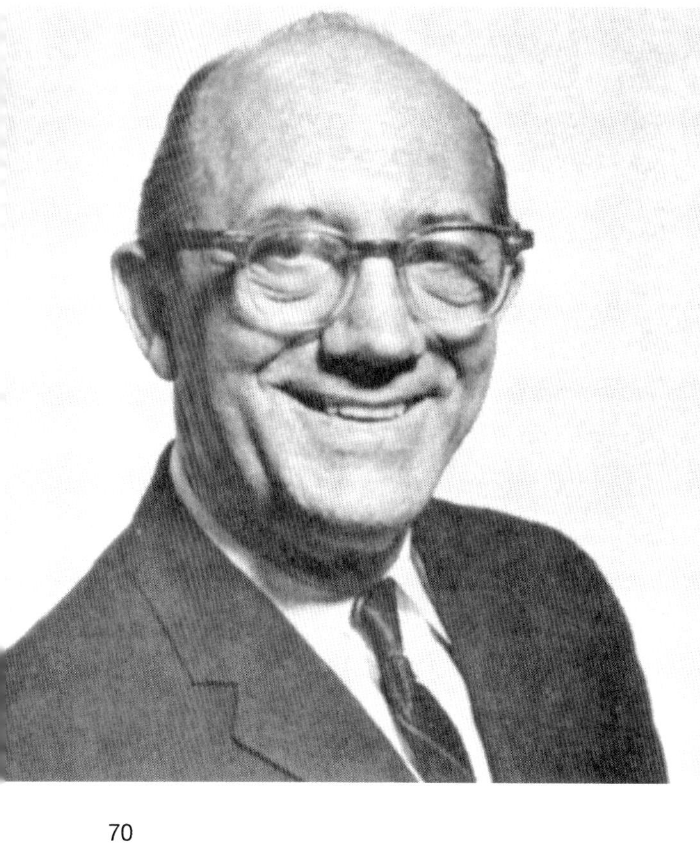

Dr. Bruno C. Schmidt, Broward County Poet Laureate

A German émigré, Bruno Schmidt came to the United States in 1926, eventually settling in Fort Lauderdale in 1951. Schmidt published *Songs of Broward*, a book of poems, in 1960 and had a regular column in the *Fort Lauderdale News*. After composing 500 verses about Fort Lauderdale, Dr. Schmidt was named Broward County Poet Laureate in 1969. A major benefactor for Nova University and Holy Cross Hospital, he was the recipient of the World of Poetry Golden Poet Award in 1987.

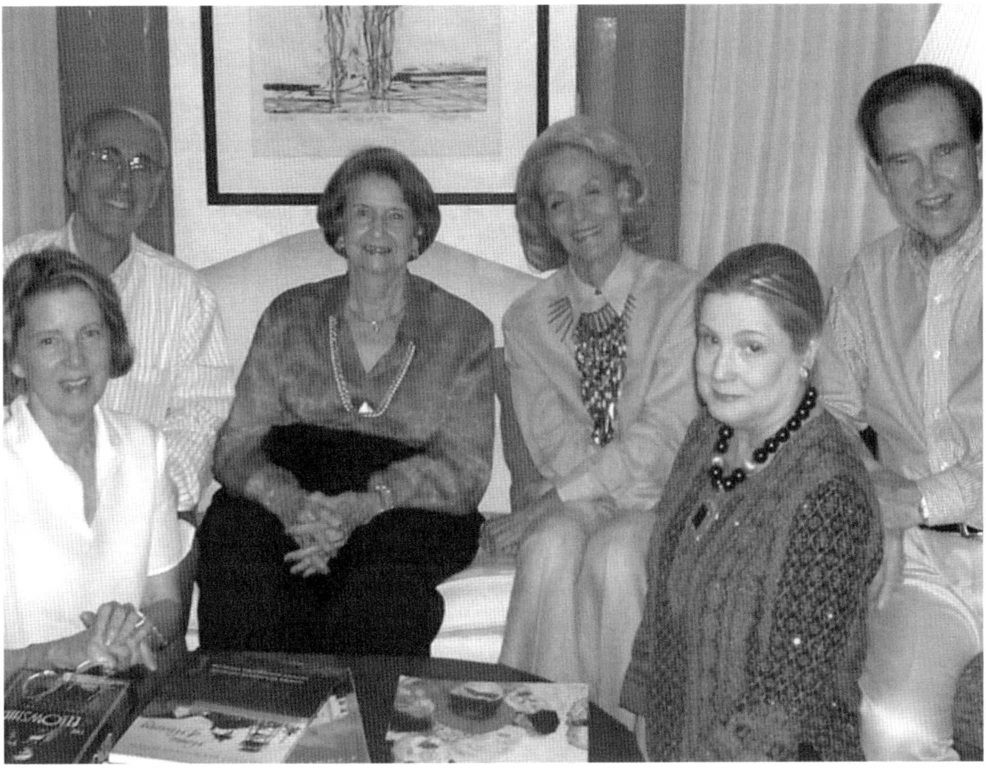

Anna Toms McDaniel (center), Museum of Art Patron

Anna McDaniel was a longtime community arts activist. She began by volunteering for the Fort Lauderdale community concerts and later served as president of the Charity Guild and assisted with the symphony and opera. During her 30 years with the Museum of Art, McDaniel served as a docent, president, interim director, and on the board of directors. In 1993, she was named chairwoman of the Florida State Arts Council. As her daughter stated, "She cared deeply about the arts in Fort Lauderdale. She devoted her life to it. That was her passion." (Courtesy of Mr. and Mrs. William Crawford.)

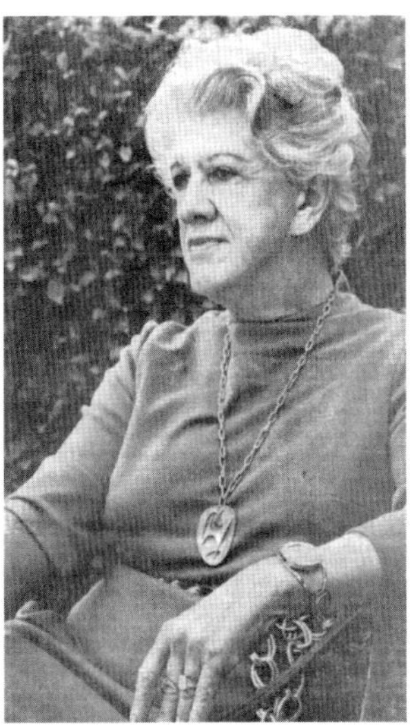

Mary McCahill, Museum of Art Patron

Mary McCahill arrived in 1958 and set about to build the reputation of the city's arts and academic institutions. She joined the board of directors of the Museum of Art in 1967 and became its president in 1969. During her tenure, which lasted until 1986, McCahill guided the growth of the museum from a remodeled hardware storefront to a new $7.5 million museum building. In 1973, she became the first woman appointed to the board of trustees of Nova University and in 1975, its first woman chairman.

Benjamin "Bob" Clark, Writer, Director, and Producer of *Porky's* and *A Christmas Story*
Born in New Orleans, Bob Clark lived in Birmingham, Alabama, until his family moved to Fort Lauderdale in the 1950s. He received a football scholarship to Hillsdale College in Michigan, where he played quarterback. Clark turned down several offers to play professional football but did briefly play semipro for the Fort Lauderdale Knights. He studied theater at the University of Miami. Clark started out as a writer, director, and producer in the horror genre. His movie *Children Shouldn't Play with Dead Things* (1972) was bought and distributed by Quadrant of Canada. This began Clark's career as one of Canada's most artistically and commercial filmmakers. He followed up with *Deathdream* (1972) and *Black Christmas* (1974), considered one of the seminal slasher films. In 1975, Clark produced *Moonrunners*, which later was reworked into the television series *The Dukes of Hazzard*. He received critical acclaim, a Genie Award for Best Achievement in Direction for the 1979 Sherlock Holmes film *Murder by Decree*. Clark is best remembered for *Porky's* (1982), the highest-grossing Canadian film of all time, and is credited with launching the genre of teen sex comedy. *Porky's* is loosely based on Clark's teenage experiences in Fort Lauderdale. Another film that he is known for is *A Christmas Story* (1983), which he cowrote, directed, and produced.

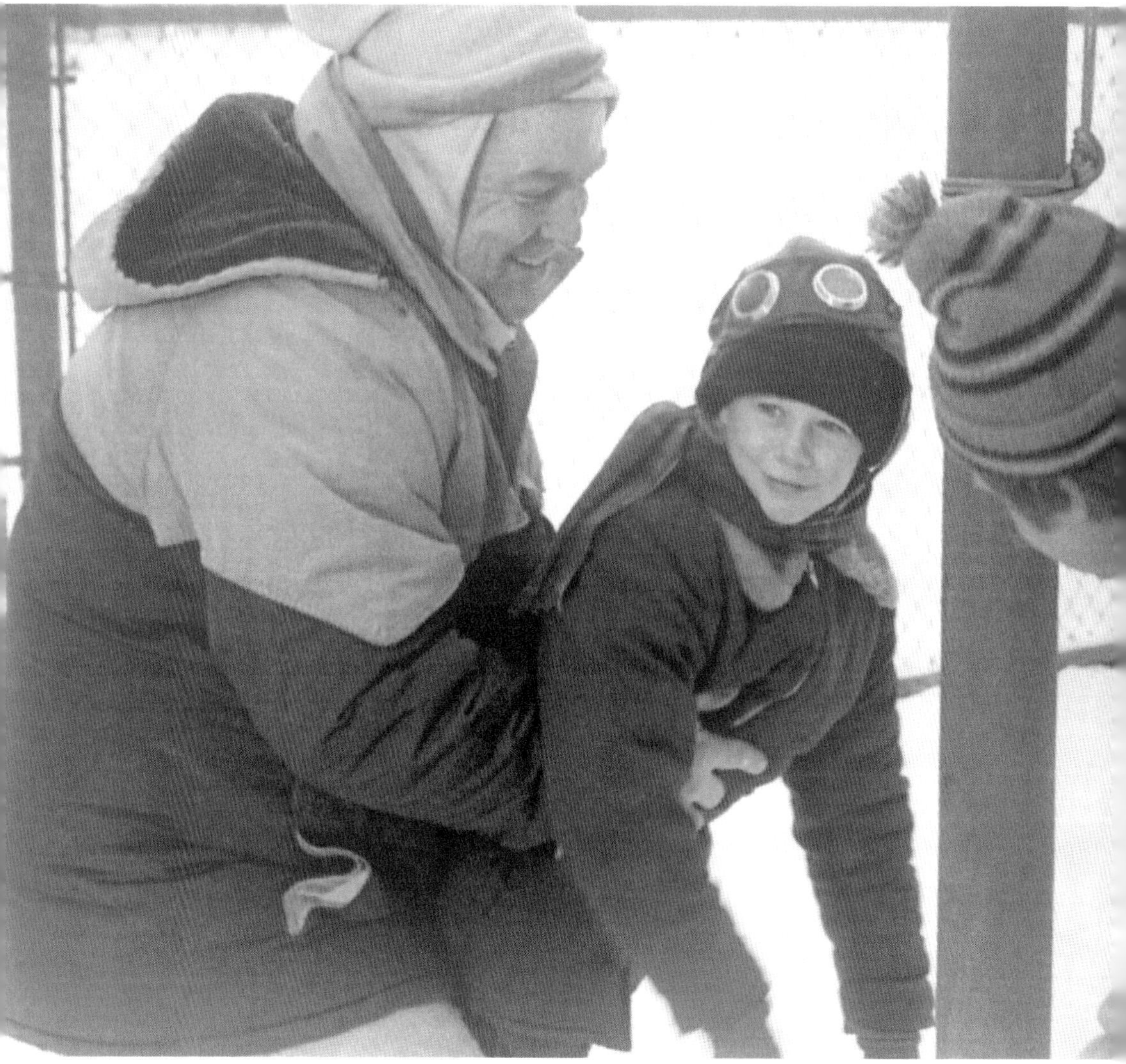

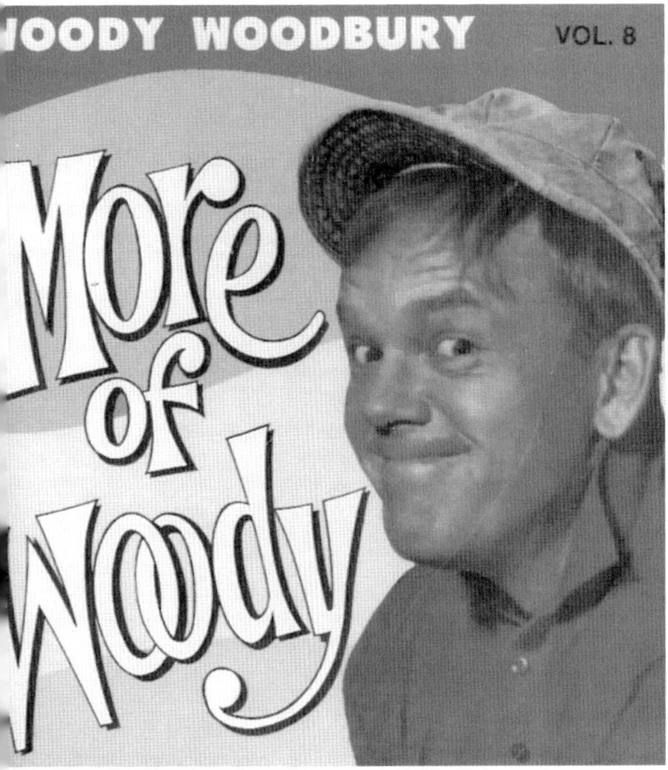

Robert D. "Woody" Woodbury, Comedian
Woody Woodbury was a flight instructor during World War II, and he would do stand-up comedy at the service clubs. By 1948, he was working at the Clover Club in Miami. Woodbury came to Fort Lauderdale in 1956 and conducted his shows at the Bahama Hotel. In 1962, Woodbury lost out to Johnny Carson as host of *The Tonight Show.* His syndicated show, *The Woody Woodbury Show*, ran for two years, from 1967 to 1969. In 1972, he returned to Fort Lauderdale, where he still conducts shows today.

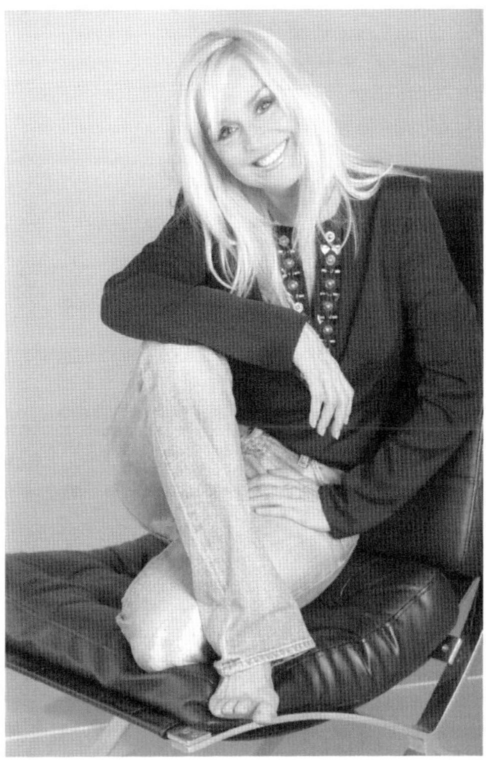

Catherine Hickland, Actress and Hypnotist
Born and raised in Fort Lauderdale, Catherine Hickland graduated from Fort Lauderdale High School in 1974. She worked as a flight attendant for National Airlines, and after making a commercial for the airline, she left for Los Angeles to study acting. Hickland secured roles in several daytime soap operas including *Texas*, *Capitol*, and *Loving*. She portrayed Lindsay Rappaport for 10 years on *One Life to Live*. In 1984, Hickland married David Hasselhoff of *Knight Rider* and *Baywatch* fame. She is a certified hypnotherapist and performs over 200 comedy hypnosis shows a year.

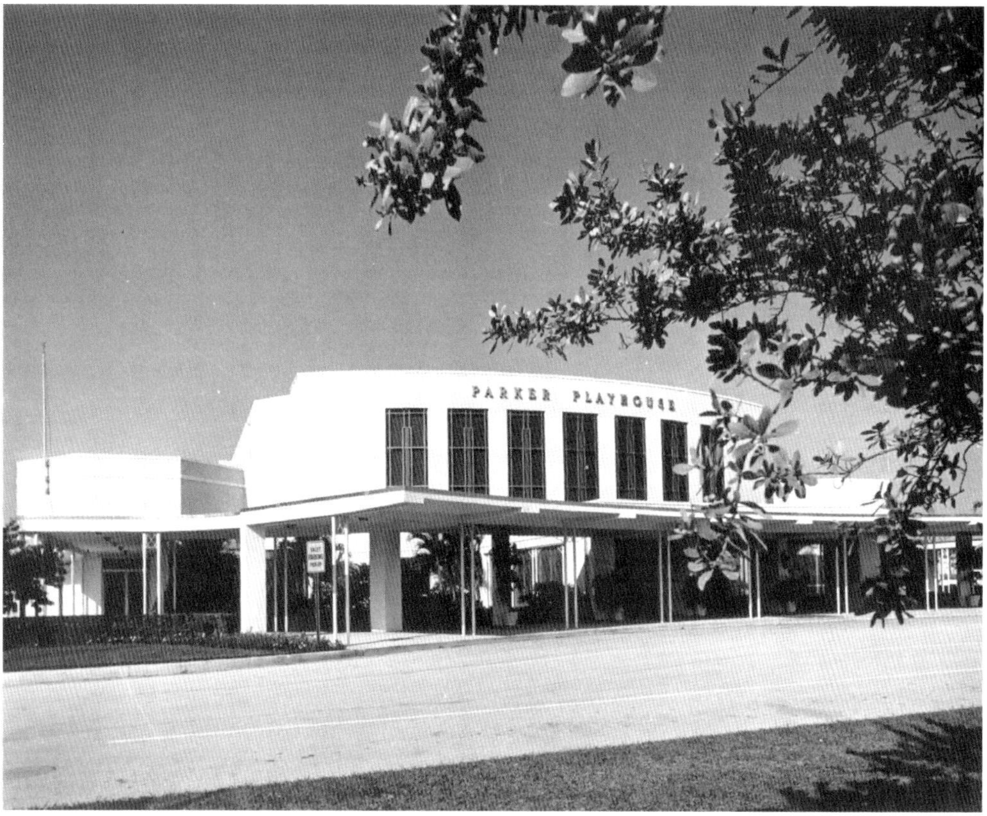

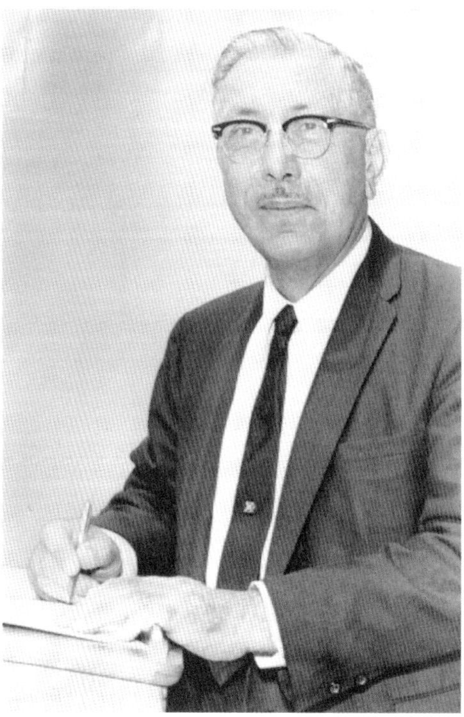

Louis W. Parker, Inventor and Founder of Parker Playhouse

Born Lazlo Kolozsy in Hungary in 1906, Louis Parker immigrated to the United States in 1923. He taught himself English by reading the subtitles of silent movies and became an inventor. At age 12, Parker received his first of over 250 patents for a reusable circuit breaker. In 1947, he invented the intercarrier sound system, which allowed for the simultaneous transmission of television audio and video signals. Within 15 years, 100 million televisions worldwide used Parker's system, and he was a multimillionaire. In 1959, he moved to Fort Lauderdale. A lover of arts, Parker built the Parker Playhouse in 1966 for $1 million and then donated the building to the city. All the proceeds from the performances were donated to Broward County arts and cultural groups. He also pledged $1 million for the construction of the physical sciences building (one of the first three buildings) at Nova University. In the 1960s, Parker invented a meter that monitored oxygen on the Apollo astronaut spacesuits. He was inducted into the National Inventors Hall of Fame in 1988.

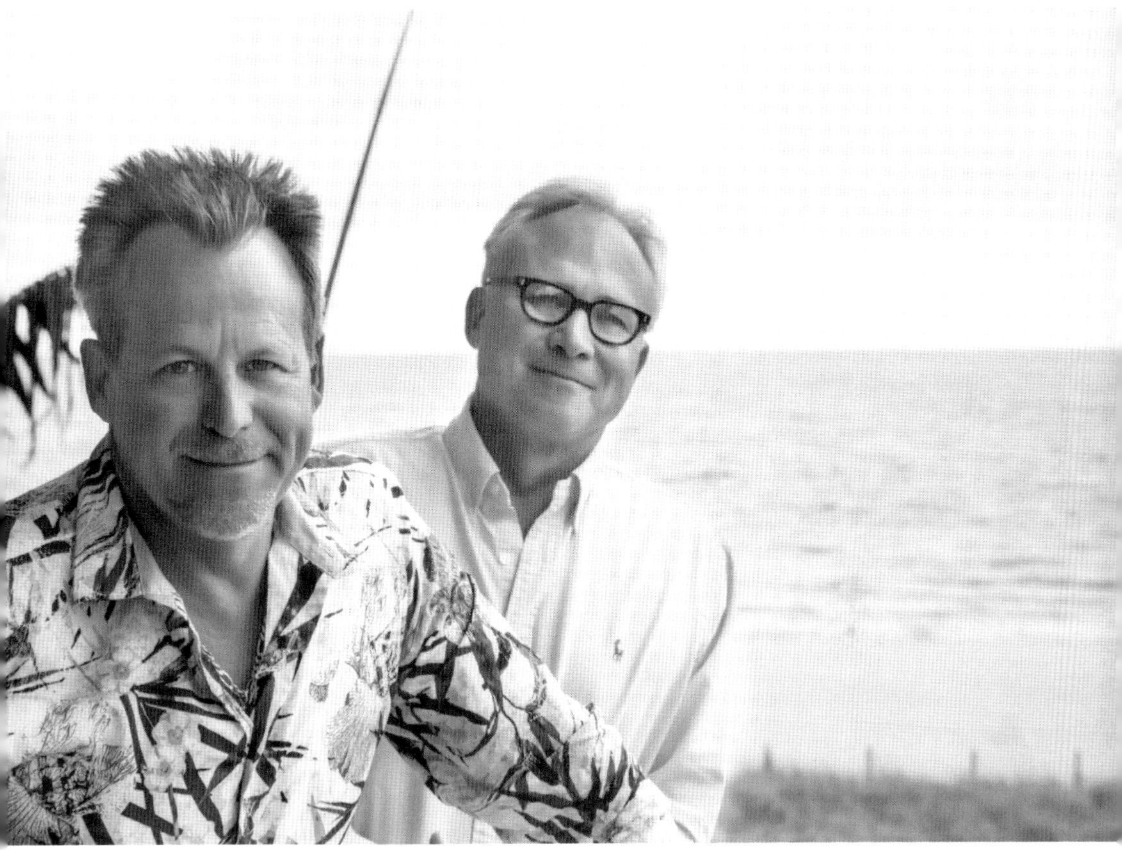

Kin and Wil Shriner, Television Personalities

Twin sons of humorist and television host Herb Shriner, Kin and Wil grew up in Fort Lauderdale during the 1960s. The boys attended Cardinal Gibbons High School. However, following their parents' death in 1970, they moved to Texas to live with their grandmother and finish school. Kin and Wil returned to Fort Lauderdale, driving cabs for a few years before moving to Los Angeles. Kin, the eldest by six minutes, is best known for his role as Scotty Baldwin on the television soap opera *General Hospital*. Kin has been nominated 13 times for Daytime Emmy and Soap Opera Digest Awards, winning twice. He also voiced Green Arrow on *Justice League Unlimited*. Wil attended film school at UCLA and got his start writing for David Letterman. He had his own Emmy-nominated talk show and eventually directed many top television shows including *Frasier*, *Everybody Loves Raymond*, and *Gilmore Girls*. In 2006, Wil produced and directed *Hoot*, set in South Florida. Today, he can be heard weekly on the *Paul and Young Ron Show* on Big 105.9. (Courtesy of Middle River Arts.)

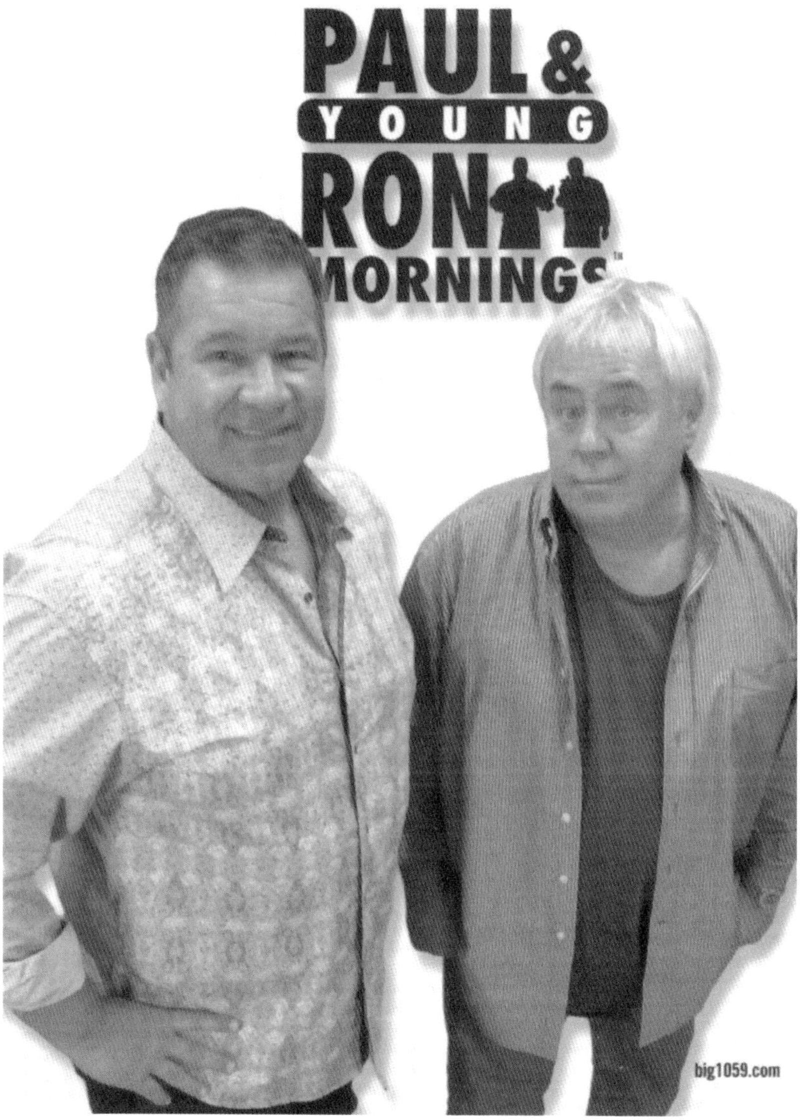

Paul Castronovo and Young Ron Brewer, Radio Personalities

Paul Castronovo and Ron Brewer have been hosting their morning comedy talk show on the Fort Lauderdale airwaves for 25 years. Originally paired together in 1989 at WSHE, they now call WBGG home. *The Paul and Young Ron Show* is one of the longest-running, most successful morning radio programs in South Florida. They are known for their comedic takes on stories and have numerous local and national celebrities visiting the show weekly. Comedian Wil Shriner, ESPN's Dave Lamont, and filmmaker Billy Corben have weekly spots, and it is not unusual for comedians Ralphie May, Dom Irrera, Billy Gardell, or Lisa Lampanelli to call in or visit the studio. The show is the No. 1 rated program in the 18–25 and 25–45 male demographics. Paul and Ron say the best thing about their job is that they get to laugh at work and reach cross-generational audiences. Aside from the radio show, Paul and Ron are actively involved in charity events around South Florida. Their most successful charity project is an annual food drive that has collected over 16 million pounds of food. They are also supporters of the annual Dolphins Cycling Challenge for cancer research. (Courtesy of iHeartMedia.)

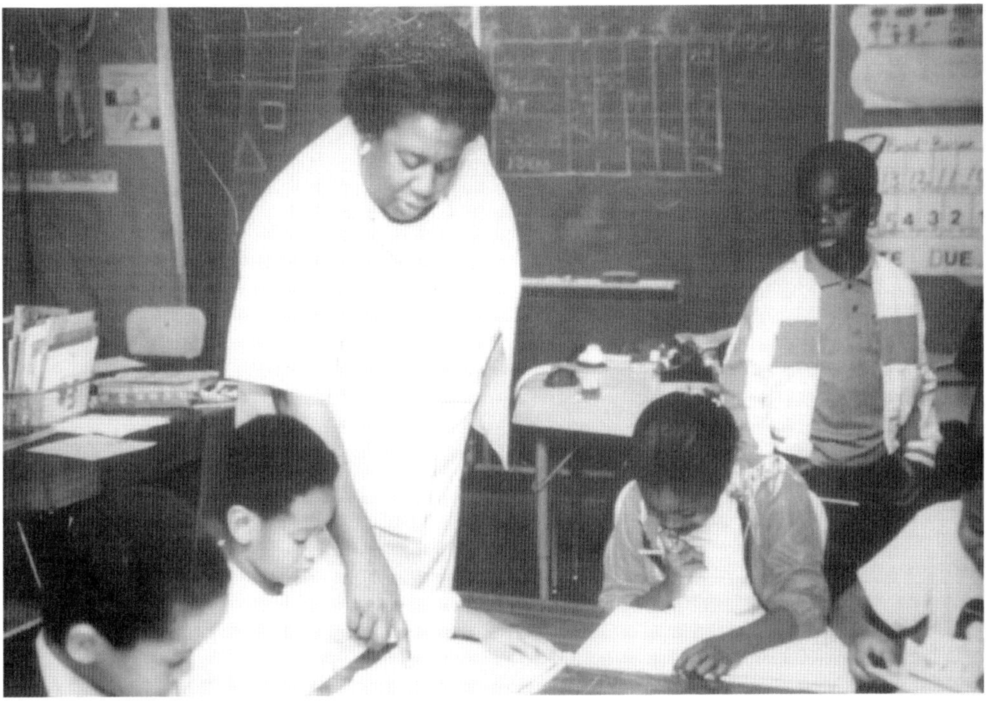

Mary L. Smith, Founder of the Black Historical Society

Mary Smith's family came to Fort Lauderdale in 1916, and she was a 1953 graduate of Dillard High School. After graduating from Bethune-Cookman College in 1957, Smith returned to Fort Lauderdale to teach at Walker Elementary. Smith taught there until the school system was integrated and then taught at Plantation Park Elementary, a predominately white school. In 1976, she became the founder and president of the Black Historical Society. Smith also assisted in the restoration of the Old Dillard School and its 1991 induction into the National Register of Historic Places. (Courtesy of Old Dillard Museum.)

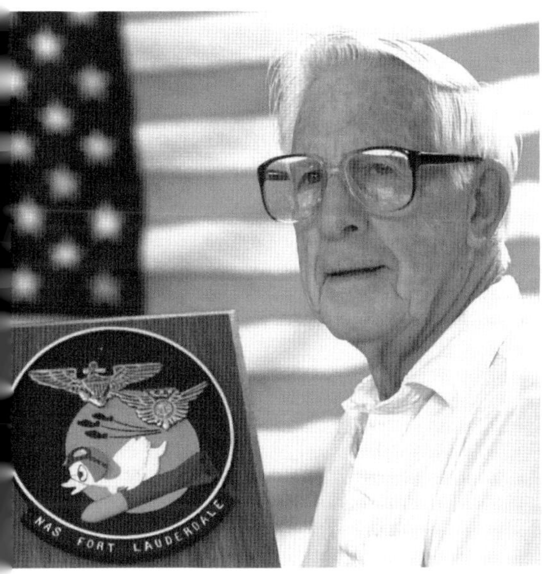

Allan F. McElhiney, Founder of Naval Air Station Fort Lauderdale Historical Museum

In 1979, former US Navy sailor Allan McElhiney helped form the Naval Air Station Fort Lauderdale Historical Association with the goal to save at least one building from the former air station. After moving and restoring the Link Trainer Building, it opened as the Naval Air Station Fort Lauderdale Museum. For over 30 years, McElhiney served as the curator, collecting documents, photographs, and artifacts. In 1989, he started the annual Flight 19 Memorial Ceremony. McElhiney received the Broward Navy Days Freedom Award in 2012. Shortly before his passing in 2014, McElhiney participated in the Honor Flight of World War II veterans to Washington, DC. (Courtesy of *Sun-Sentinel*.)

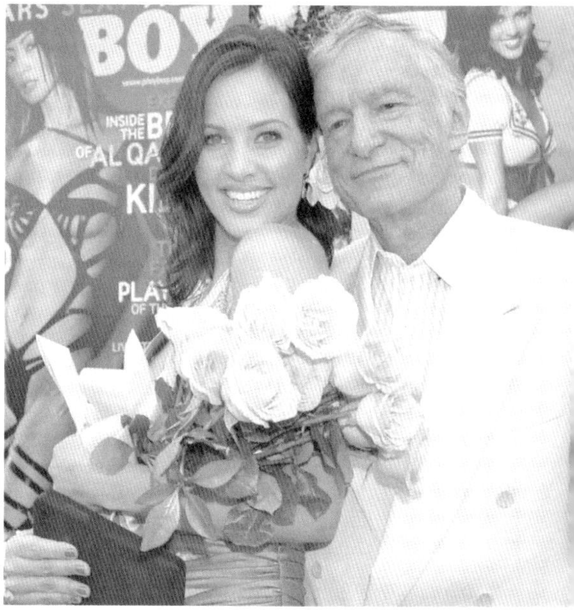

Tiffany Fallon, 2005 Playmate of the Year
Tiffany Fallon attended Fort Lauderdale High School, where she was homecoming queen and senior class president; she also played volleyball, soccer, and ran track. In the late 1990s, she was a cheerleader for the Atlanta Falcons. Fallon was Miss Georgia and second runner-up for Miss USA in 2001. She was *Playboy* Playmate of the Month for December 2004 and was named *Playboy's* Playmate of the Year for 2005. Fallon married Joe Don Rooney of the country group Rascal Flatts in 2006.

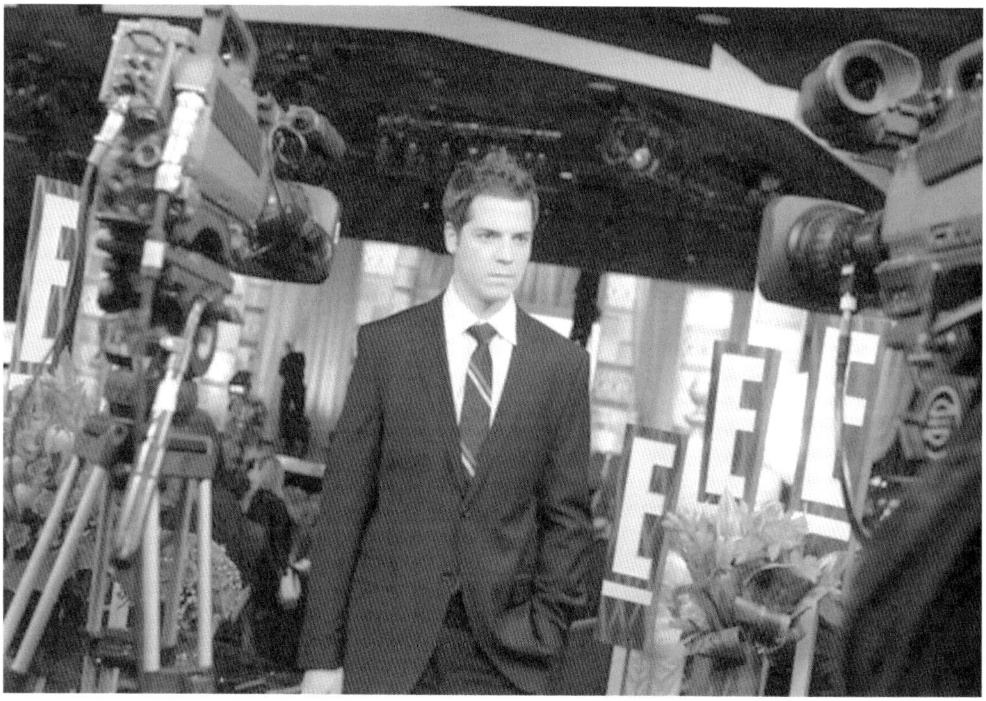

Jason Kennedy, E! Network Correspondent
Jason Kennedy graduated from Westminster Academy and the University of Miami (UM). As a pre-teen, he would produce a mock-news show he edited in his own home studio. While at UM, Kennedy won several awards, including the Associated Press Award for Best News Feature in the state of Florida. In 2004, he moved to Los Angeles and landed a job on the TV Guide Channel. Kennedy then became a correspondent for the E! network. In 2012, he was name coanchor of *E! News Weekend* and host of the series *Live from E!*

CHAPTER SEVEN

Community Activism

Churches have always been an important social draw, especially in a settlement's early development. Churches sponsored many early events. The first congregation that formed in Fort Lauderdale was the First Methodist Church in 1903. The black pioneers founded First Baptist Church Piney Groves (1904) and the Mount Herman African Methodist Episcopal Church (1906) to meet their communal needs. Mount Herman hosted the first local NAACP meeting in 1945 and served as the organization's first headquarters. In 1907, the First Baptist Church began services.

The All Saints Episcopal Church and the First Presbyterian Church were both founded in 1912. All Saints began ministering to low-income Latino immigrants in 2006. First Presbyterian outreach programs include the Thanksgiving Project (providing meals to the needy), blood drives, and constructing houses with Habitat for Humanity. In the 1920s, St. Anthony's Catholic Church (1922) and Temple Emanu-El (1926) formed. There has always been an exchange between church and neighborhood, and today, the churches offer many services, including daycare, food pantries, classes, and counseling.

In 1922, a "color line" was established in town (no blacks east of the railroad tracks after dark), and by 1927, the town was segregated with black businesses and residences restricted to the northwest quadrant of the city. Separate beaches and schools were established. Eula Johnson and Dr. Von Mizell organized a series of "wade-ins" at the "whites only" beaches in 1961, and Judge Ted Cabot ended the beach segregation in 1962. Even though school segregation was declared unconstitutional in 1954 with *Brown v. Board of Education*, Fort Lauderdale and Broward County schools did not desegregate until the early 1970s, following a lawsuit by George Allen on behalf of his children.

Throughout the years, Fort Lauderdale organizations and individuals have been at the forefront of tackling community issues. The Woman's Club and the Junior League have undertaken projects to improve conditions for the needy, the hungry, children, and those in healthcare services. Arnold Abbott feeds the hungry and took on the city in 2014 after they passed an ordinance regarding outdoor food distribution.

Fort Lauderdale has a large LGBT community and is at the forefront of LGBT rights issues. The area is gay-friendly and has been a popular vacation spot since the 1970s. Both Broward County and Fort Lauderdale have passed ordinances banning discrimination based on sexual orientation. There are over 150 LGBT-owned businesses in the county. The Marlin Beach Hotel became the first gay resort hotel in the mid-1970s, and the Greater Fort Lauderdale Convention and Visitors Bureau instituted the first dedicated ad campaign for LGBT visitors in 1996.

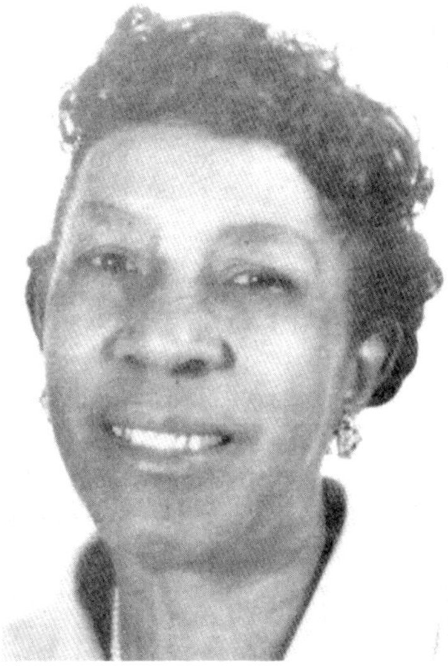

Lucretia Jordan Jackson, "Mother of the Church"

Lucretia Jackson came to Fort Lauderdale in 1904. A talented organizer, she was one of the founders of the First Baptist Piney Grove Church (the first black church). Jackson was a trained nurse and was involved in the public health of the black community. She was also an entrepreneur, owning and operating the Jordan Gospel Music Store, the Lewis Hotel, the Stranahan Grocery, and the West End Employment Bureau. Jackson was a promoter of voter registration campaigns and was one of the first African Americans to register and vote in Broward County. (Courtesy of the African-American Research Library and Cultural Center.)

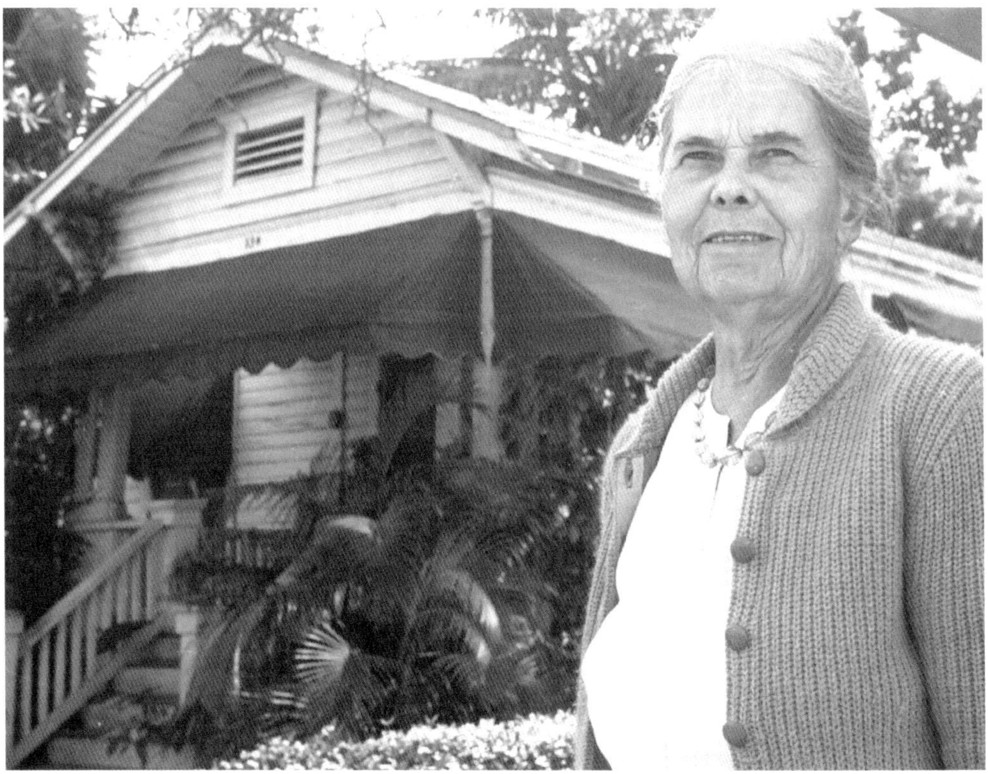

Annie Beck, Community Clubs Organizer

Annie and her husband, A.J. Beck, came in 1916 and owned and operated Beck's Drug Store until 1949. Beck was active in many early cultural clubs. In 1916, she started the Alpha Bridge Club and later started the 1919 Study Club. Beck was a member, and later president, of the Woman's Club and a founder of the All Saints Episcopal Church. After the 1926 hurricane, she started the Garden Club to replenish the city's greenery. Beck started the first city library in her home and was one of the founders of the Fort Lauderdale Historical Society.

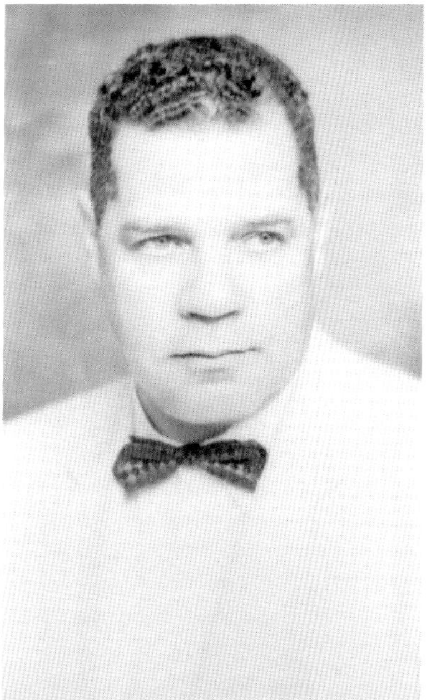

Dr. Von Mizell, First Black Surgeon and Civil Rights Activist

The eldest of 14 children, Von Mizell was raised in Dania (just south of Fort Lauderdale) and graduated from Meharry Medical College in Tennessee in 1936. He returned to Fort Lauderdale in 1938, becoming the second black doctor in the area and the first black surgeon in South Florida. That same year, Dr. Mizell joined with Dr. Sistrunk to found Provident Hospital (below), the first black hospital in Fort Lauderdale. In 1945, he founded the Fort Lauderdale chapter of the National Association for the Advancement of Colored People (NAACP). During 1947, Dr. Mizell led a march on city hall that resulted in the hiring of the first two black policemen in town. He also ran for the school board that year, becoming the first African American in Broward County to run for public office. During his lifetime, Dr. Mizell fought for better housing, integrated schools, equal recreational opportunities, and his right to practice medicine. In 1961, along with Eula Johnson, he helped to organize the "wade-ins" at the "whites only" beach.

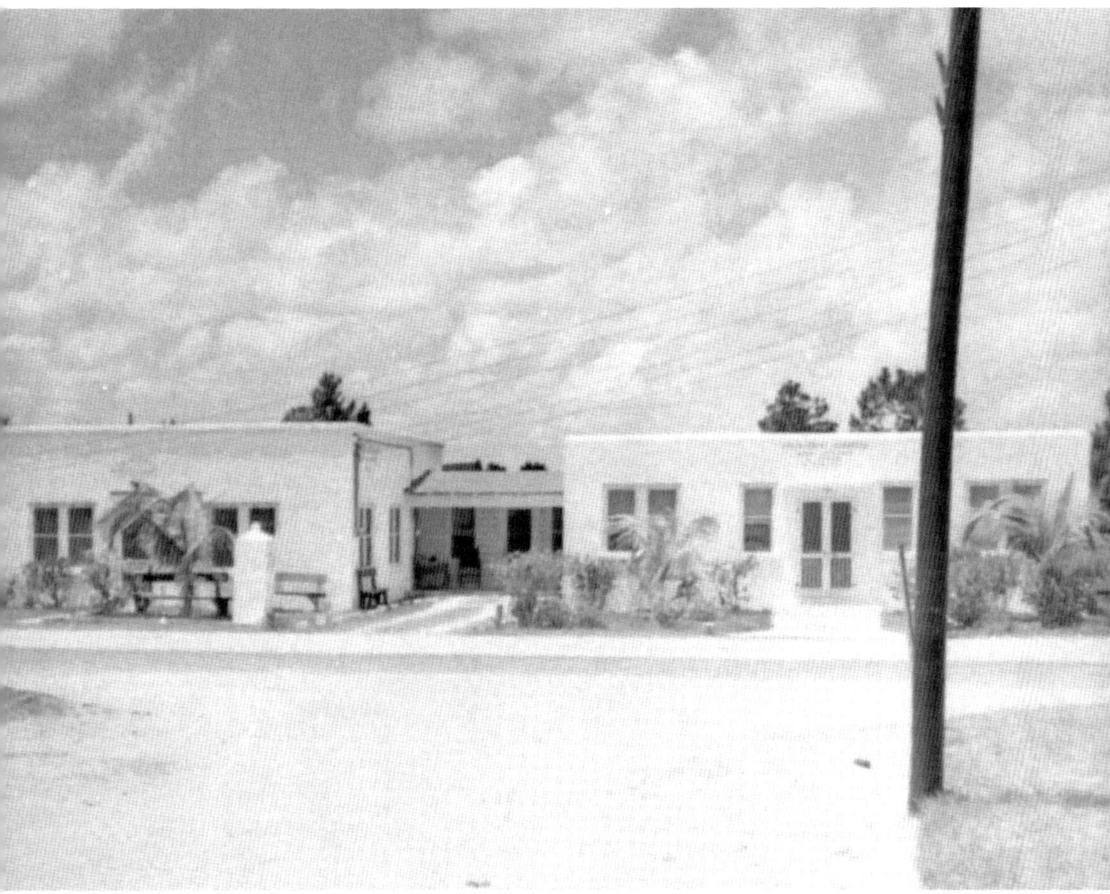

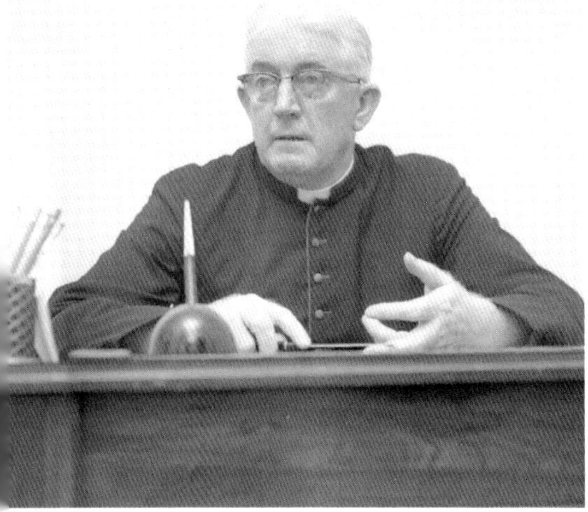

Msgr. John J. O'Looney, Longtime Pastor of St. Anthony's Church

Msgr. John O'Looney arrived in 1928 to become the pastor of St. Anthony's Church, Fort Lauderdale's first Roman Catholic church. During his 42 years at St. Anthony's, the young Irish priest with the flaming red hair was a driving force for Catholic education. For years, O'Looney hand-delivered report cards to the students at St. Anthony's School. He was instrumental in the establishment of Central Catholic High School (now St. Thomas Aquinas) in the early 1950s. O'Looney also originated the fund drive to construct Holy Cross Hospital, which opened in 1953. Moreover, he founded the Emerald Society, Broward County's oldest Irish Heritage nonprofit, in 1951. In addition to overseeing the construction of a new St. Anthony's Church in 1949, he was also involved in the building of Annunciation Church and St. Sebastian Church. It is estimated that O'Looney baptized 6,000 babies, heard 500,000 confessions, spoke at 4,000 funerals, and united 5,000 couples in marriage during his career. (Left, courtesy of the Fort Lauderdale Historical Society, Gene Hyde Collection.)

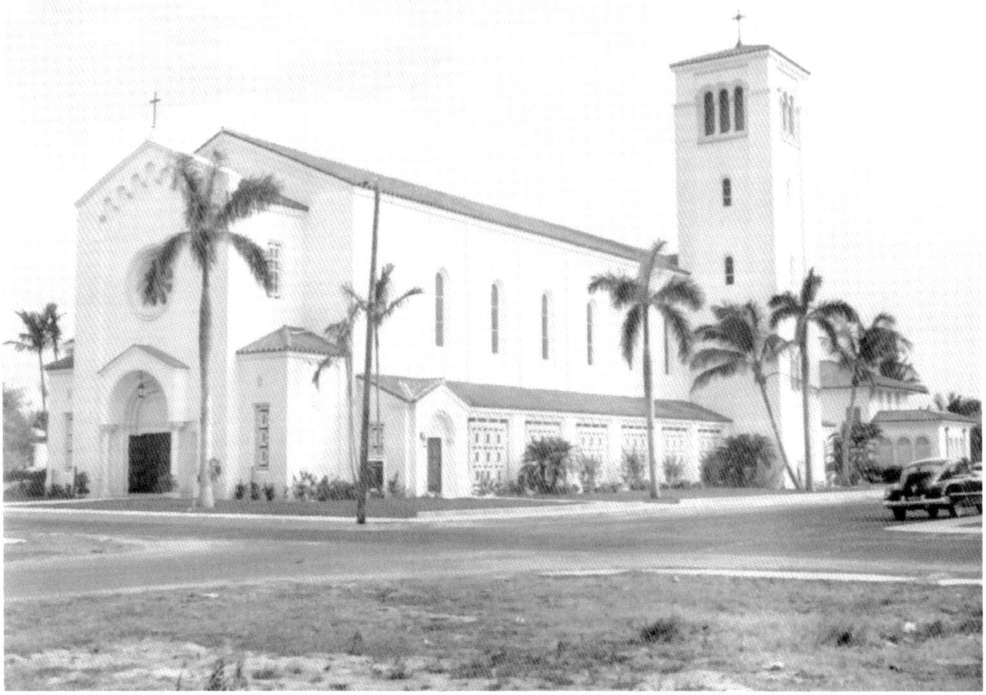

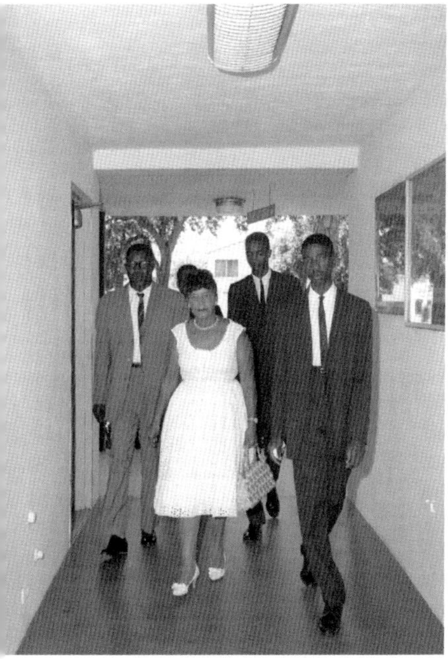

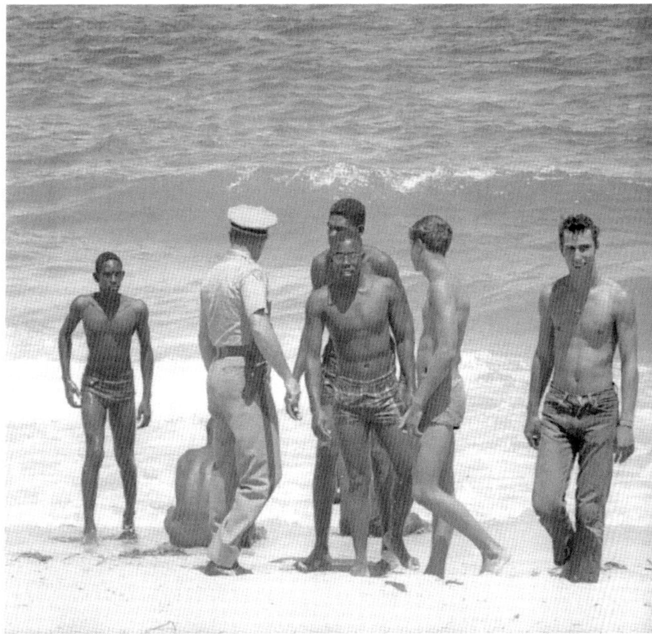

Eula Johnson, Civil Rights Activist and "Wade-in" Organizer

Born in Georgia, Eula Johnson and her family moved to Fort Lauderdale in 1935. There, they owned a small grocery store and two gas stations in the northwest section of town. In the early 1950s, she was widowed, and armed only with a GED, she continued to run the businesses and raise her three children. Johnson became the first female president of the Fort Lauderdale chapter of the National Association for the Advancement of Colored People (NAACP) in 1959, and during her tenure, she made it her mission to reverse the Jim Crow laws of segregated Broward County. She felt that everyone should be treated equally and with respect. Using her home as an unofficial command center, she planned protests for the desegregation of restaurants, hotels, schools, and movie theaters. Johnson brought national exposure to the civil rights issues in Fort Lauderdale when she, Dr. Von Mizell and some Dillard High School students staged a "wade-in" at the "whites only" beach at Las Olas Boulevard on July 4, 1961. Fort Lauderdale's beaches had been segregated since 1927, and the six-week series of "wade-ins" forced the issue. The city sued Johnson for inciting chaos and being a public nuisance. In 1962, state judge Ted Cabot ruled in her favor and against the city's segregation policies. Despite repeated arrests, threats, and bribes, the "Rosa Parks of Broward County" persevered. Today, her home on Sistrunk Boulevard is a museum, welcome center, and headquarters of the Fort Lauderdale/Broward County NAACP. (Both, courtesy of the Fort Lauderdale Historical Society, Gene Hyde Collection.)

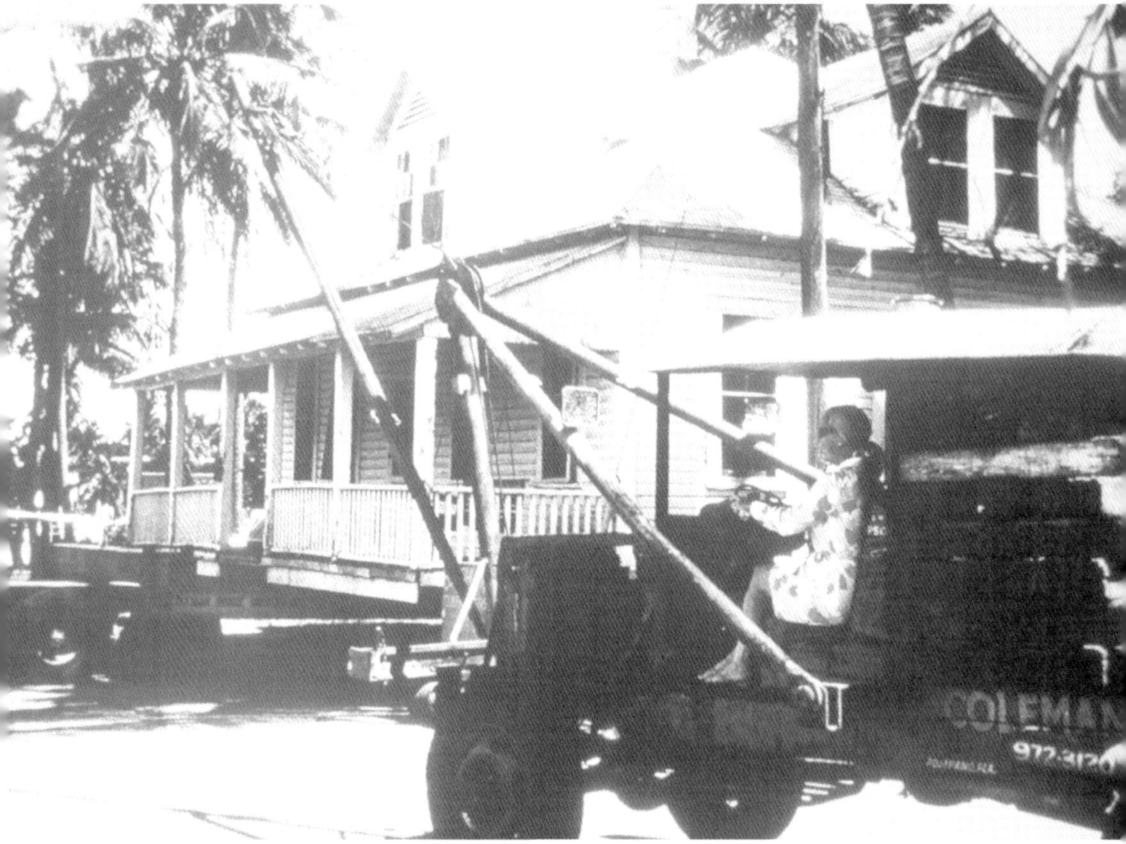

Junior League of Greater Fort Lauderdale

Founded as the Fort Lauderdale Junior Service League in 1937, the Junior League is a nonprofit organization of women committed to promoting volunteerism and improving the community through effective action and leadership. Their Legacy projects have included the establishment and funding of the Jack and Jill Children's Center (1942), the Henderson Mental Health Clinic (1954), the Museum of Art (1958), the Museum of Discovery and Science (1974), Kids in Distress (1978), SOS Children's Village (1988), the Susan B. Anthony Recovery Center (1992) and the Fort Lauderdale Independence Training and Education (FLITE) Center (2009). In 1971, the Junior League initiated the first historic preservation project in Fort Lauderdale with the relocation and restoration of the 1907 King-Cromartie House. The home of Edwin King, the city's first building contractor, it was moved to the site of the New River Inn and the Philemon Bryan home and today is part of the Fort Lauderdale History Center complex.

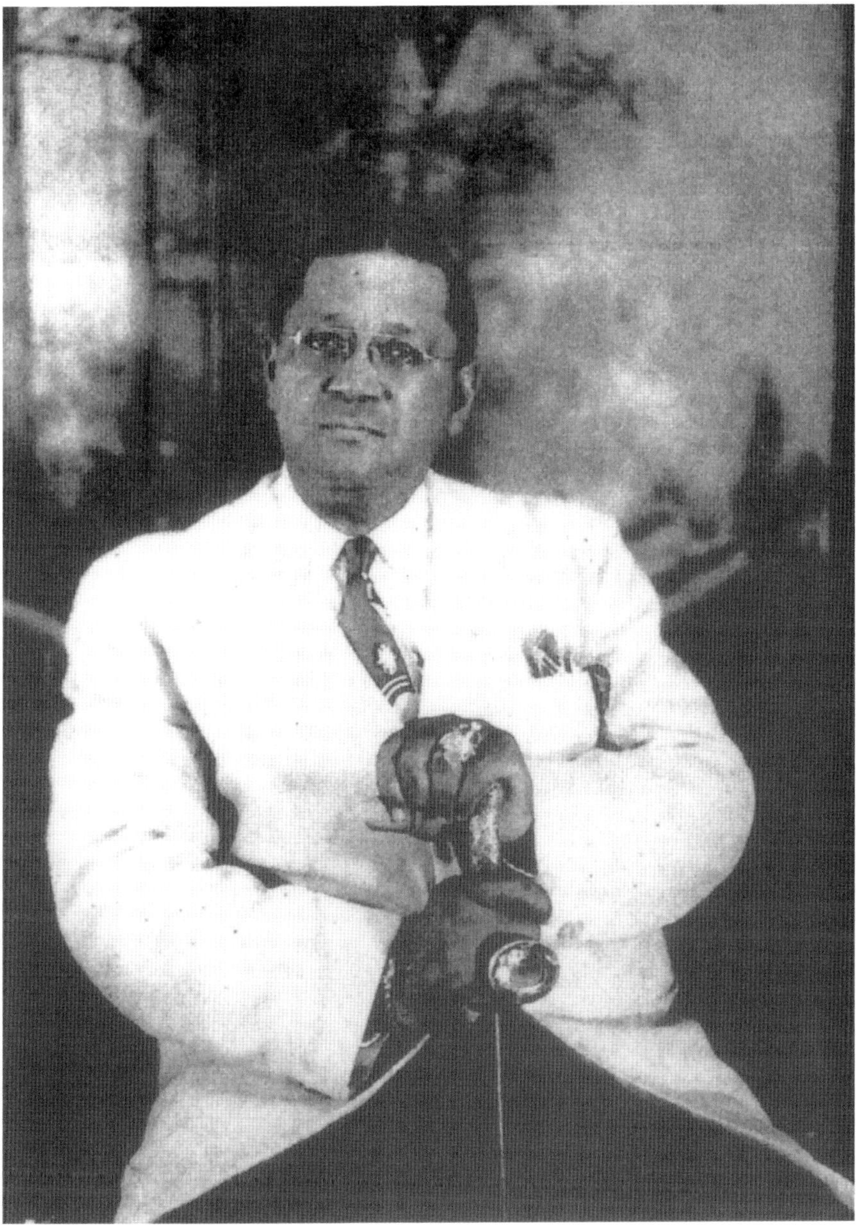

Dr. Harry G. Sweeting, Black Philanthropist

Of Bahamian descent, Dr. Harry Sweeting owned a chain of drugstores in Dade County before moving to Fort Lauderdale in 1941. Here, he operated a sundry and dry goods store. An ordained minister with a doctor of divinity and a degree in psychology, Sweeting was interested in education and philanthropy. He aided young businessmen, founded the Northwest Merchants Association and established the Sweeting Foundation to provide scholarships. On his nine-acre waterfront property on the North Fork of the New River, he built an estate that housed a museum of artifacts from his world travels. Sweeting also opened his estate for annual Easter morning sunrise services. He was a sponsor of the annual Christmas parade in the black section of town and would ride a fire truck and toss out candy. Sweeting also donated the first $1,000 to start the Sistrunk Historic Festival.

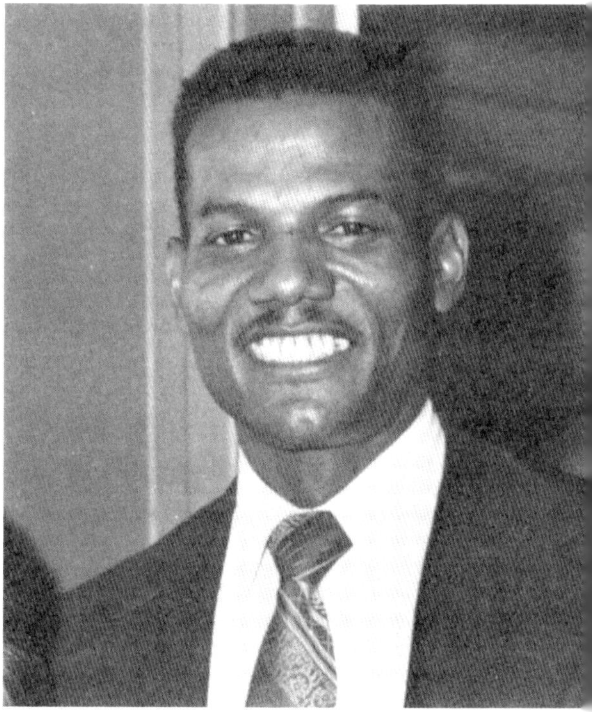

Levi Henry Jr., Founder of the *Westside Gazette*

Levi Henry Jr. came to Fort Lauderdale in 1956, and after an assortment of odd jobs, Levy began selling advertising for the black radio station, WRBD. He participated in the "wade-ins" to integrate the beaches. In 1971, Levy began publishing the *Westside Gazette*, Broward County's oldest black newspaper. The *Westside Gazette* publishes "positive news." Son Bobby Levy now runs the paper. Levy was also the founder of We Help Ourselves (WHO), a drug rehabilitation program. (Courtesy of the African-American Research Library and Cultural Center.)

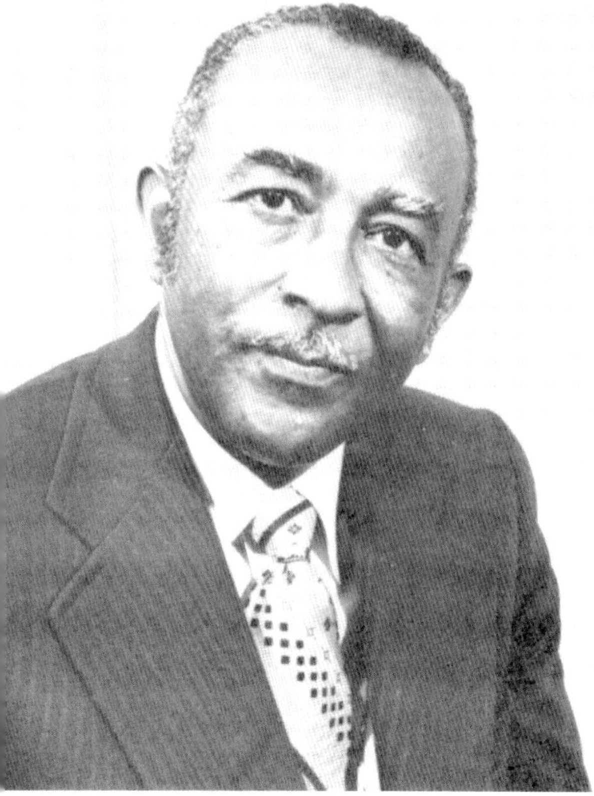

Rev. George Edward Weaver, New Mount Olive Baptist Church

George Weaver graduated from Paine College in Georgia with a bachelor of arts in religion and philosophy. In 1962, Reverend Weaver became the pastor of the New Mount Olive Baptist Church in Fort Lauderdale. Under his leadership, the church built a new building and the Mount Olive Child Care Center was established. The G.E. Weaver Scholarship Fund was established for students in need. Reverend Weaver led the effort to integrate the Greater Fort Lauderdale Ministerial Association and served as its first black president. He also organized the Broward County Baptist Ministers Brotherhood. (Courtesy of the African-American Research Library and Cultural Center.)

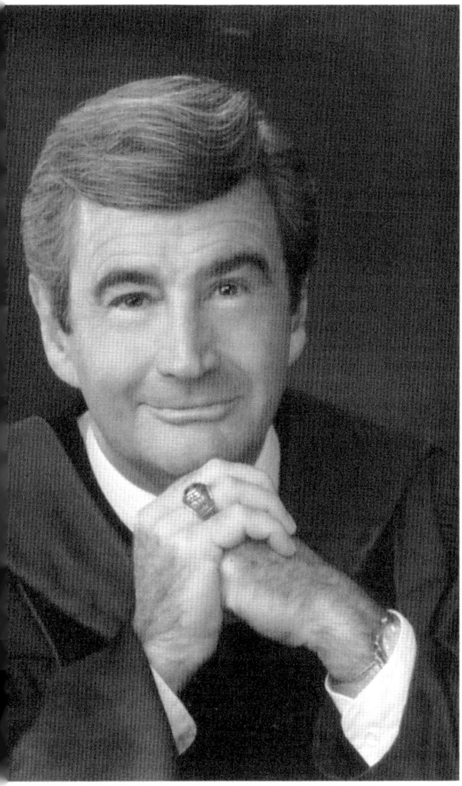

D. James Kennedy, Coral Ridge Presbyterian Church Televangelist
D. James Kennedy, a former dance instructor at the Arthur Murray Dance Studio, received his master of divinity in 1955. Kennedy became the founding pastor of the Coral Ridge Presbyterian Church in 1960. He began broadcasting *The Coral Ridge Hour*, a weekly television program, in 1974. It had a peak weekly audience of 3.5 million in 200 countries. In 2003, Kennedy was inducted into the National Religious Broadcasters Hall of Fame. In 1971, he founded the Westminster Academy, a private Christian school.

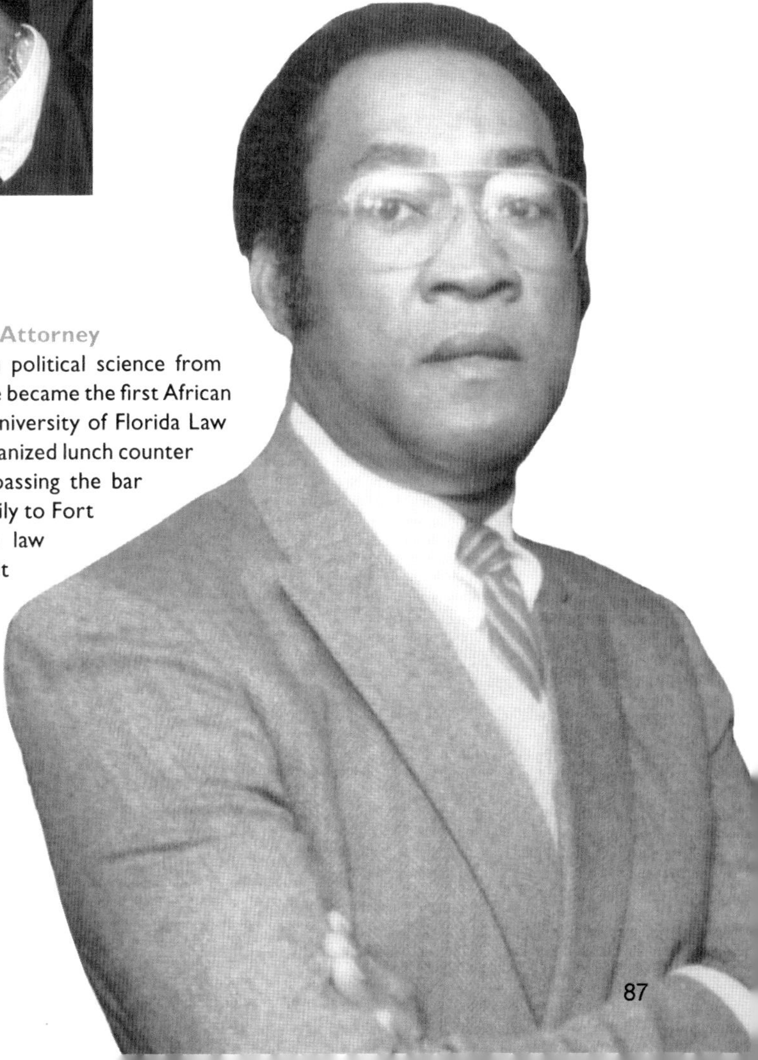

W. George Allen, Civil Rights Attorney
George Allen earned a degree in political science from Florida A&M University. In 1962, he became the first African American to graduate from the University of Florida Law School. While in law school, he organized lunch counter sit-ins around Gainesville. After passing the bar exam in 1963, Allen moved his family to Fort Lauderdale and started his own law practice. In 1970, he won a lawsuit against the Broward County School District to desegregate the schools in compliance with *Brown v. Board of Education* (1954). Allen was inducted into the National Bar Association's Hall of Fame in 2003. (Courtesy of *Sun-Sentinel*.)

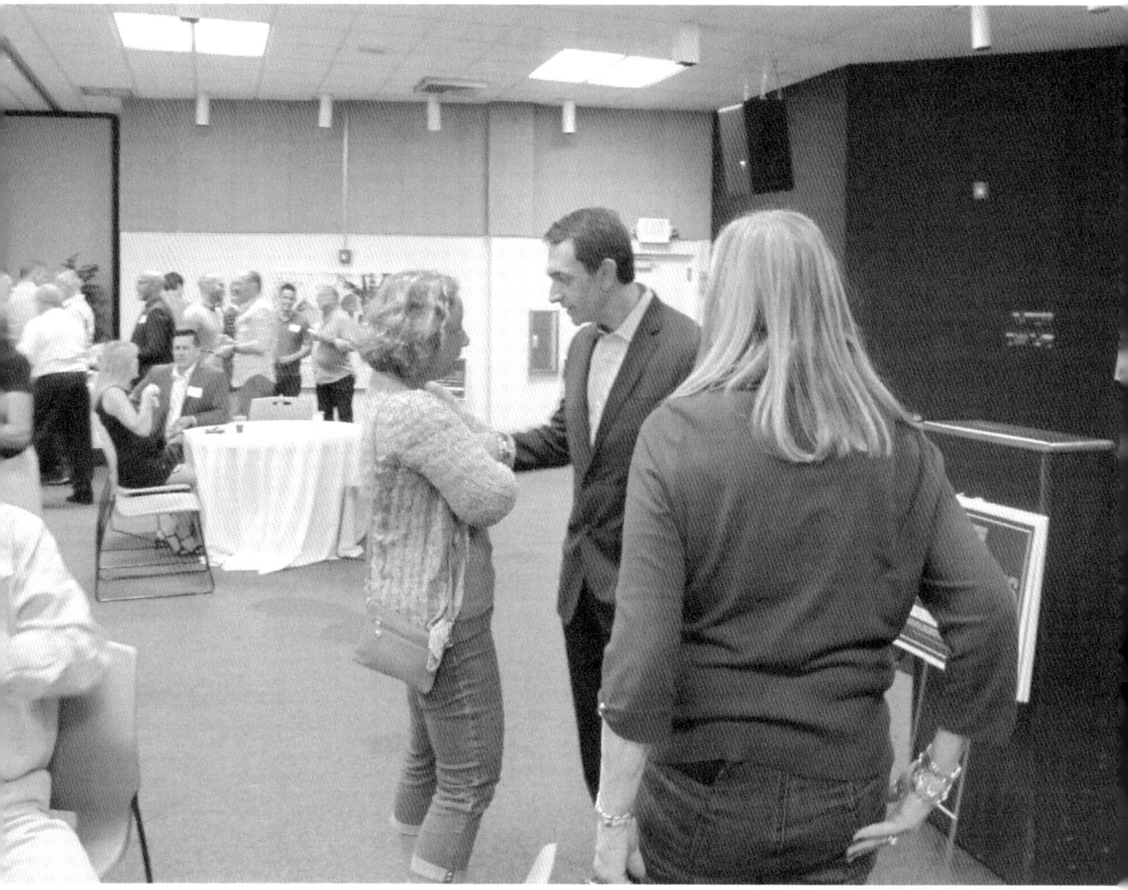

Dean Trantalis, First Openly Gay City Commissioner
Born and raised in Norwich, Connecticut, Dean Trantalis graduated from Boston University with a degree in political science. He received his law degree from Stetson University School of Law in 1979 and studied international law in London and Russia. Trantalis began practicing law in Broward County in 1982 and became chair of Broward United Against Discrimination in 1993. The group organized to stop the American Family Association from inducing communities to pass restrictive anti-gay legislation. In 1995, Trantalis served as cochair of Americans for Equality and aided in the enactment of the Broward County Human Rights Ordinance. He cowrote and assisted in the passage of Broward County's domestic partnership law in 1999. Trantalis was elected to the Fort Lauderdale City Commission in 2003, serving a three-year term. He was vice mayor in both 2005 and 2006. Trantalis was reelected to the commission in 2013 to finish commissioner Charlotte Rodstrom's term and was reelected in 2015.

"Chef" Arnold Abbott, Feeder of Homeless and Media Celebrity

Decorated World War II veteran and former traveling salesman Arnold Abbot moved to Florida in 1970. He and his wife, Maureen, operated a jewelry business, and their humanitarian aid started with offering food and money to homeless people in the city. After Maureen's passing in 1991, Abbott formed the Love Thy Neighbor organization, an interfaith group that provides meals and a culinary skills training program for the homeless. It is estimated that they have served more than 500,000 meals during their weekly Wednesday night dinners. Love Thy Neighbor provides a balanced and nutritional four-course meal. Abbott became an international celebrity following his citations in November 2014 for his insistence on feeding the homeless of Fort Lauderdale in defiance of a new city ordinance regulating feeding sites. The Farver Foundation named him their 2014 Humanitarian of the Year. (Courtesy of *Sun-Sentinel*.)

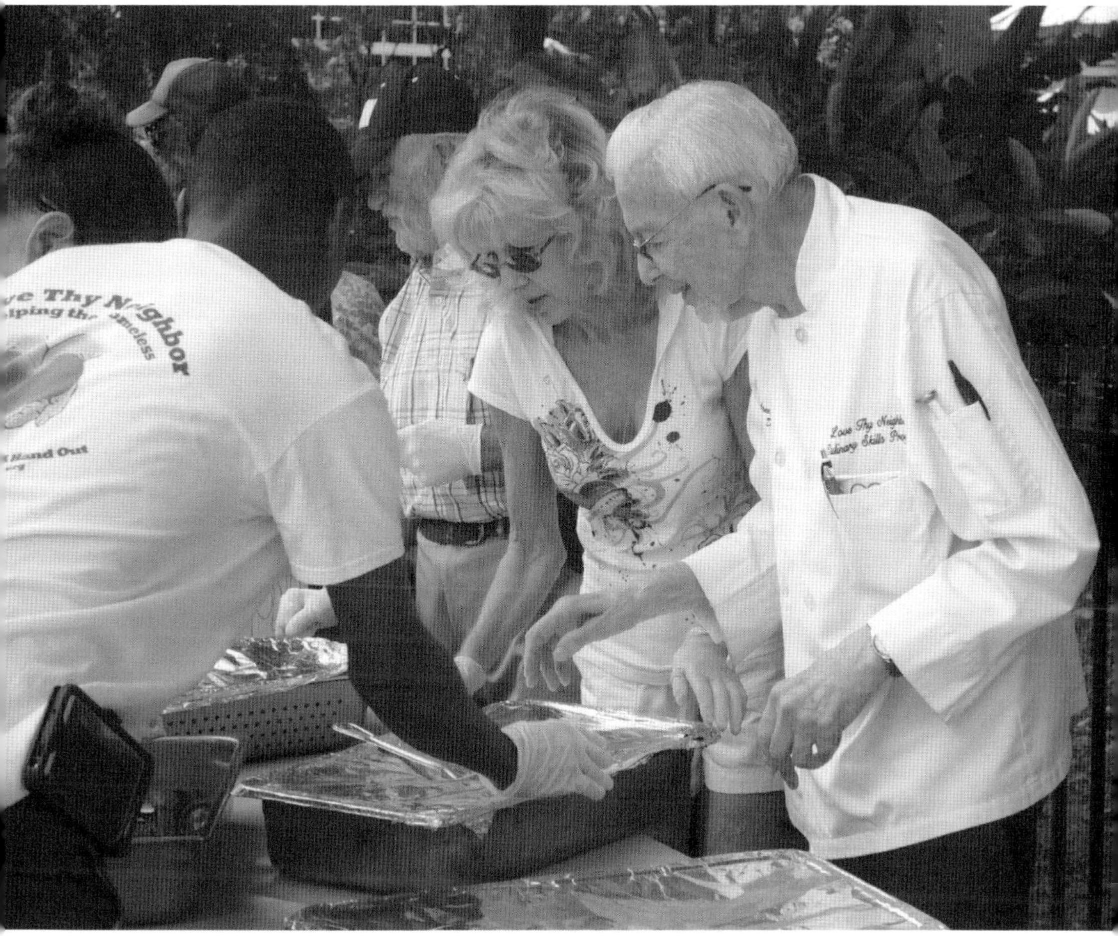

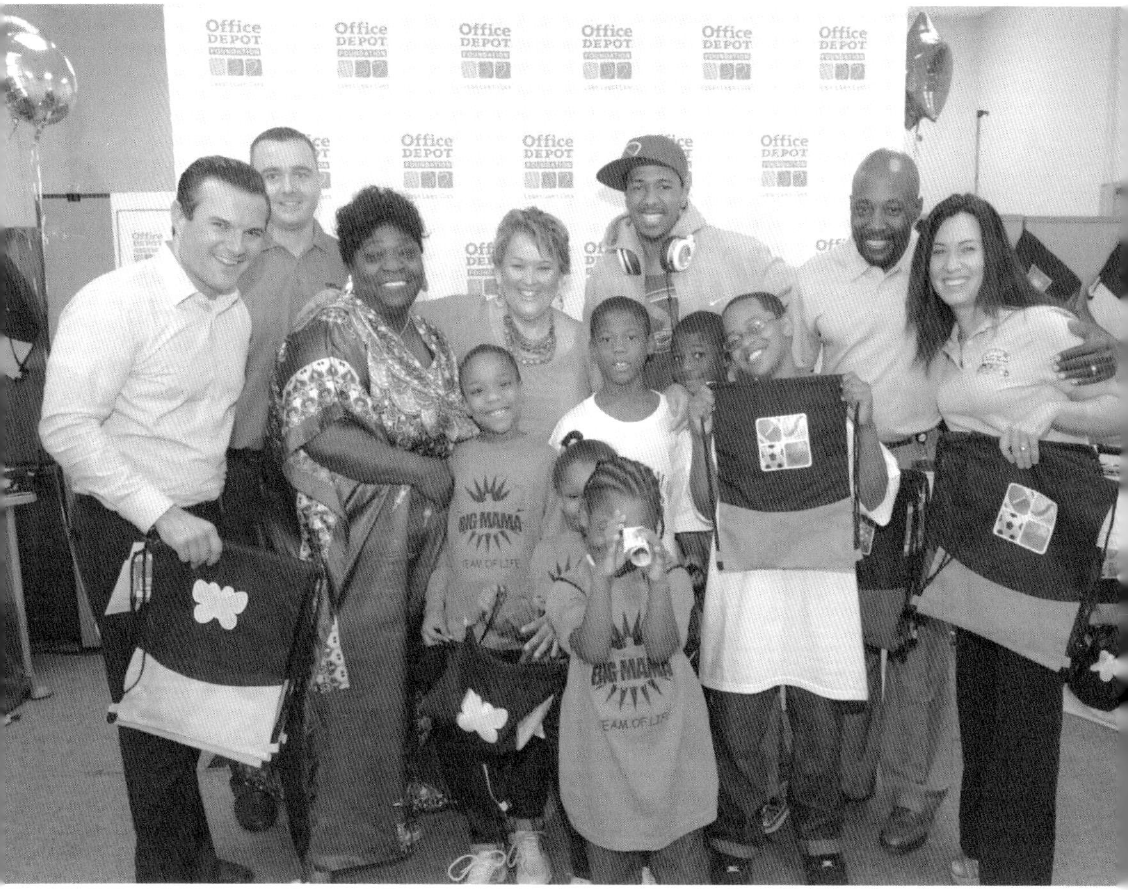

Essie "Big Mama" Reed (third from left), Team of Life Founder

Essie Reed's efforts to assist the community's less fortunate children arose from her own personal adversity. In the 1980s, her husband walked out, leaving her with three sons. For three years, they slept on the floor of the fish market that she owned. While benefactors provided her family with aid, they also showed her how she could help others. In 1989, "Big Mama" opened a youth ministry to help children whose family lives were marred by drug and alcohol problems, poverty, and violence. Today, her Team of Life organization—with corporate sponsors such as Starbucks, Office Depot, and American Express—provides school supplies, Thanksgiving turkeys, and immunizations to children whose families cannot afford them. This well-respected dynamo of concern, kindness, and action of the community has received numerous awards, including the 2001 Vanguard Chronicle Community Activist of the Year, 2006 Broward County School Social Workers Association Citizenship Award, and 2009 Fort Lauderdale Citizen of the Year. In 2006, ABC's *Extreme Makeover: Home Edition* built a community center for Big Mama to provide a refuge for neighborhood kids.

CHAPTER EIGHT

Athletics

Athletics have been a part of Fort Lauderdale life since the beginning. The town fielded its first baseball team in 1909 and won the East Coast League pennant in 1924. Fort Lauderdale High School won the 1917 Boys Track state championship. In 1921, the city constructed a nine-hole golf course, where a "hijacked" President-elect Harding played with city leaders. The Casino Pool opened in 1928, and since 1930, Fort Lauderdale swimmers and divers have dominated the state team championships. National Champion and Olympian Katherine Rawls trained at the pool. Les McNeese was selected for the 1936 Olympic baseball team.

On the high school level, Fort Lauderdale public and private schools have achieved over 300 state championships and hosted countless individual state champions. St. Thomas Aquinas High School leads the way with 98 state titles and has been awarded the Broward County all-sports trophy by the *Sun-Sentinel* for 27 consecutive years. The other high schools have also established dynastic periods: Fort Lauderdale High School—boys cross-country (1956–1962), boys and girls swimming and diving (1930–1956), boys tennis (1945–1950); Stranahan High School—wrestling (1971–1975); Dillard High School—boys basketball (2000–2003), girls basketball (2010–2015); Cardinal Gibbons High School—boys tennis (1985–1988, 1995–2002), girls tennis (1996–2003), girls volleyball (1975–1998); Pine Crest Preparatory School—boys basketball (2008–2012), boys and girls swimming and diving (1957–1990), girls volleyball (2001–2003); and Westminster Academy—boys cross-country (1983–1988).

Local athletes have gone on to play at every collegiate level and have played professionally in football, basketball, baseball, racing, golf, and soccer. They have also represented the United States in the Olympics and at national and international track and swimming events. Several players and coaches have been honored in their respective halls of fame.

Fort Lauderdale has been home to minor league baseball and professional soccer. The 1940 Tarpons, an affiliate of the Pittsburgh Pirates, won the Florida East Coast League championship. The Fort Lauderdale Yankees of the Florida State League (Class A) played at the Fort Lauderdale Municipal Stadium from 1962 to 1992 and won the league championship seven times. The New York Yankees (1962–1995) and Baltimore Orioles (1996–2009) held spring training in Fort Lauderdale, and the locals got to see the likes of Mickey Mantle, Roger Maris, Thurman Munson, Reggie Jackson, Don Mattingly, Derek Jeter, Cal Ripken Jr., and Jeff Conine play. The Fort Lauderdale Strikers, in various iterations, have played in town since 1977. Soccer star Christiano Ronaldo joined the ownership group in 2014.

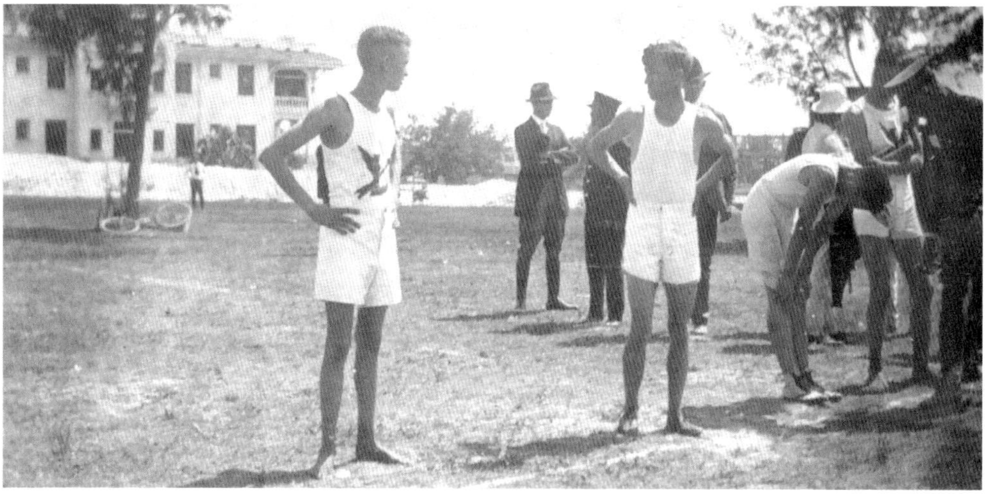

Charlie Rodes Jr., Track and Golf Star

Charlie Rodes Jr. (left) was a member of the Fort Lauderdale High School 1921 state track runner-up team. He won the mile race with a time of 4:58.0, while running barefoot on a cinder track. The team wore an "L" on their uniforms, and during the race, someone commented, "Look at that Flying L." The nickname stuck, and since then, the Fort Lauderdale High School mascot has been the "Flying L." Rodes was also a tennis player and baseball pitcher. He won 10 city golf championships.

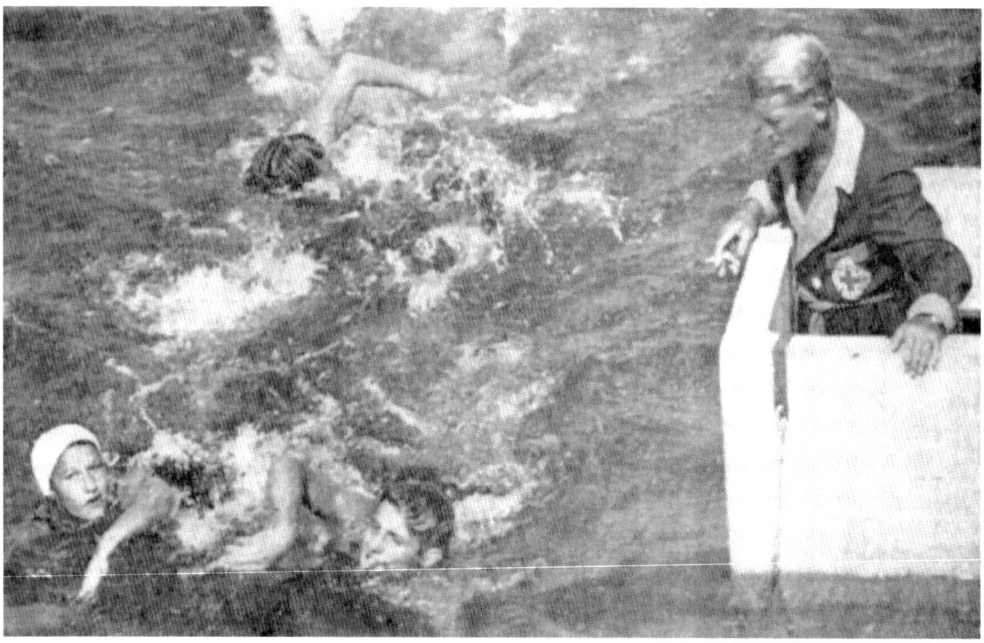

"Aquatic Al" Gordon, Swim Coach and Founder of the Collegiate Aquatic Forum

Al Gordon was the manager of the Casino Pool from 1929 to 1938 and founded the first Fort Lauderdale swimming team. In 1935, with August Burghard of the chamber of commerce and Sam Ingram of Colgate University, Gordon helped to establish the annual Collegiate Aquatic Forum. From 1938 to 1960, he was the swim coach at Pine Crest Preparatory School. Gordon is believed to be the first to invent the submarine observation station, a way to observe swimmers from underwater.

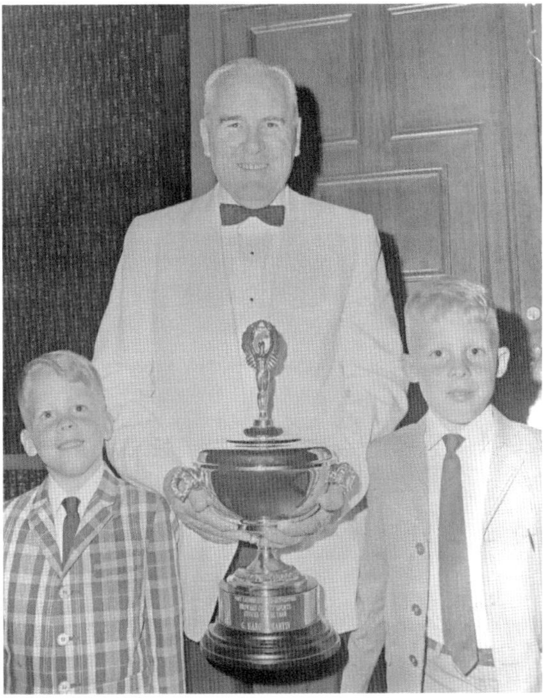

G. Harold Martin, Father of Recreation

Harold Martin came to Fort Lauderdale in 1925 and served as a municipal judge from 1932 to 1936. He pushed for the construction of the Casino Pool and helped promote the Collegiate Aquatic Forum. During the 1930s, Martin founded the Dad's Club at Fort Lauderdale High School to promote the school's athletic teams. In the 1940s, he pushed for the development of Holiday Park and the formation of a citywide recreation board. Martin received a special citation as the city's "Father of Recreation" in 1958 and was the 1969 Broward County Sports Citizen of the Year.

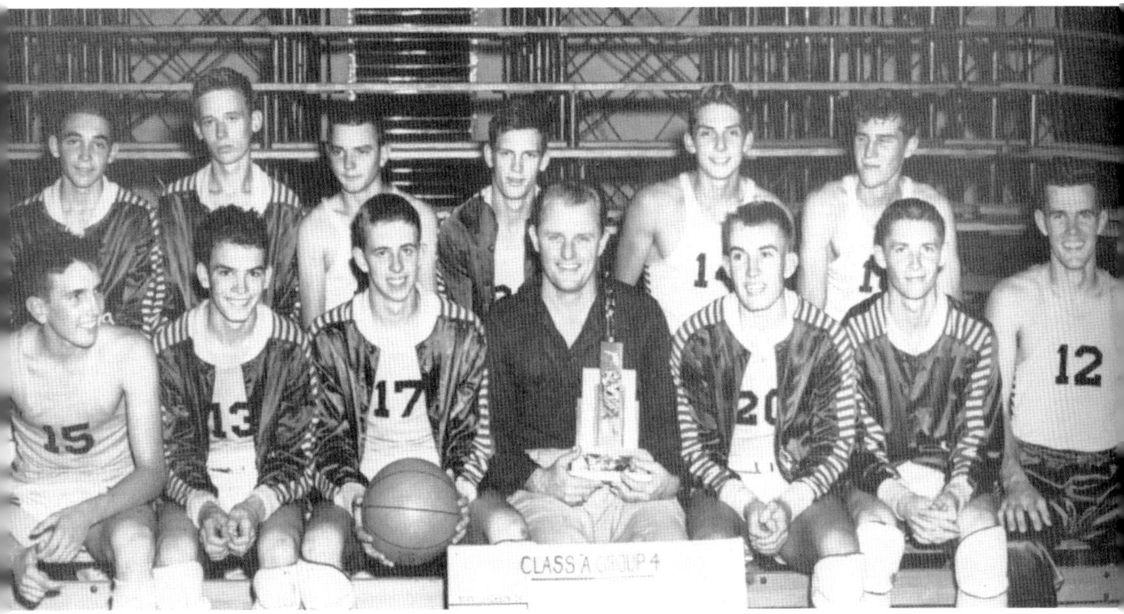

Clois Caldwell, Championship Boys Basketball Coach

Clois Caldwell was a standout basketball player at Millsaps College (Mississippi), where, in 1934, he had a 25-point scoring average. Between 1941 and 1954, he was a top basketball coach in the state, taking 12 Fort Lauderdale High School teams to the state tournament and winning the title in 1943, 1946, and 1953. Seven of his teams won 20 or more games, and the 1953 team was 25-1. Caldwell's 13-year record was 244-55. In 1955, he became the school's athletic director, holding the post until his retirement in 1976.

Katherine Rawls, Champion Diver and Swimmer

Born into what became a swimming and diving family, Katherine Rawls moved to Fort Lauderdale in 1932 at the age of 15 and began training at the Casino Pool. Nicknamed "The Minnow," she won 28 swimming and five diving US Nationals titles during the 1930s. Rawls was a member of the 1932 and 1936 Olympic teams, winning a silver medal in springboard diving both times and a bronze medal in 1936 as part of the freestyle relay team. In 1937, she was named the Associated Press Female Athlete of the Year when she won an unprecedented four individual swimming titles at the US Nationals, all of which she retained the following year. Rawls retired from swimming in 1939 after marrying Theodore Thompson and began working at the Thompson School of Aviation. Qualified as a pilot, she was one of the initial 25 pilots of the Women's Auxiliary Ferrying Squadron (WAFS) in 1942, assisting in transporting aircraft from the factories to military bases. In 1965, Rawls was an inaugural inductee into the International Swimming Hall of Fame.

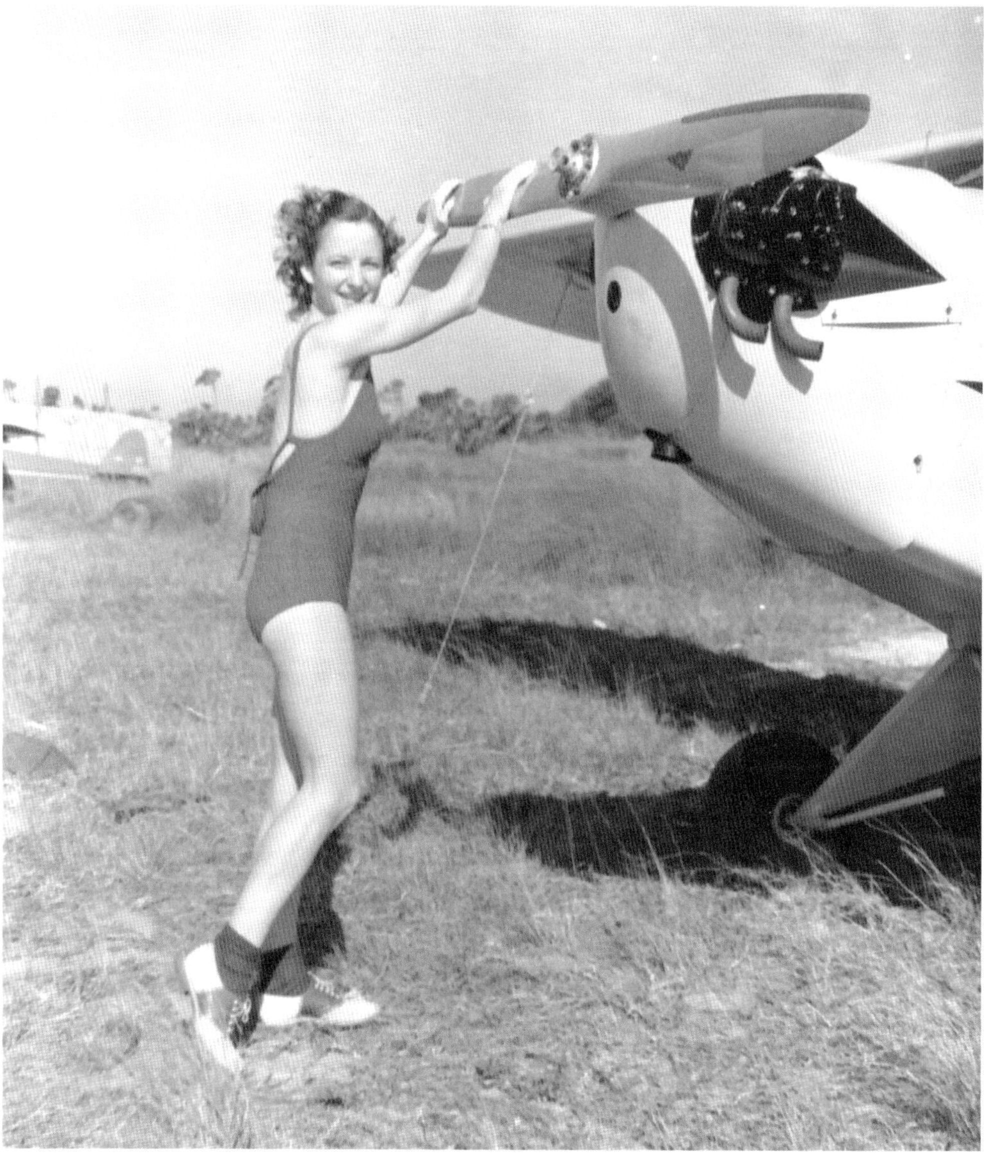

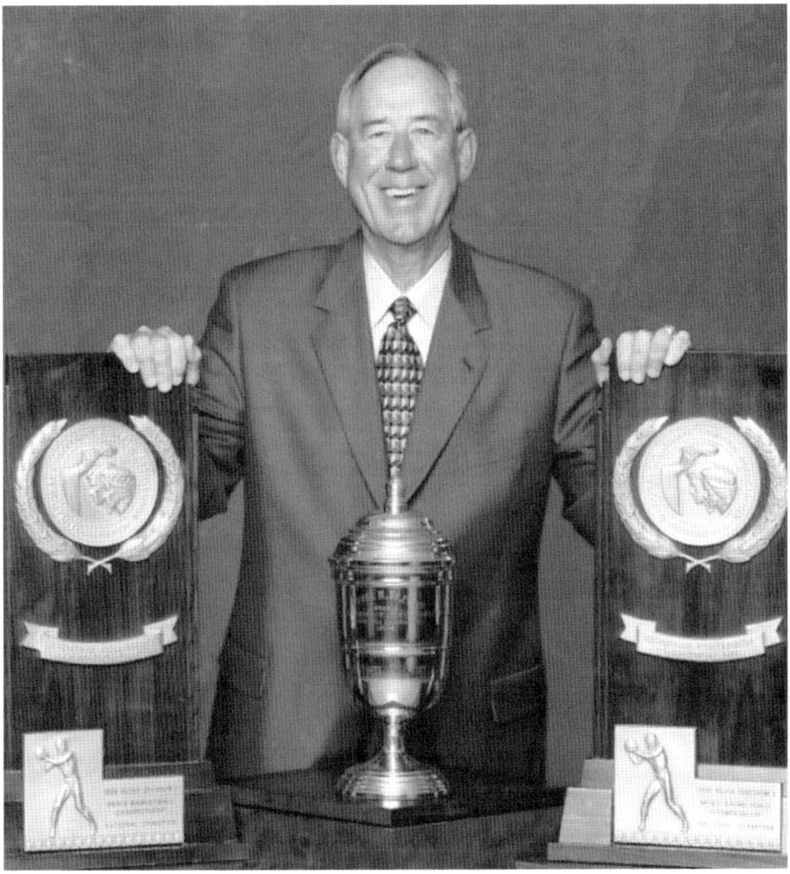

Charles M. Newton, Three-Sport Star, Basketball Coach, and University of Kentucky Athletic Director

A three-sport, all-state player at Fort Lauderdale High School, Charles Newton helped the school win state basketball (1946) and baseball (1947) championships. Recruited by Adolph Rupp, Newton played on Kentucky's 1951 national championship basketball team. After college, he became the coach at Transylvania University (Kentucky) and played three years in the minor leagues with the New York Yankees. Newton remained at Transylvania until 1968, compiling a 169-137 record. As coach, he recruited the school's first black player, James Hurley. One day, Newton received a call from Paul "Bear" Bryant asking him to be the coach at Alabama. Newton took the job and, in his first year, signed Wendell Hudson, the first black scholarship athlete in University of Alabama history. From 1969 to 1980, Newton compiled a 211-123 record, winning three straight SEC titles between 1974 and 1976. He was named SEC Coach of the Year in 1972 and 1976. From 1975 to 1985, he served on the NCAA Rules Committee and helped to usher in the shot clock and the three-point shot. In 1980, Newton resigned to become associate commissioner of the SEC. Vanderbilt University came calling in 1981, and Newton coached there for the next eight seasons. During that time, he also served as an assistant coach on the 1984 US Olympic men's basketball team. In 1989, Newton's alma mater, the University of Kentucky, hired him as athletic director to turn around the basketball program. He hired Rick Pitino, and Kentucky won the national championship in 1996. When Pitino left for the NBA, Newton hired Tubby Smith, the first black basketball coach at Kentucky, and the team won the 1998 national championship. During this time, he was also president of USA Basketball (1992–1996), overseeing the creation of the 1992 US Olympic basketball "Dream Team." In 2000, Newton retired from Kentucky and was also enshrined in the Naismith Memorial Basketball Hall of Fame. (Courtesy of the University of Kentucky.)

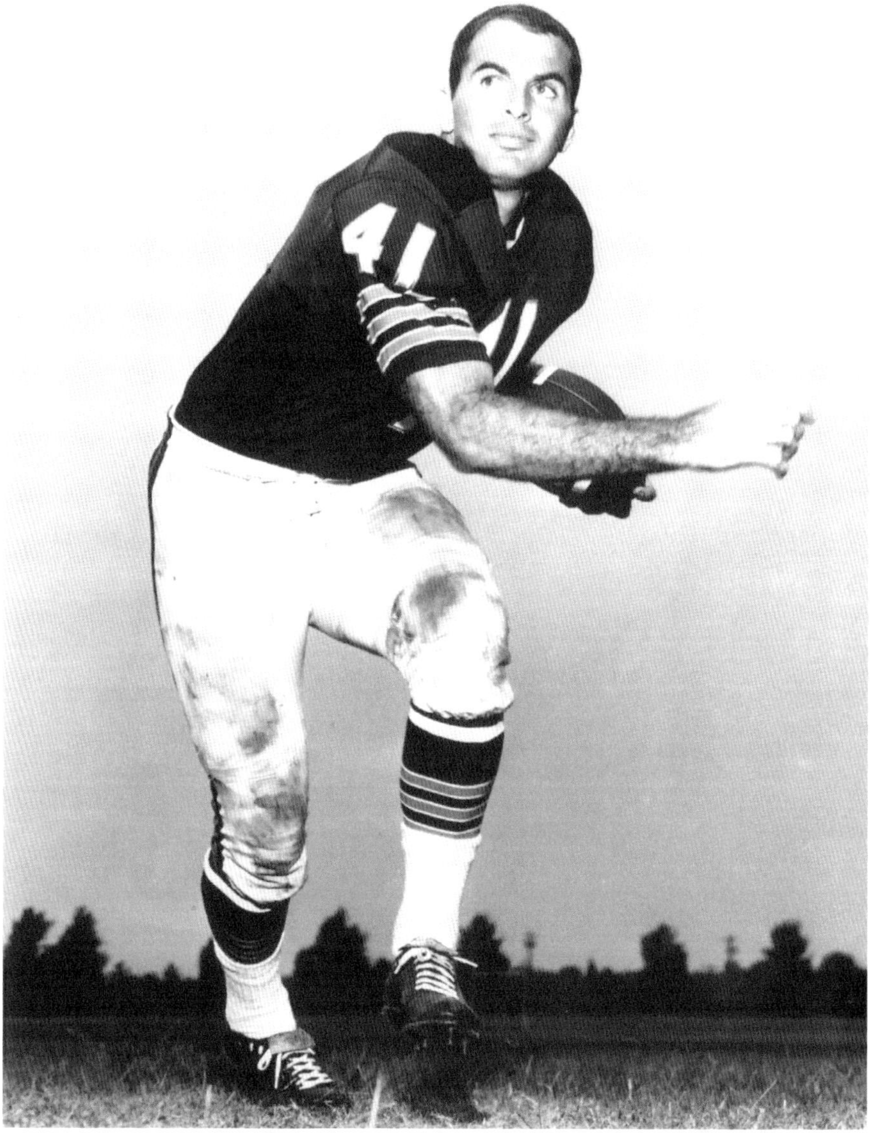

Brian Piccolo, NFL Player

In 1947, the Piccolo family moved to Fort Lauderdale when son Brian was three. His favorite sport was baseball, and he was a Little League star. Piccolo also played youth football, making every local all-star team in both sports. He was a star running back for St. Thomas Aquinas High School (then named Central Catholic High School), graduating in 1961. Piccolo went to Wake Forest and led the nation in rushing and scoring. He was named Atlantic Coast Conference (ACC) Player of the Year in 1964. Piccolo went undrafted to the NFL but joined the Chicago Bears as a free agent. By 1967, he was backing up tailback Gale Sayers and, in 1969, was named the starting fullback. Sayers and Piccolo were the first black and white men to room together in the NFL. In November 1969, Piccolo was diagnosed with embryonal carcinoma and passed away on June 16, 1970. His story was immortalized in the 1971 TV movie *Brian's Song*. In his honor, the Chicago Bears retired Piccolo's No. 41, and the St. Thomas Aquinas High School football stadium is named for him. Both the Bears and the ACC present the Brian Piccolo Award to their most courageous player. (Author's collection.)

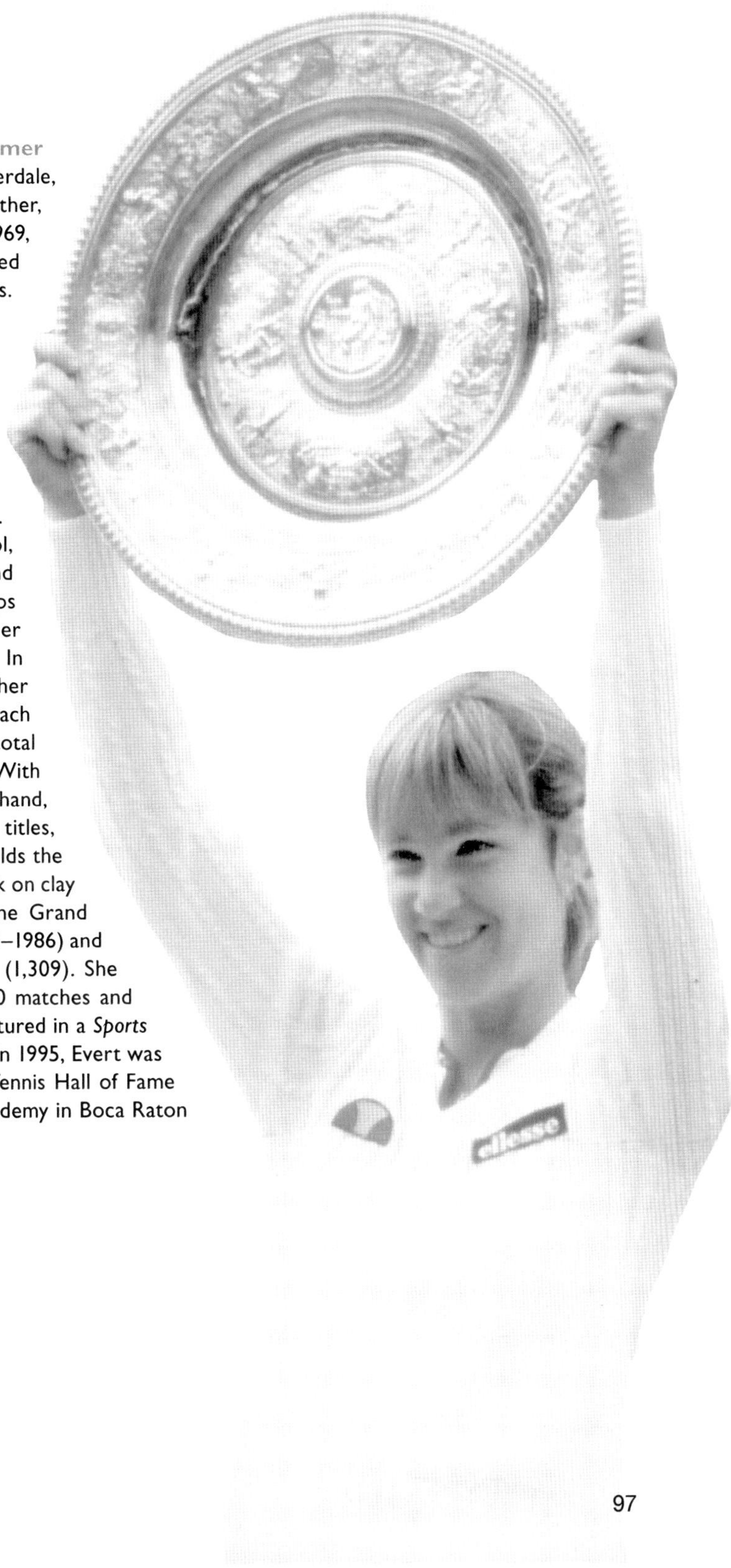

Chris Evert, Tennis Hall of Famer
Born and raised in Fort Lauderdale, Chris Evert was trained by her father, Jimmy, at Holiday Park. By 1969, she had become the No. 1 ranked under-14 girl in the United States. In 1970, Evert won the national 16-and-under championship and beat the world's No. 1, Margaret Court, in an exhibition. She burst onto the national scene in 1971 when, at age 16, she reached the semifinals of the US Open. While a student at St. Thomas Aquinas High School, Evert won three state singles and two state doubles championships and six US junior titles. On her 18th birthday, she turned pro. In November 1975, Evert achieved her first No. 1 ranking. She would reach No. 1 eight additional times for a total of 260 weeks (No. 3 all-time). With her trademark two-handed backhand, Evert would win 157 singles titles, including 18 Grand Slams. She holds the records of a 125-match win streak on clay (1973–1979), winning at least one Grand Slam every year for 13 years (1974–1986) and the total number of match wins (1,309). She was the first player to win 1,000 matches and the first woman athlete to be featured in a *Sports Illustrated* television commercial. In 1995, Evert was inducted into the International Tennis Hall of Fame and opened the Evert Tennis Academy in Boca Raton in 1996. (Author's collection.)

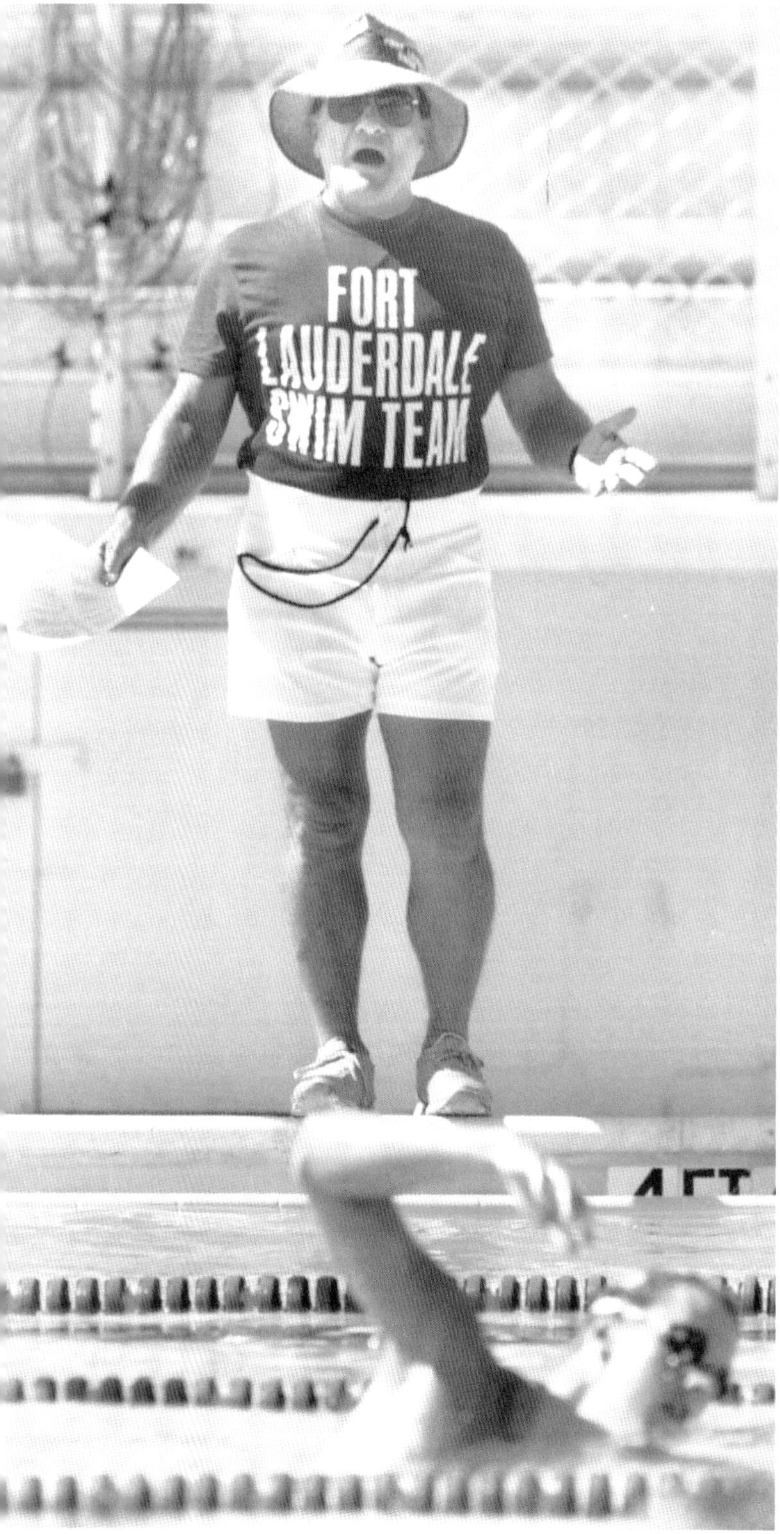

Jack Nelson, Fort Lauderdale Swim Team Coach
Born in Georgia, Jack Nelson moved to Fort Lauderdale in 1950 and began work as a lifeguard. After a stint in the US Air Force, where he was a member and coach of the swim team, Nelson participated in the 1956 Olympics, finishing fourth in the 200-meter butterfly. From 1957 to 1960, he attended the University of Miami (UM), where he was an All-American in 1958 and UM Athlete of the Year in 1959. From 1960 to 1986, Nelson was the swim coach for three different high schools, including Pine Crest and Fort Lauderdale High School, leading them to 30 state championships. In 1966, he founded the Jack Nelson Swim Team (later the Fort Lauderdale Swim Team), which he ran until his retirement in 2004. He was the 1976 US Women's Olympic swim team head coach. Nelson has also coached eight US national teams, 44 Olympians, and 460 All-Americans. He was inducted into the International Swimming Hall of Fame in 1994.

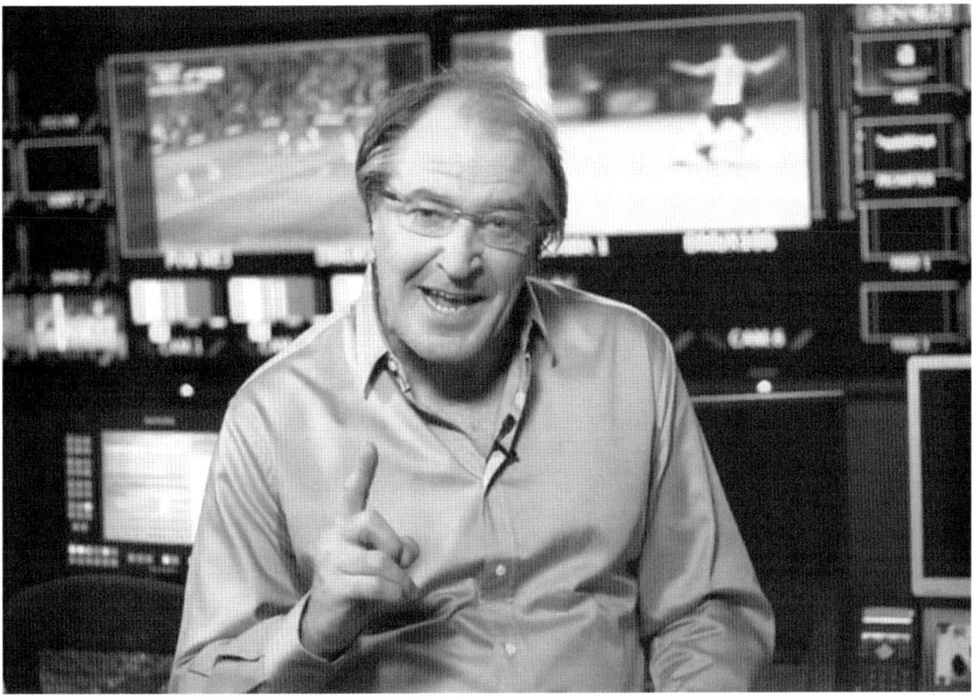

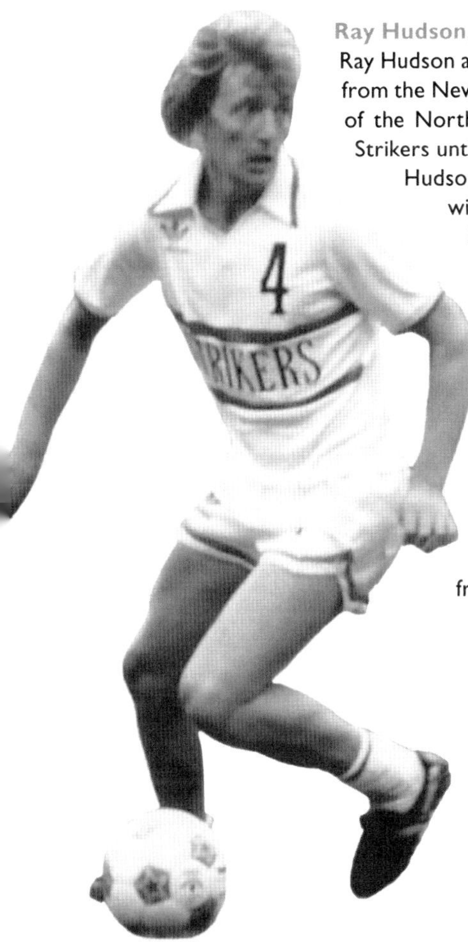

Ray Hudson, Strikers Soccer Star and Broadcaster

Ray Hudson arrived in Fort Lauderdale in 1977, as a 21-year-old on loan from the Newcastle United soccer club to the Fort Lauderdale Strikers of the North American Soccer League (NASL). He played with the Strikers until 1984 (the last year in Minnesota after the team moved). Hudson was named to five All-NASL squads. He played four years with the Minnesota Strikers of the Major Indoor Soccer League. In 1988, Hudson returned to the Fort Lauderdale Strikers of the newly formed American Soccer League, helping them win the league championship in 1989. His last year as a player was in 1991. Hudson was named the Miami Fusion (Major League Soccer) head coach in 2000 and coached them for two years. In 2002, he was hired as the coach of D.C. United. Beginning in 2004, Hudson started as a soccer commentator for GOL TV. His commentary has been described as flowery, clever, comical, and a mix of John Madden, Dick Vitale, and Don Cherry. In 2012, he was hired by beIN Sports. Hudson is able to do all of his play-by-play commentary from a small studio in Fort Lauderdale.

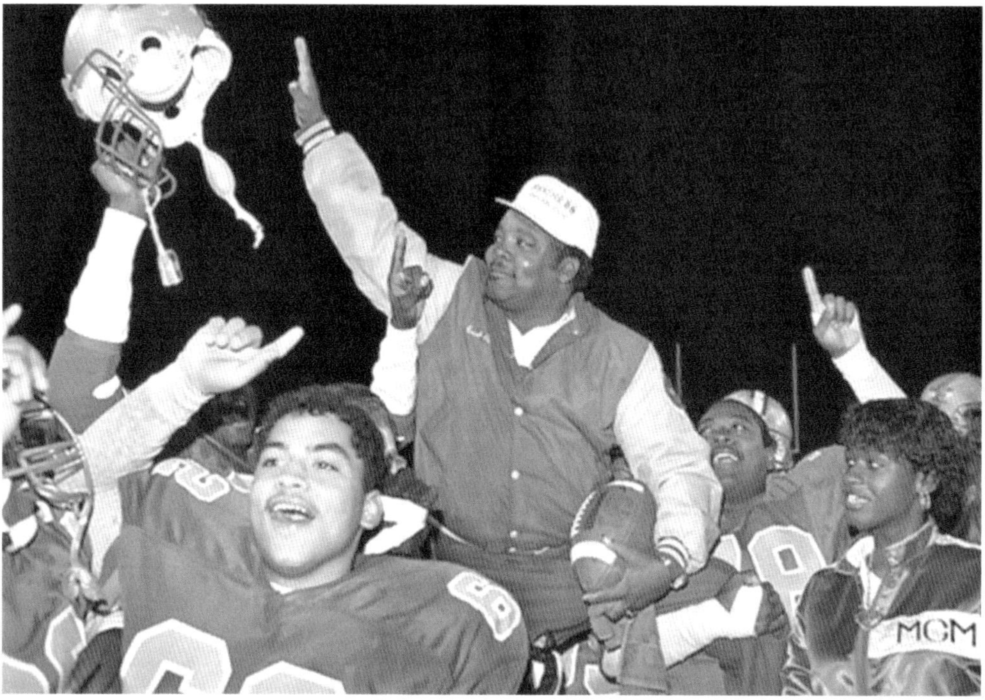

Otis Gray Jr., Dillard High School Football Coach

A former Dillard High School graduate, Otis Gray Jr. returned to his alma mater in 1979 to take over a struggling inner city school football team. During a 13-year career, he turned the team into a state power (two championships) and compiled a 107-55 record. Gray is only one of three football coaches in Broward County history to win multiple state titles. His 1990 team was ranked in the Top 25 in the nation by *USA Today.* In 2008, the Dillard High School football stadium was rededicated the Otis Gray Jr. Memorial Stadium.

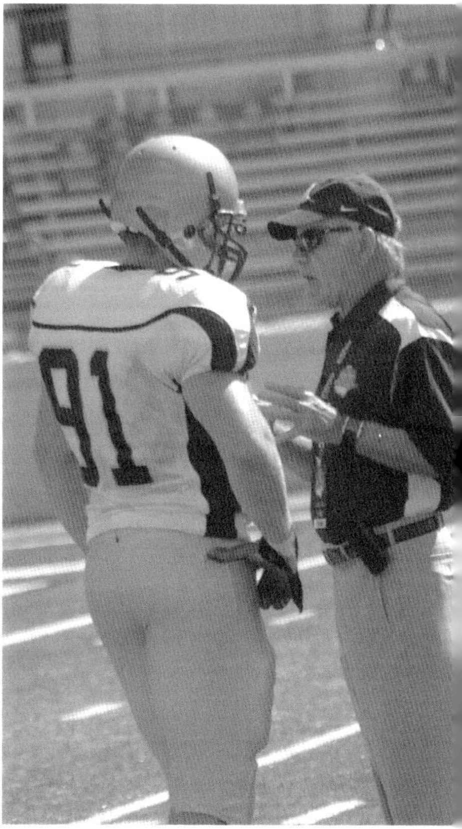

George Smith, St. Thomas Aquinas High School Football Coach

As the football coach for St. Thomas Aquinas, George Smith led his teams to 361 wins in 34 years. They went to 13 state title games, winning six. St. Thomas Aquinas also won the national championship in 2008 and 2010. Smith had more than 580 players play college ball, with 30 of them reaching the NFL. He was named the 2008 *USA Today* Coach of the Year. Smith was a 2005 inductee into the Florida High School Athletic Association Hall of Fame. (Courtesy of St. Thomas Aquinas High School.)

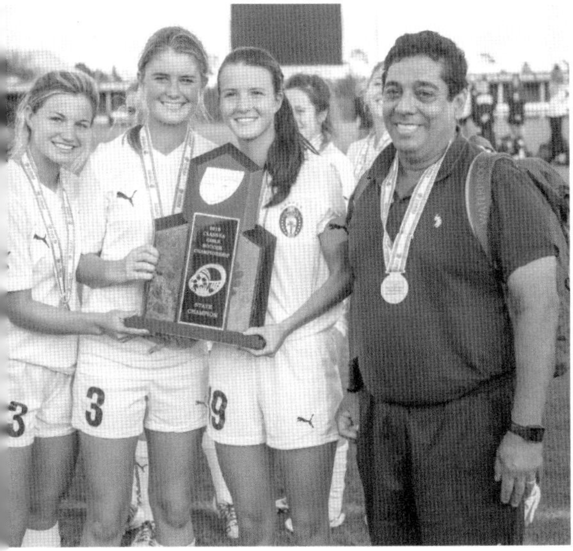

Carlos Giron, St. Thomas Aquinas Girls Soccer Coach
Since taking over the St. Thomas Aquinas girls soccer team in 1983, Carlos Giron has led them to 733 wins, 14 state titles, and seven national titles. He and his teams hold five national records, including most goals scored in a season (238), longest unbeaten win streak (158), and most wins by a coach. Winner of numerous awards, including 2007 Girls Soccer National Coach of the Year, Giron has also been honored with the Lifetime Achievement Award from the Florida Athletic Coaches Association. (Courtesy of St. Thomas Aquinas High School.)

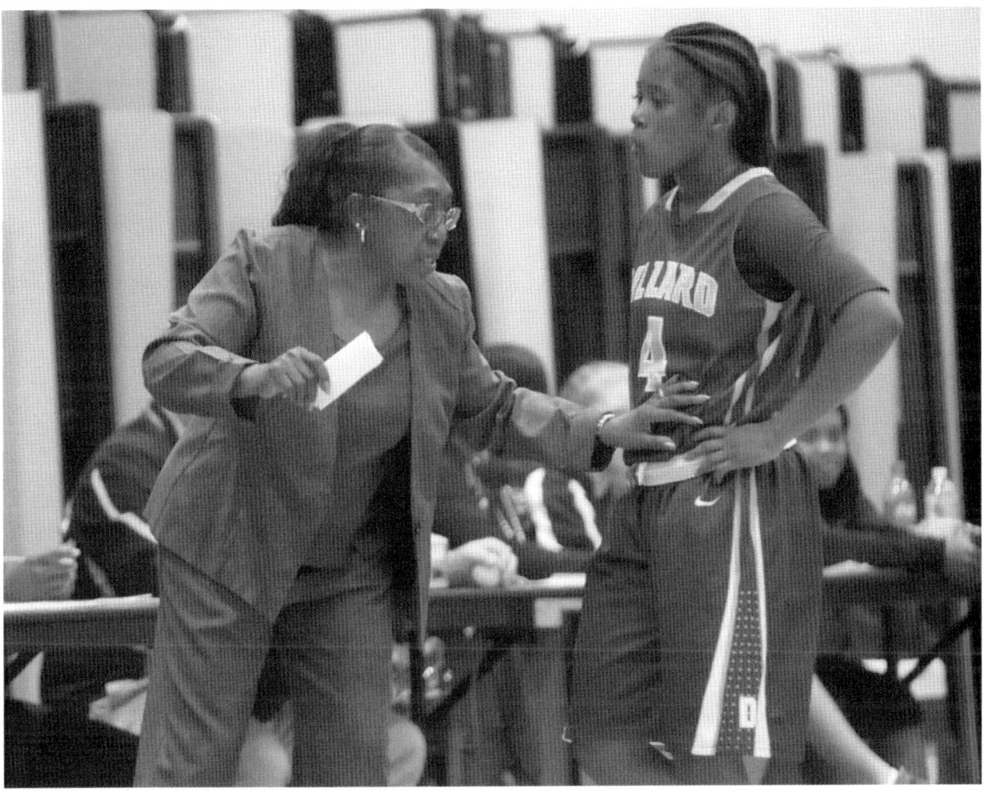

Marcia Pinder, Dillard High School Girls Basketball Coach
Since becoming the Dillard High School girls basketball coach in 1977, Marcia Pinder has led the team to 884 wins and nine state titles. Her current win total is the most by any Florida prep basketball coach, and she has the most state titles by a girls basketball coach. Pinder's win total places her in the national top 15 all-time. She was the 2013 National High School Athletic Coaches Association (NHSACA) Coach of the Year and was a 2014 inductee in the NHSACA Hall of Fame. (Courtesy of *Sun-Sentinel*.)

Michael Irvin, NFL Hall of Fame Receiver

Born in Fort Lauderdale, Michael Irvin graduated from St. Thomas Aquinas High School (All-State selection, 1983) before attending the University of Miami (UM). While at UM, Irvin set school records for receptions (143), receiving yardage (2,423), and touchdown receptions (26). He was a member of the 1987 national championship team. Irvin was selected 11th in the 1988 NFL Draft by the Dallas Cowboys and played for them for 12 years. Along with Troy Aikman and Emmitt Smith, he helped the Cowboys win three Super Bowls. Irvin finished his career with 750 receptions, 11,904 receiving yards, and 65 touchdowns. At the time of his retirement, he held or was tied for 20 Cowboys receiving records. Following his NFL career, Irvin went into broadcasting as a NFL analyst. In 2007, Irvin was elected into the Pro Football Hall of Fame and named to the Florida High School Athletic Association (FHSAA) all-century football team. (Author's collection.)

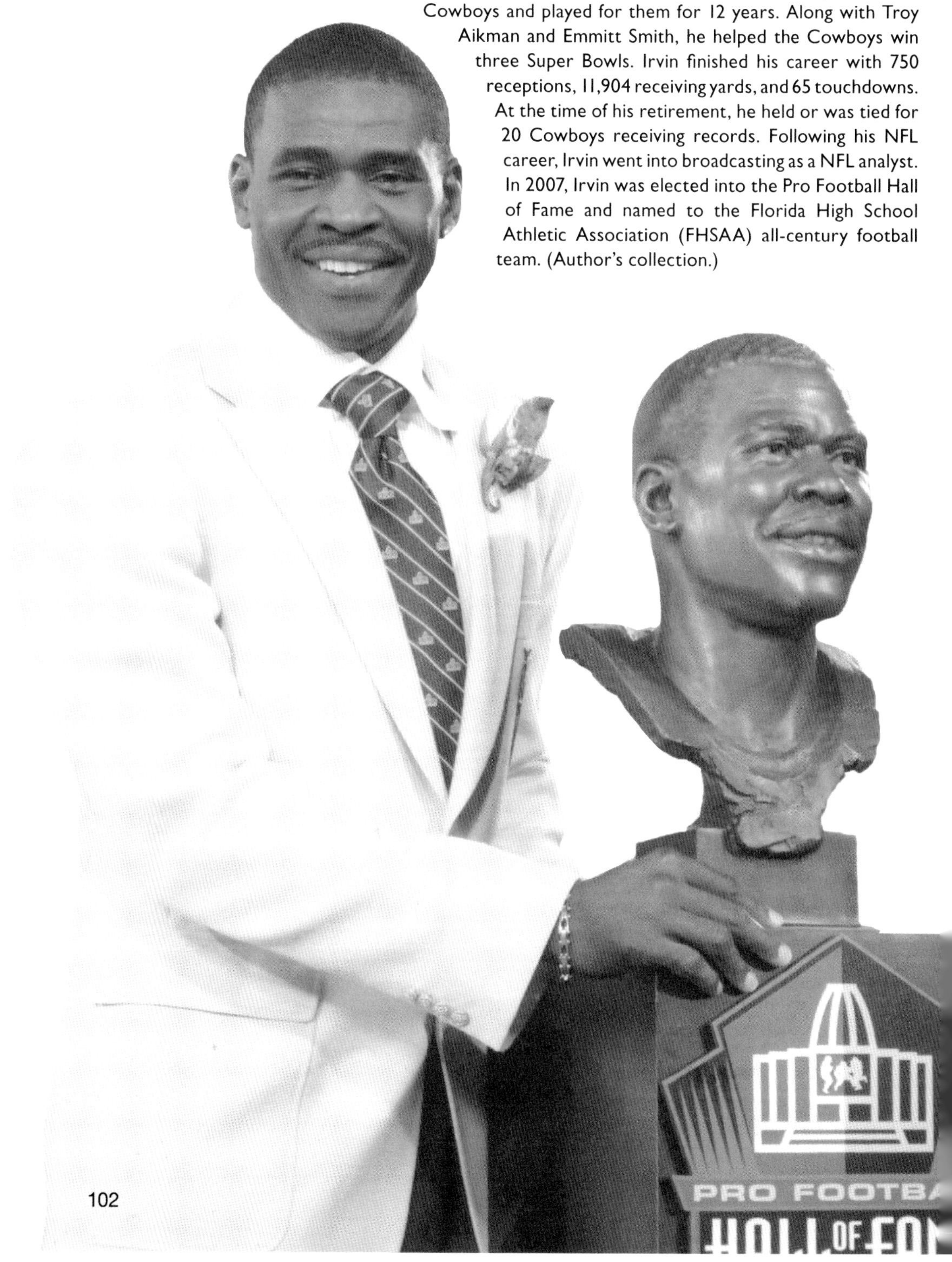

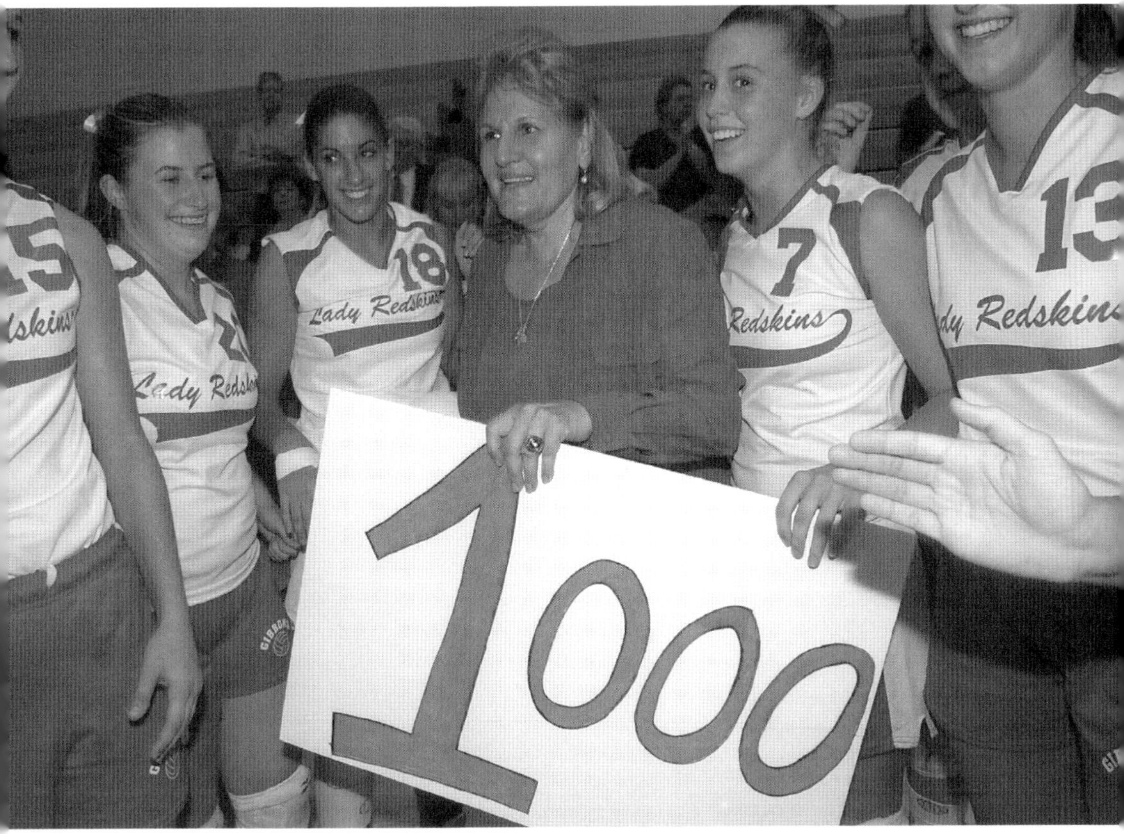

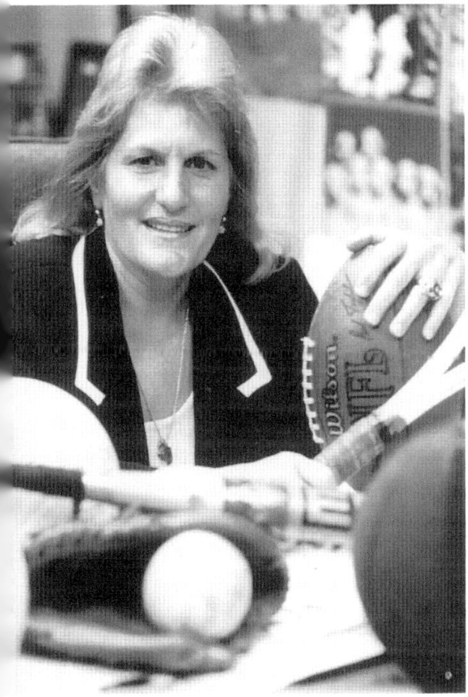

Louise Crocco, Cardinal Gibbons High School Volleyball Coach

During Louise Crocco's two years at Cardinal Gibbons High School, she helped to start varsity volleyball, basketball, and softball and was captain and MVP in all three sports. After graduating from Florida Atlantic University in 1969, she returned to Cardinal Gibbons to coach the volleyball, basketball, and softball teams. In 1981, Crocco was named athletic director and later stopped coaching basketball and softball. As the volleyball coach for 39 years, she compiled a 1,132-123 record and captured a Florida record of 18 state championships. Crocco was named National Coach of the Year four times, Florida Athletic Coaches Association Coach of the Year 18 times, and was inducted into the American Volleyball Coaches Association Hall of Fame in 2005. She was also the first woman to be inducted into the Florida Athletics Coaches Association Hall of Fame. Crocco retired as the volleyball coach in 2007 but remained the athletic director until 2009. (Above, courtesy of *Sun-Sentinel*; left, courtesy of Louise Crocco.)

Sanya Richards-Ross, Track and Field Olympian

Born in Jamaica, Sanya Richards-Ross moved with her family to Fort Lauderdale when she was 12. Running since she was age seven, Richards-Ross won nine individual state titles while at St. Thomas Aquinas High School. A 2002 graduate and a member of the National Honor Society, she was named the Gatorade National High School Girls Track & Field Athlete of the Year, the National High School Female Athlete of the Year, the USA Track and Field's Youth Athlete of the Year and the *Track and Field News* Women's Prep Athlete of the Year, during her senior year. That same year, Richards-Ross won a silver medal in the 400-meter event and a bronze in the 200-meter event at the World Championships. In 2003, she became the NCAA 400-meter champion. During the 2004, 2008, and 2012 Olympics, Richards-Ross was a member of the gold medal-winning 400-meter relay team. Also at the 2012 Olympics, she won her first individual gold medal in the 400-meter event. Richards-Ross is attempting to qualify for the 2016 Olympics and is a 2015 inductee into the Florida High School Athletic Association's Hall of Fame. (Author's collection.)

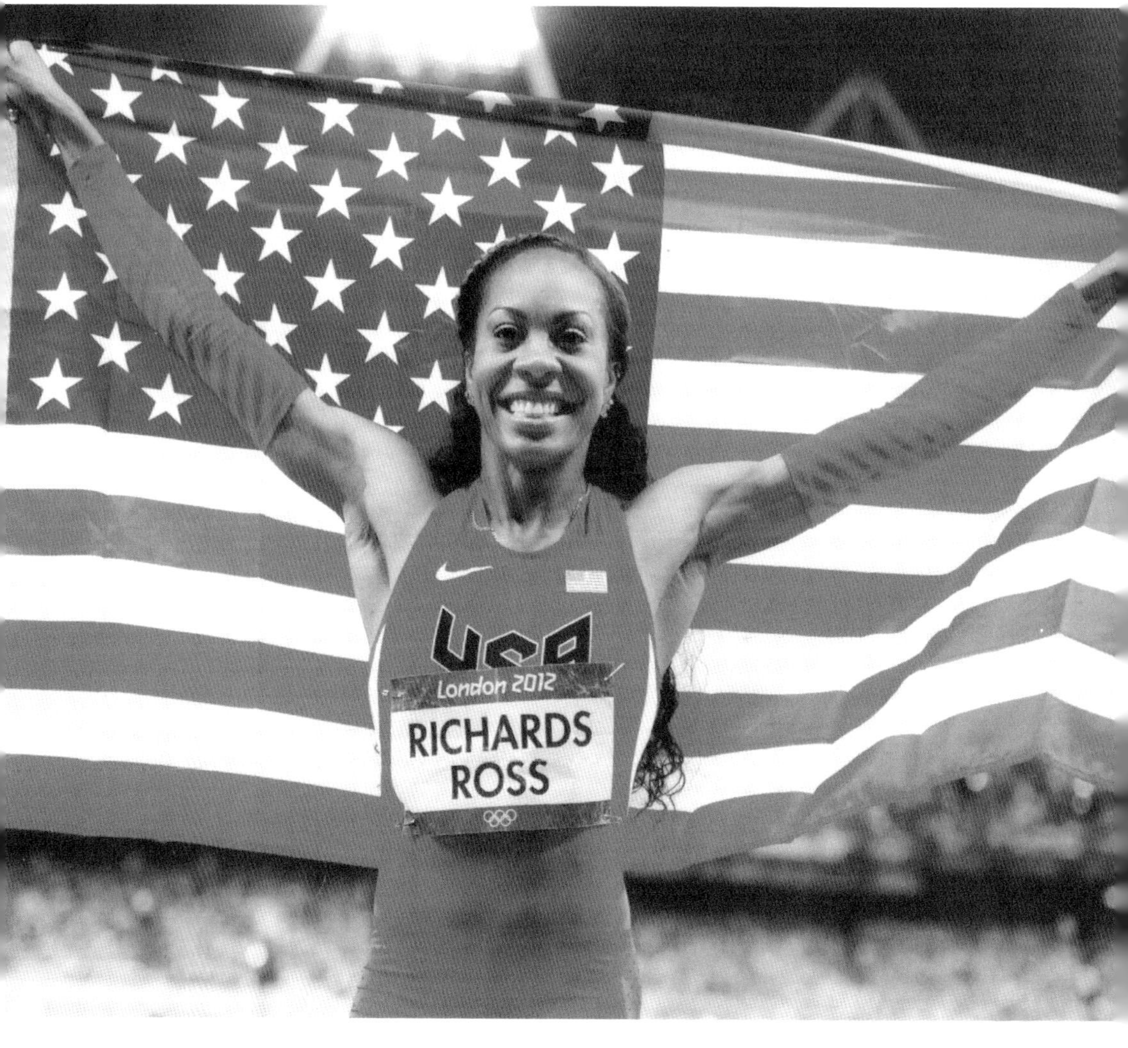

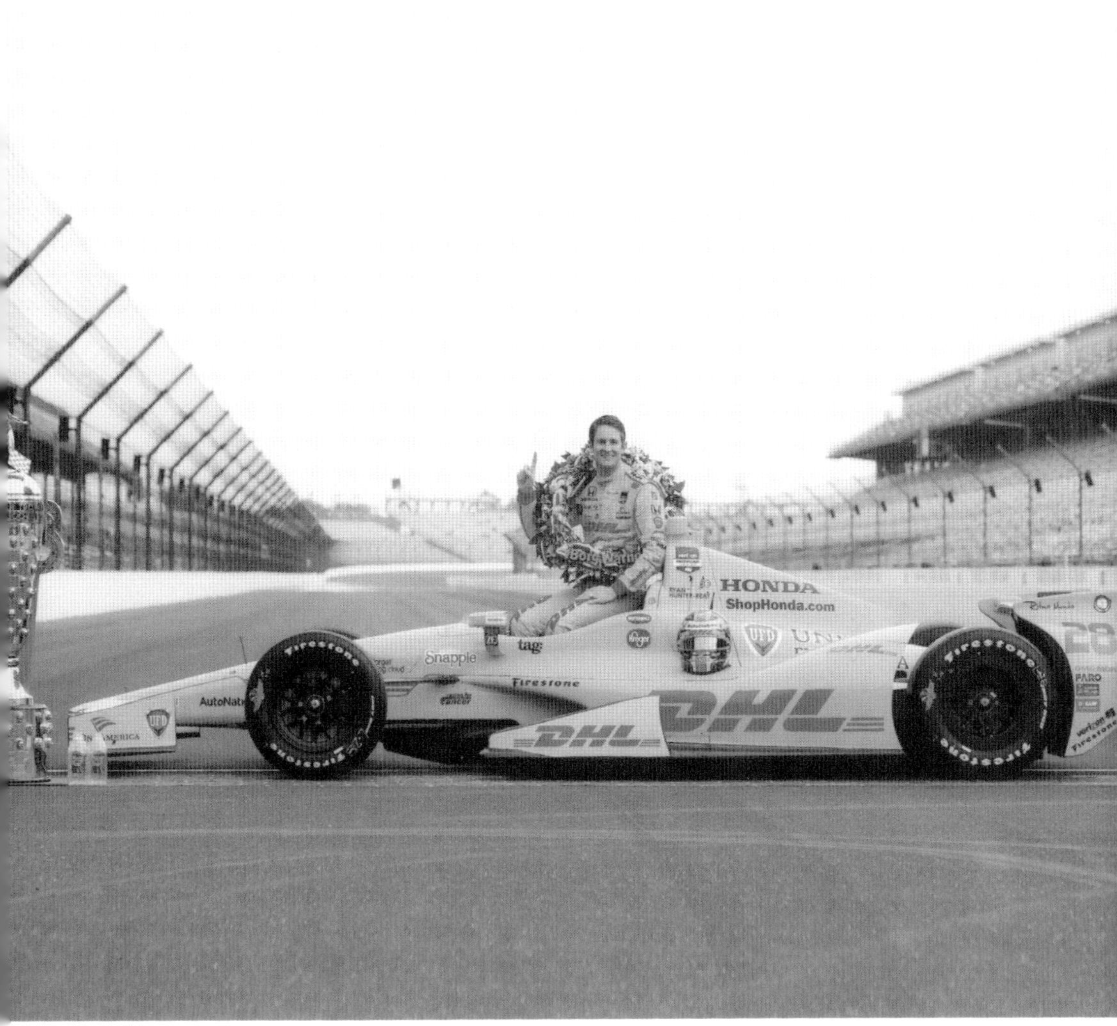

Ryan Hunter-Reay, 2014 Indianapolis 500 Winner

In the late 1990s, before he even graduated from Cardinal Gibbons High School, Ryan Hunter-Reay burst onto the racing scene. He won six national karting championships before turning his attention to open-wheel cars. In 2003, Hunter-Reay moved up to the Champ Car World Series, winning two races. He joined the Verizon IndyCar Series in 2007, signing with Rahal Letterman Racing. Hunter-Reay was the Rookie of the Year in 2007 and the Indianapolis 500 Rookie of the Year in 2008. Now driving for Andretti Autosport, he was the 2012 Verizon IndyCar Series champion and winner of the 2014 Indianapolis 500. Through the 2014 season, Hunter-Reay had 14 career victories and won the ESPY Award for Best Driver in 2013 and 2014. He feels that South Florida traffic prepared him for the racetrack, saying, "I-95 rush hour is harder than any Indy 500!" Hunter-Reay also spearheads fundraising efforts for the fight against cancer through his Racing for Cancer foundation. (Author's collection.)

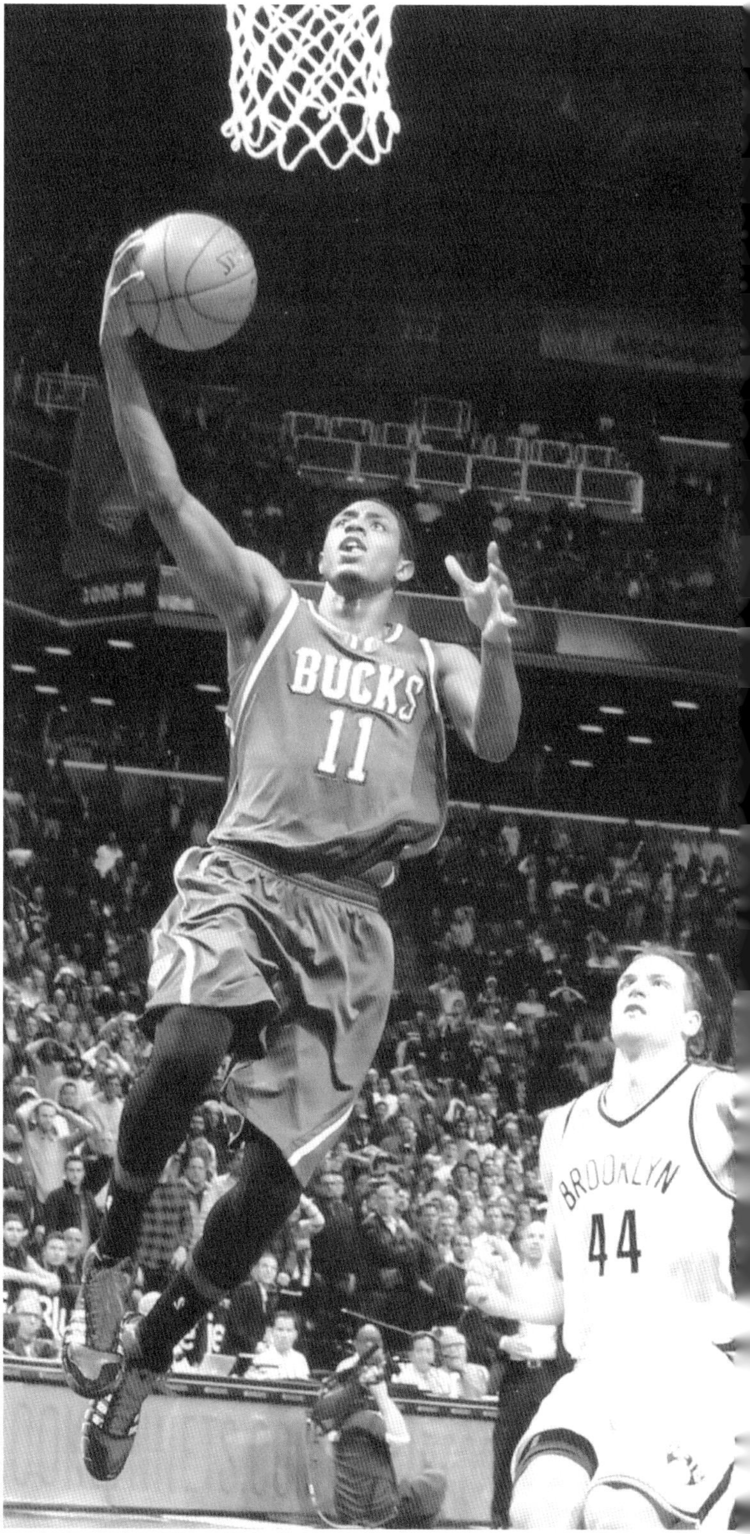

Brandon Knight, NBA Player
Brandon Knight attended Pine Crest Preparatory School, where he was a two-time Gatorade National Boys Basketball Player of the Year (2009–2010) and 2010 Gatorade National Male Athlete of the Year. He led the school to consecutive state titles in 2008 and 2009 and the finals in 2007 and 2010. Knight was the 2009 Florida Mr. Basketball and is second all-time on the state scoring list with 3,515 points. He signed with the University of Kentucky, playing only one year. Knight was named to the SEC All-Freshman Team and First Team All-SEC. He led the team to the SEC Championship and the NCAA Final Four. Knight was the No. 8 pick in the 2011 NBA Draft by the Detroit Pistons. He was named to the NBA All-Rookie First Team. Knight has also played for the Milwaukee Bucks and the Phoenix Suns. (Author's collection.)

CHAPTER NINE

Education

Formal education in Fort Lauderdale began in a one-room, wooden schoolhouse with nine students in 1899. Eighteen-year-old Ivy Cromartie, who had just passed the state teacher's exam with a 98 percent rating, was sent by Dade County school superintendent Z.T. Merritt at the request of Edwin King. It served as the only school until a two-story, four-room, concrete block building was constructed in 1910. The Central High School opened in 1915 on land donated by the Stranahans and had its first graduating class (five boys) that same year. Colored School No. 11 was established in 1907, and Mrs. Thigpen and supervisor W.B. Burns welcomed 10 students to the one-room wooden schoolhouse.

The Broward County School District was established in 1915, after the county was formed from Dade County. James Rickards (1920–1929) and Ulrich J. Bennett (1931–1952) served as longtime superintendents. High school students from all outlying areas of Broward County were transported to Fort Lauderdale, as it was the only high school between Miami and West Palm Beach. As the population of Fort Lauderdale grew in the late teens and early 1920s, four neighborhood or ward elementary schools were opened. The North Side Elementary School building from 1927 is still in use. A new Colored School building, later renamed Dillard School, opened in 1924 on land purchased from the Stranahan's for $1. The first Catholic school, St. Anthony's Catholic School, opened in 1926.

The 1930s saw the opening of private schools such as Pine Crest Preparatory School by Dr. Mae McMillan and Fern Hall by Edna Herriott. The Tanglewood School for handicapped students opened in 1938. Dillard High School, under the direction of principal Clarence Walker from 1937 to 1942, held its first graduation in 1938. A new Dillard High School campus was built in 1950. The late 1940s saw Harryette Johnson and Avis McSmith forming preschools for white and black students, respectively.

In 1952, Central Catholic High School, later renamed St. Thomas Aquinas High School, separated from St. Anthony's. Fort Lauderdale's second public high school, Stranahan High School, opened in 1953 as an elementary school before converting to a high school in 1957. A new Fort Lauderdale High School campus opened in 1963, and a second Catholic high school, Cardinal Gibbons, opened in 1961.

Today, the Broward County Public School District is the second largest public school district in Florida and the sixth largest in the nation. Fort Lauderdale has 16 elementary schools, four middle schools, and three public high schools. Additional high schools include St. Thomas Aquinas, Cardinal Gibbons, Pine Crest, Westminster Academy, and Calvary Christian Academy. On the collegiate level, the Art Institute, Broward College, and Florida Atlantic University also call Fort Lauderdale home.

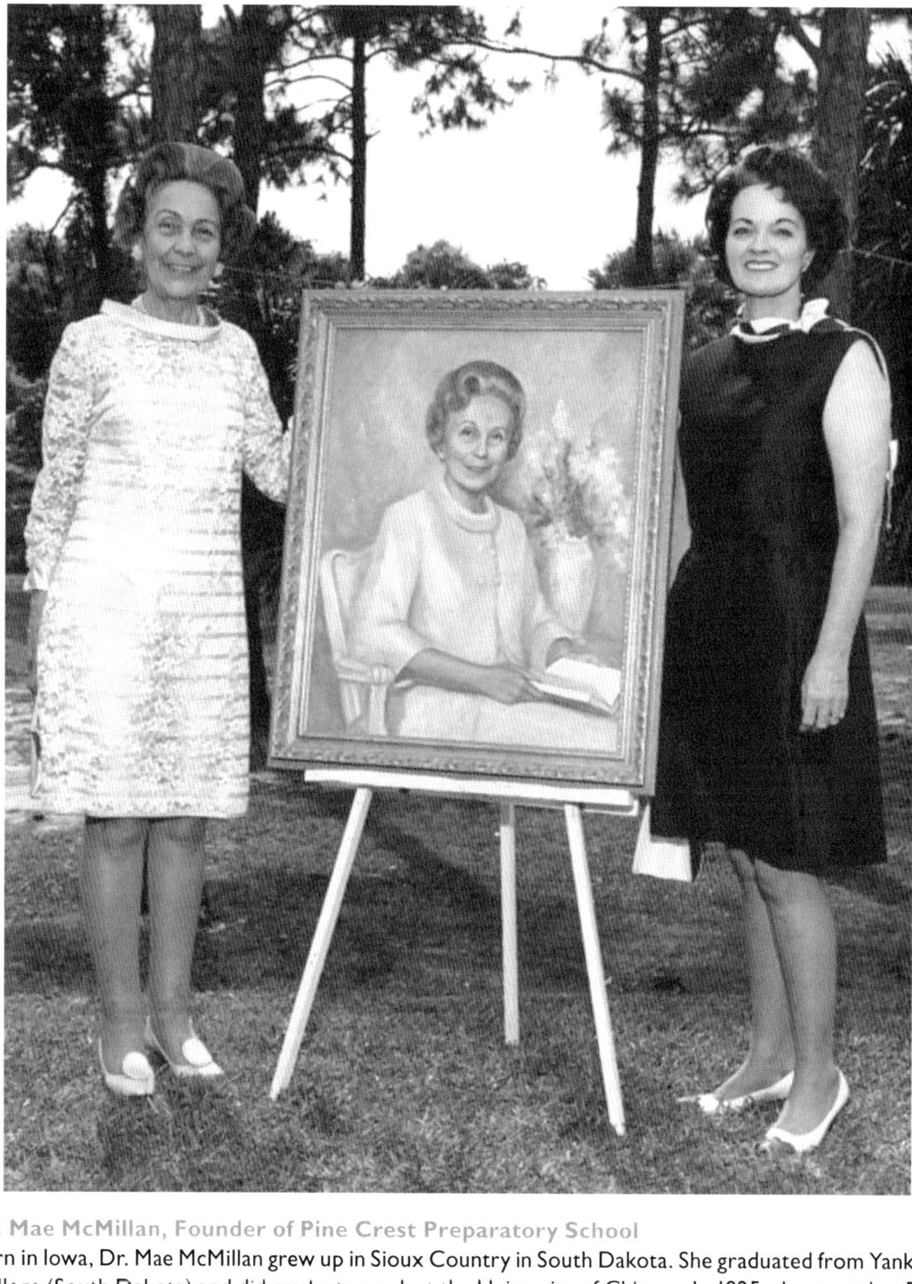

Dr. Mae McMillan, Founder of Pine Crest Preparatory School

Born in Iowa, Dr. Mae McMillan grew up in Sioux Country in South Dakota. She graduated from Yankton College (South Dakota) and did graduate work at the University of Chicago. In 1925, she moved to Fort Lauderdale with her husband, Albert. McMillan taught at Dania High School until the 1926 hurricane and the Great Depression forced people to move back north and she lost her job. In the early 1930s, she began to tutor students who were vacationing in Fort Lauderdale during the winter. McMillan founded Pine Crest School in 1934, with the classes held in the old Fort Lauderdale School building. In 1939, the school of 100 students relocated to the old Pine Crest Sanatorium (Maxwell Hospital) on Broward Boulevard. By 1965, the school had outgrown the small campus and moved to a new 49-acre location in northeast Fort Lauderdale. McMillan remained active at the school for 51 years. Today, over 1,700 students attend Pine Crest.

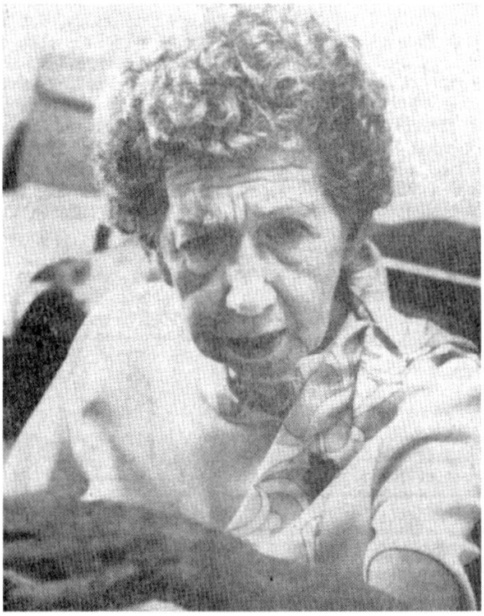

Edna Herriott, Founder of Fern Hall School
Edna Herriott arrived shortly after the 1926 hurricane. She taught at a local school before founding Fern Hall, the city's first private school, in 1932. It originally catered to tourist students who wanted to keep up with their studies. Originally located at the Bivans Hotel, Fern Hall relocated to the Maxwell Arcade in 1936. Herriot charged $2 a week for elementary education and $6 a week for high school education. Later, in 1950, she built a new school building on southeast Ninth Street. Fern Hall closed in 1971.

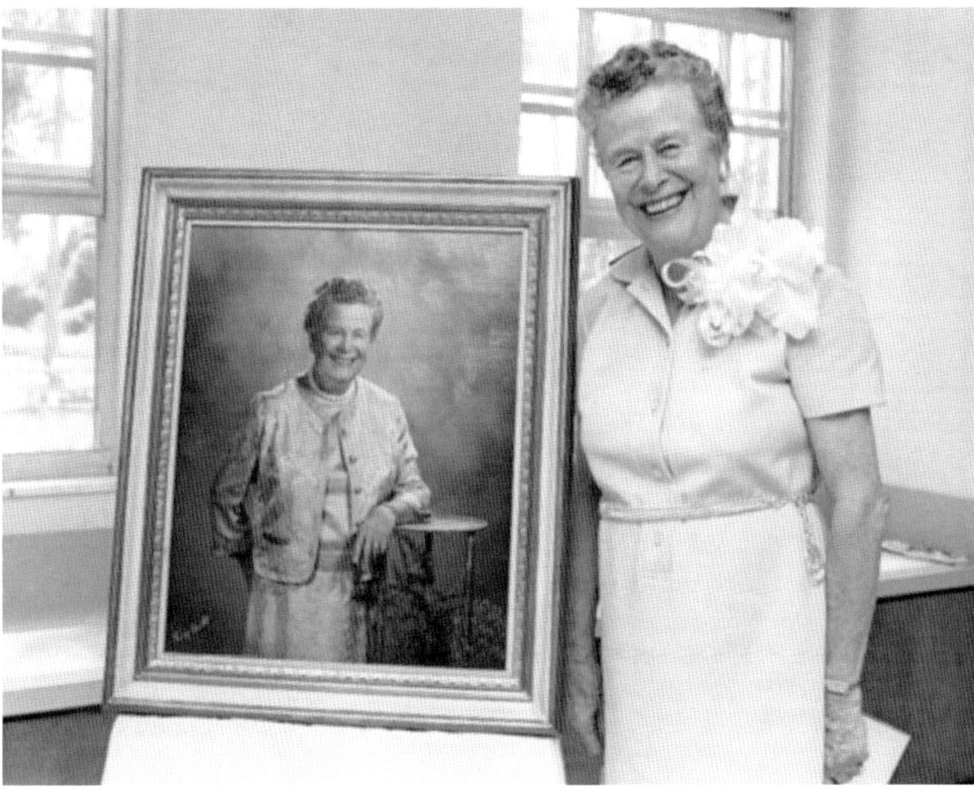

Marjean Packard, Longtime Principal at Pine Crest Elementary School
Marjean Packard was a graduate of the Teachers College, Miami University and taught school in Ohio and Illinois. In 1938, she moved to Fort Lauderdale, where she was offered a position at the Pine Crest School. In 1951, Packard became the principal of the elementary school and held that position until she retired in 1973. She was honored with a new building, the Marjean Packard Learning Center, on the Pine Crest campus in 1972.

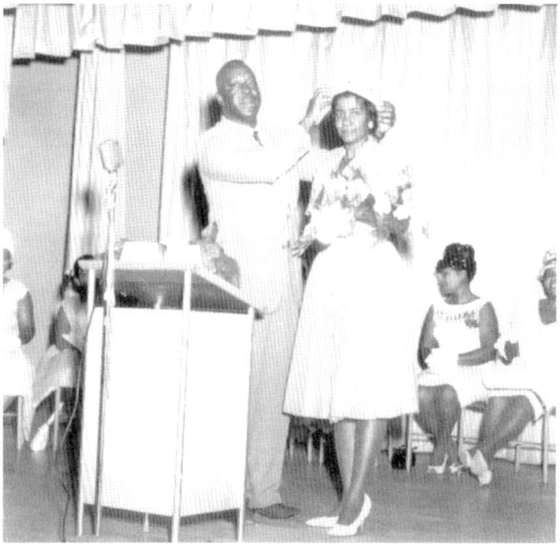

Cato Roach Jr., Walker Elementary School Principal

Cato Roach Jr. arrived in 1946 to teach science and math at Dillard High School. He was also the basketball and football coach. Roach spent eight years at Dillard, three of them as assistant principal. Roach helped improve the curriculum and developed the first vocational program in Broward County. In 1954, he became the principal at Walker Elementary School, serving there for 11 years. Following this, Roach became the first black county-level supervisor of elementary education. In 1966, he became the director of the Head Start Program. (Courtesy of Old Dillard Museum.)

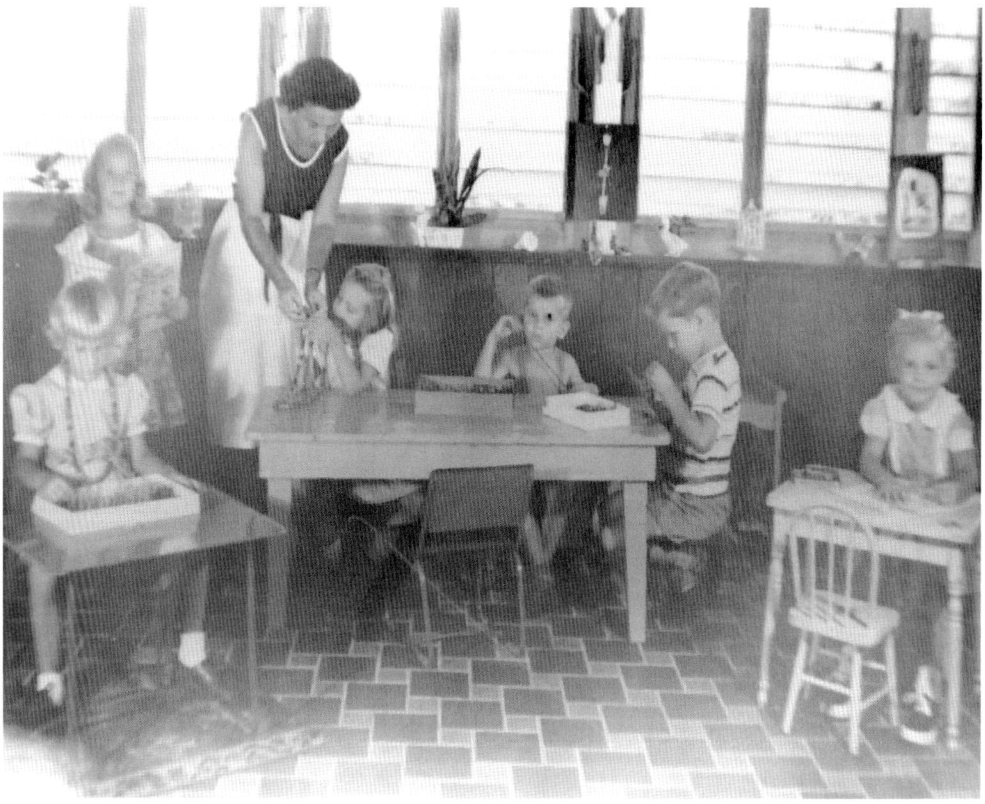

Harryette Johnson, Nursery School Teacher

Harryette Johnson arrived in town in the mid-1940s. After teaching for a couple of years at Fort Lauderdale High School, she opened a three-room school for four and five year olds in 1947. She taught for 37 years in a building behind her home. Beginning in 1952, her students put on an annual Thanksgiving play. In addition to teaching the students their ABC's and manners, Johnson also served as the bus driver, picking up all 16 students with her station wagon daily.

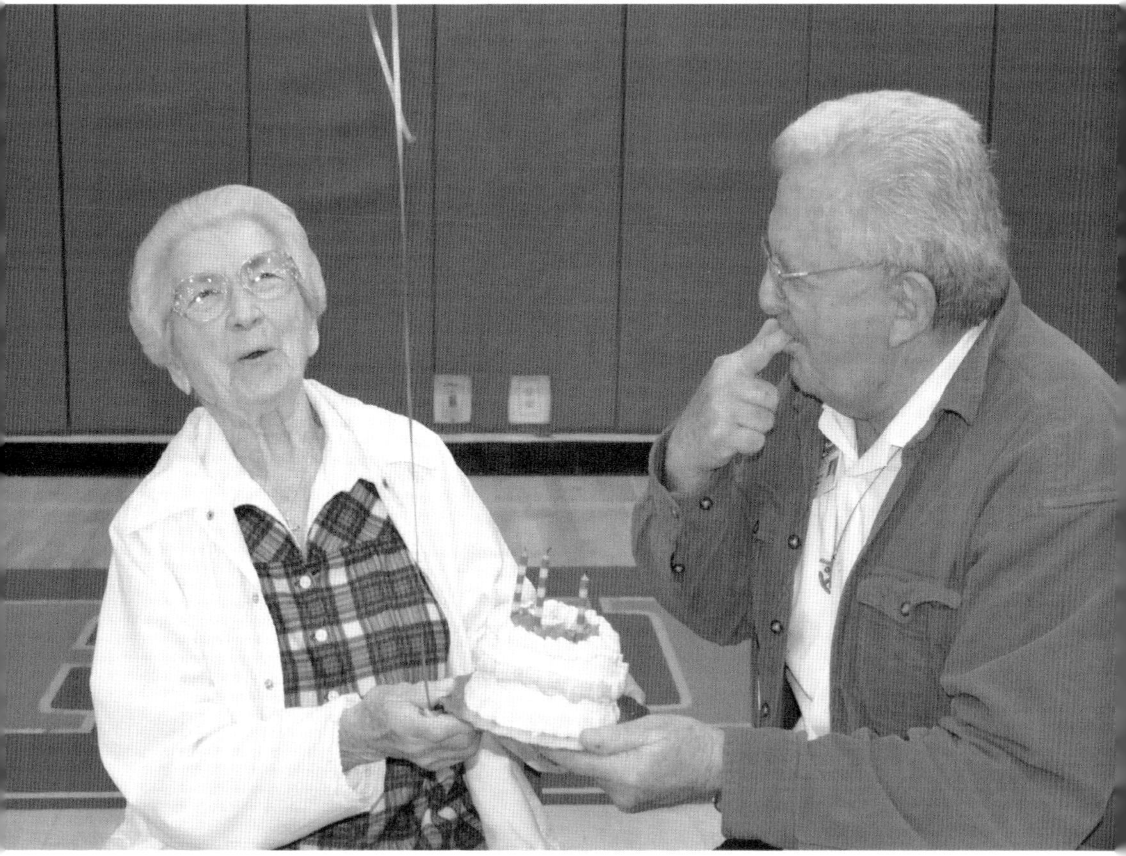

Sr. Marie Schramko, Longtime Assistant Principal of Cardinal Gibbons High School
Franciscan Sr. Marie Schramko arrived at Cardinal Gibbons High School in 1961 to serve as the first principal of girls. In 1972, when the school became co-ed, she became the assistant principal. Born in Johnstown, Pennsylvania, in 1917, Sister Schramko showed an early interest in teaching. She has an undergraduate degree in Latin from the College of St. Francis and two master's degrees, one from DePaul University and the other from Florida Atlantic University. Sister Schramko spent 23 years teaching in Illinois and Ohio before being selected for Cardinal Gibbons. She stopped teaching in 2009 at the age of 93. Sister Schramko has been a fixture at Cardinal Gibbons for over 50 years and, in addition to teaching Latin, algebra, geometry, biology, and chemistry, she has a tradition of attending all home sporting events. She has seen the school grow from an enrollment of 172 to over 1,100 and from sand-strewn, incomplete buildings to a fully developed 18-acre campus. As current principal Paul Ott stated, "Without a doubt, she is the most respected person on campus. She is the silent backbone of the institution." During her tenure, Sister Schramko has maintained a series of journals that detail the history of Cardinal Gibbons High School. In 2011, Sister Schramko was presented the Lumen Christi Award for outstanding work as a Catholic educator from the Catholic Educators Guild of the Archdiocese of Miami. The City of Fort Lauderdale declared February 10, 2012, as Sr. Marie Schramko Day.

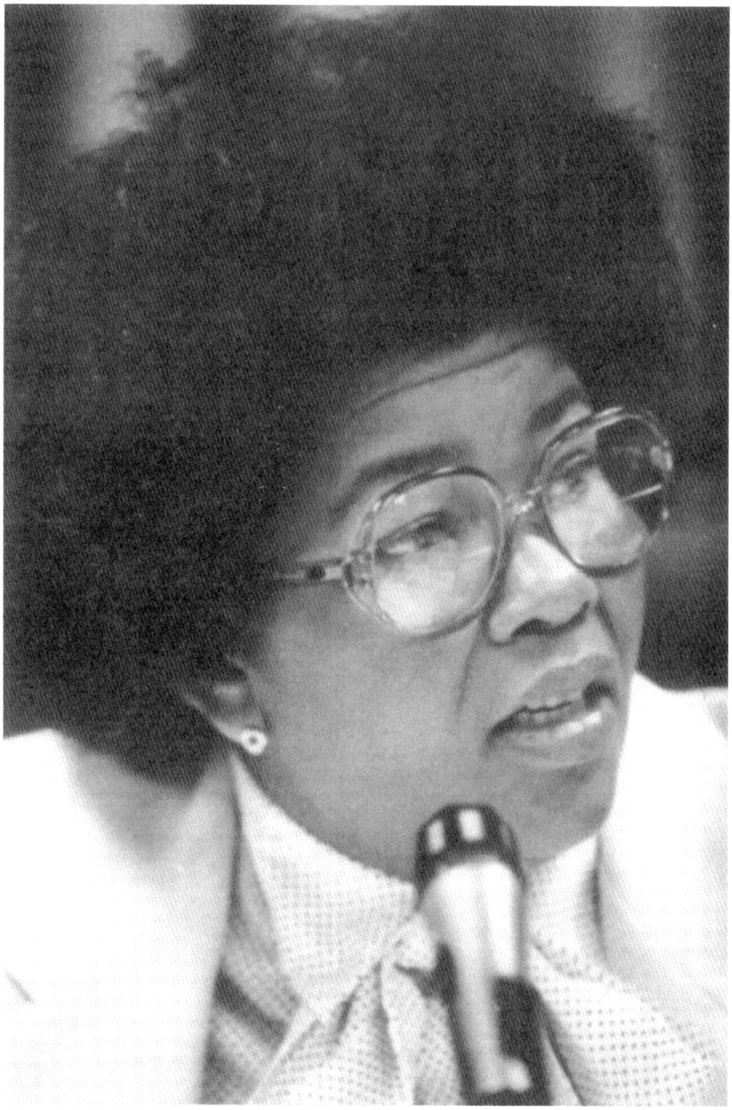

Dr. Kathleen Wright, First African American on Broward County School Board

One of 11 children born to a migrant labor foreman and a laundress, Fort Lauderdale native Dr. Kathleen Wright graduated as valedictorian of Dillard High School in 1953. She earned a bachelor's degree in social studies from Florida A&M University and a master's degree in education from Florida State University. Wright returned to Dillard High School in 1958 and taught there until 1974, when she was elected to the Broward County School Board. She was the first African American on the board and served eight years, including a stint as chairman. She advocated school integration and affirmative action. In 1980, Wright earned a doctoral degree in educational administration from Florida Atlantic University. She resigned from the school board in 1982 to run for state senate, but lost in the primary. A respected civic leader, Wright belonged to many social, political, and charitable organizations, including the Urban League, the NAACP, Delta Sigma Theta sorority, and the League of Women Voters. She was a founder of the Black Alliance for School Educators and taught bible classes at St. Christopher Episcopal Church. Following her death in 1985, the Broward County Public School District named its new administration building in her honor. (Courtesy of *Sun-Sentinel*.)

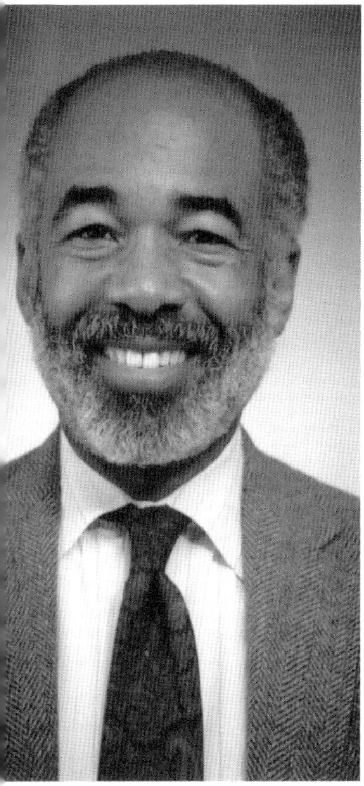

Sam Morrison, Broward County Library Director and Visionary of the African-American Research Library and Cultural Center

Born in Flagstaff, Arizona, in 1936, Sam Morrison served in the US Air Force from 1955 to 1959. After working 10 years as a manager for Lucky Supermarkets, he received a Bachelor of Arts in English from California State University-Los Angeles in 1971 and a master's degree in library science at the University of Illinois-Champaign in 1972. Morrison was hired as the assistant to the director of the Broward County Library System in 1974 and, two years later, was promoted to deputy director. In 1986, he became the chief librarian for the City of Chicago and oversaw the planning, design, and construction of the Harold Washington Library, the largest municipal library in the United States. Morrison returned to Broward County in 1990, when he was appointed the director of the Broward County Library System. In 1995, he had a vision to create a major research facility, cultural center, and historical archive for black culture in northwest Fort Lauderdale. In 2002, the African-American Research Library and Cultural Center opened. Morrison retired in 2003. He has served as part-chairman of the Greater Hollywood Arts Foundation and as a member of the board of trustees of Nova Southeastern University. He was also appointed by Governor Christ to the Children's Services Council of Broward County. (Courtesy of the African-American Research Library and Cultural Center.)

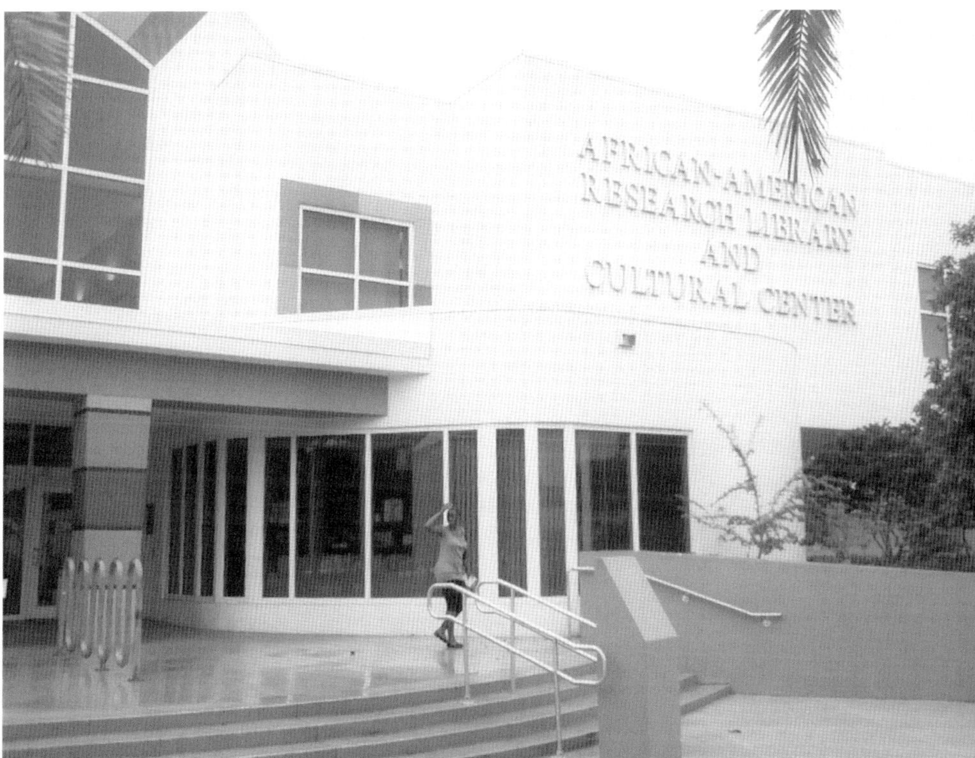

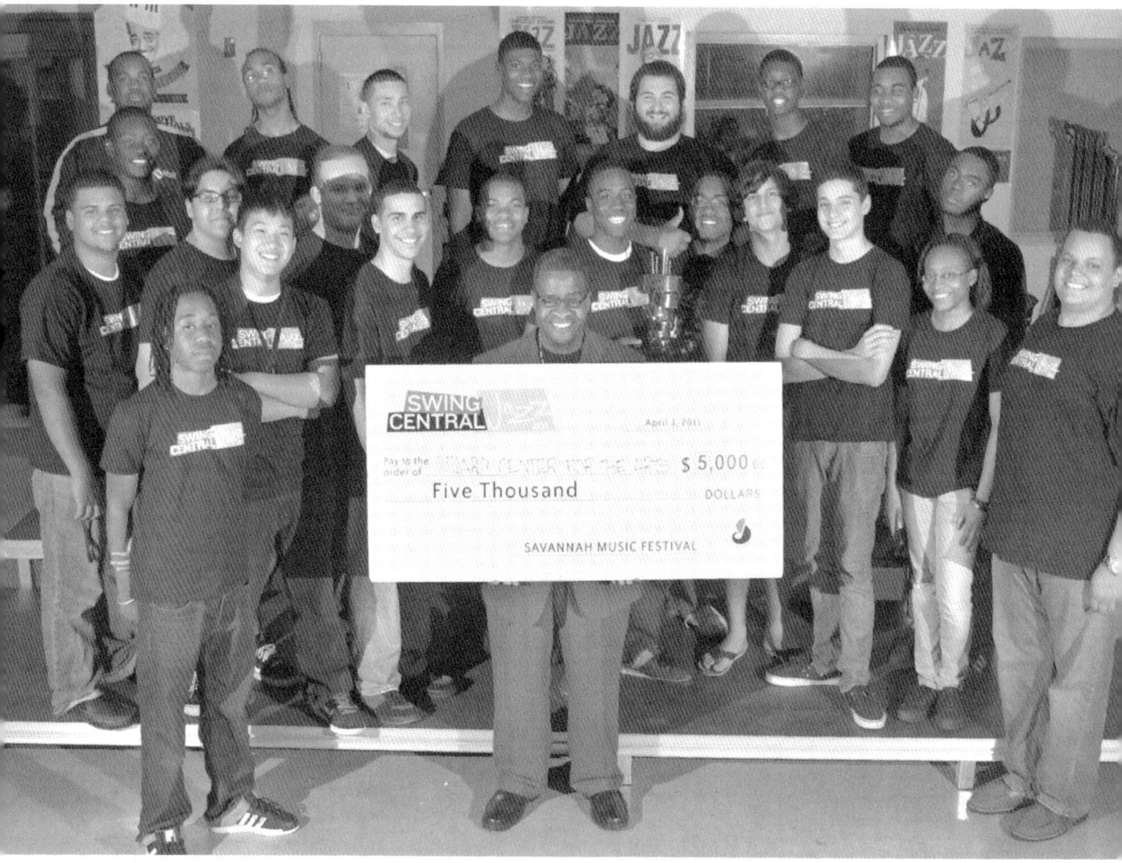

Christopher Dorsey, Dillard Center for the Arts Award-winning Jazz Ensemble Director
Since 2004, Christopher Dorsey has been the director of jazz studies at the Dillard Center for the Arts and has led the jazz ensemble to national recognition. An accomplished musician himself, Dorsey has performed with jazz greats Nat Adderley and the Roland Burns Quintet as well as Dionne Warwick and the Jason Hainsworth Orchestra. Under his leadership, the Dillard Jazz Ensemble finished first at the Savannah, Georgia, "Swing Central" jazz competition from 2010 to 2012 and took first place at the "Essentially Ellington" jazz band competition at Lincoln Center in New York City in 2011 and 2012. The ensemble finished in second place in 2010 and 2013. Dorsey has taught and nurtured young musicians for more than 26 years, and in 2011 *Jazzonian* awarded him the Excellence in Jazz Education Award. In 2013, he was a quarterfinalist for the first ever music educator award presented by the Recording Academy and the Grammy Foundation.

CHAPTER TEN

Other Notables

Throughout its history, Fort Lauderdale has been home to many individuals with interesting life stories. People from all walks of life—ages, ethnic groups, race and gender—have either grown up or relocated here. Some have been ordinary people who toiled daily to make a life for themselves and their families and others have gone on to become successful entrepreneurs and celebrities.

Previous chapters highlighted individuals who made an impact on Fort Lauderdale: founders of the town, those who assisted in the development and expansion of the town, educators, athletes, coaches, small business owners, fishermen, business magnates, commissioners, mayors, town employees, civil rights activists, religious leaders, and community needs caretakers. This chapter features those individuals that are also noteworthy but did not fit in the previous categories. Many of them are "firsts," those who participated in interesting professions, or those who were honored in some fashion for their actions or accomplishments.

There were so many people and organizations to chose from. Some of the notables that have not been included in the book are: Lt. Robert Anderson, US Army commander at Fort Sumter at the start of the Civil War; NFL players Isaac Bruce and Lorenzo White; Diana Nyad, Cuba to Florida swimmer; Nancy Stafford, Miss Florida 1976; William "Cap" Reed, three-time mayor; James Dallas Sr., educator, entrepreneur, and activist; Carl Hiaasen, lawyer for over 50 years and grandfather of writer Carl Hiaasen; Summerfield Boat Works; Leo Goodwin Sr., founder of GEICO and major benefactor and founder of Nova Southeastern University; William Dandy, activist for school integration; Brown's Good Food "pot roast table," a group of doctors, lawyers, and businessmen who had great influence in the community; Horace Alderman, rum smuggler who was hung at the Coast Guard base; Ken Burnstine, drug smuggler and pilot; Big John McLaughlin, stunt diver on James Bond movies; and Marilyn Manson, a former Broward Community College student who formed his band in 1989.

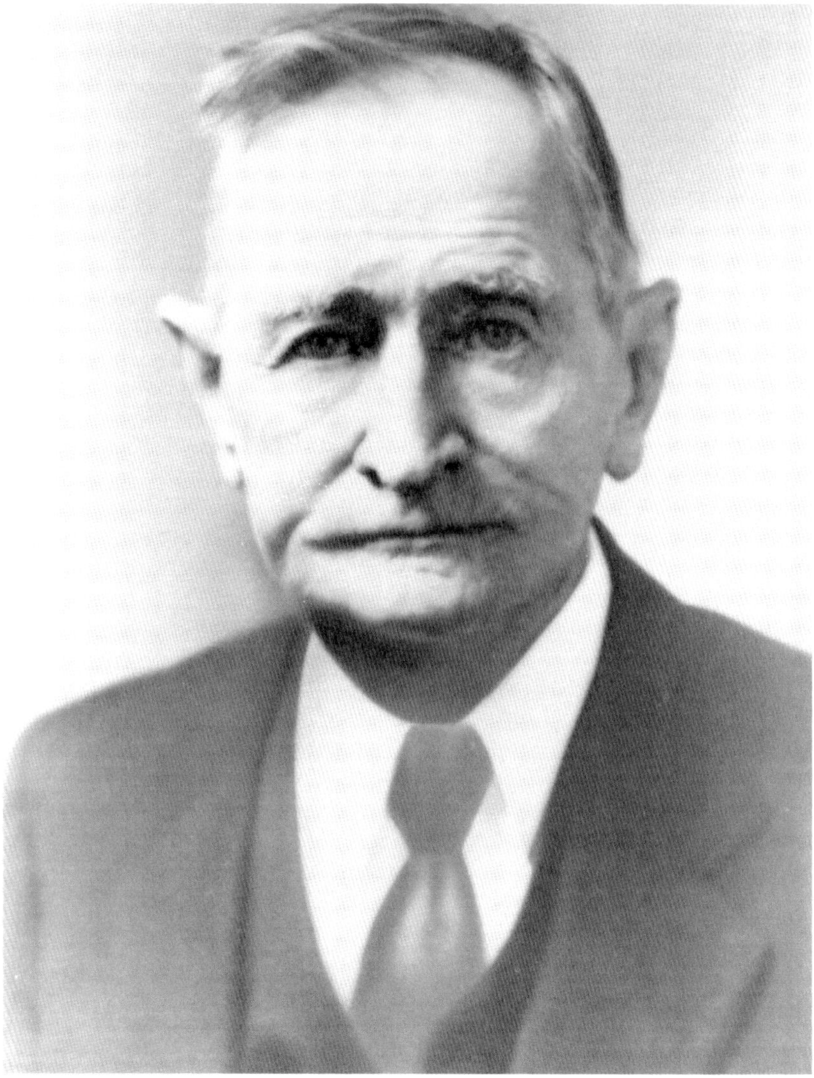

Dr. Thomas S. Kennedy, First Doctor
Originally from North Carolina, where the family homestead had been burned by General Sherman during the Civil War, Thomas Kennedy served in the Spanish-American War as a medic. In 1899, he arrived in Fort Lauderdale and became a tomato farmer. Shortly thereafter, a yellow fever epidemic broke out. With his limited medical and pharmaceutical training, Kennedy treated everyone in town, including himself, while tending his tomatoes at the same time. The Federal Bureau of Health originally wanted to charge him with practicing medicine without a license but, after investigating, determined that he had provided good treatment and paid him for his services. Kennedy used that money to get a medical degree from the University of the South (Sewanee, Tennessee). He returned to town in 1901. Kennedy made his rounds on foot, by boat, by buggy, or on horseback. He was known as "Little Doctor" due to his five-foot-five-inch stature. Kennedy was the only doctor in town until 1910, and he maintained his practice until 1938. Each month he would use his Spanish-American War veteran pension to pay off the accounts of indigent patients. He would take whatever patients could pay; he never met a man too poor for him to treat. A federal housing project was built on West Broward Boulevard in the 1930s, and it was dedicated to Kennedy in 1941.

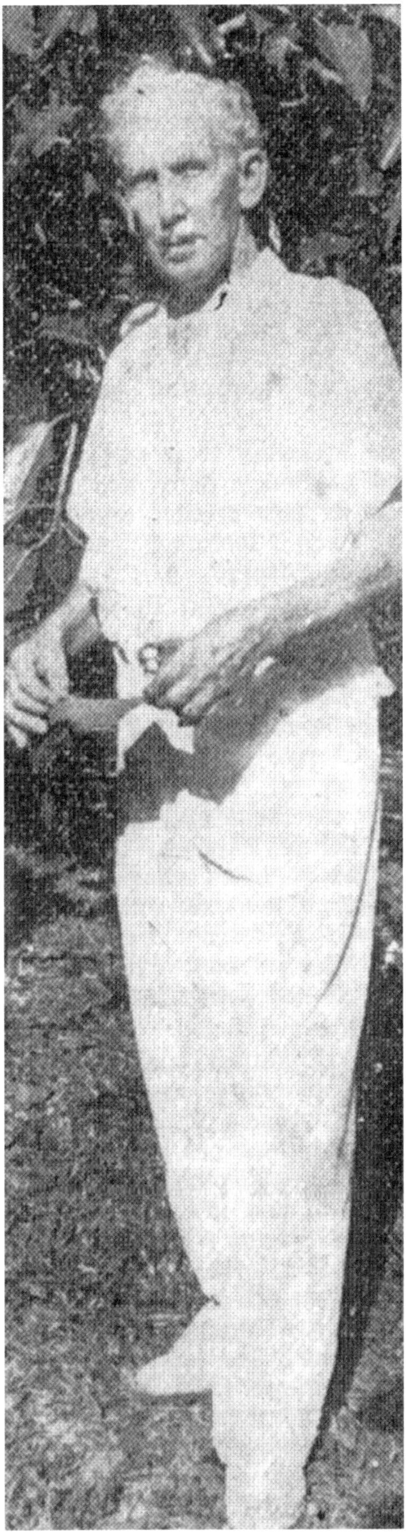

Glenn F. Bates, Horticulturist (LEFT)

Glenn Bates was known as one of Florida's finest horticulturists. A postal clerk from Michigan, he transferred to Fort Lauderdale in 1916. Bates purchased 30 acres at southwest Fourth Avenue and Twenty-Eighth Street and established Sandy Acres, one of Florida's largest collections of native and exotic plants. He developed a hybrid hibiscus. Bates was also interested in music and organized the first City of Fort Lauderdale band and was its director until the mid-1920s. After his passing, the garden center at Birch State Park was named in his honor.

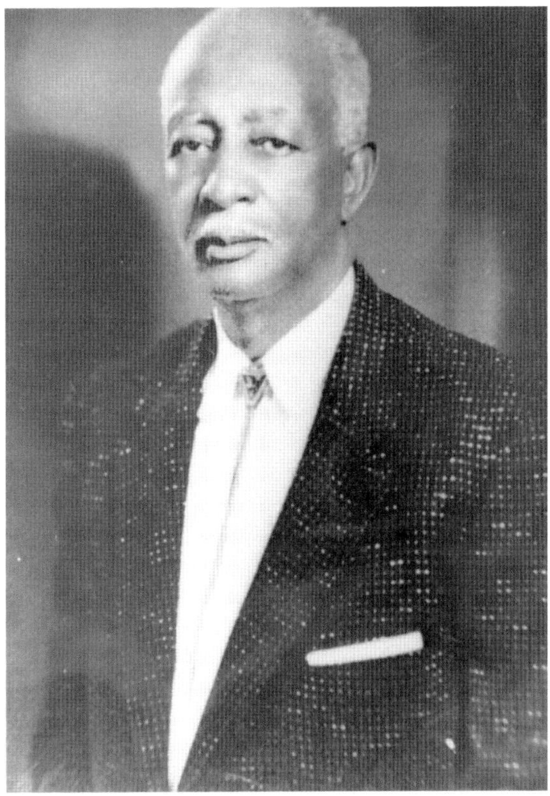

Dr. James Sistrunk, First Black Doctor (ABOVE)

James "Doc" Sistrunk graduated with honors from Meharry College (Tennessee) in 1919. Sistrunk briefly practiced in Dunnellon before arriving in Fort Lauderdale in 1922. He was the first black doctor in town and remained as such until 1938, when Dr. Von D. Mizell arrived. Together, they established Provident Hospital, the first hospital for black residents. By the time Doc Sistrunk retired in 1966, it was estimated that he had delivered 5,000 babies. In 1971, northwest Sixth Street (Sistrunk Boulevard) was renamed in his honor.

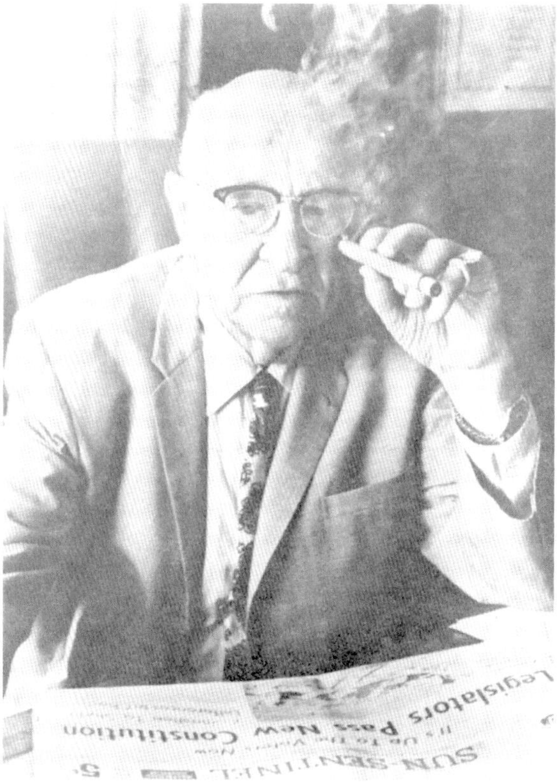

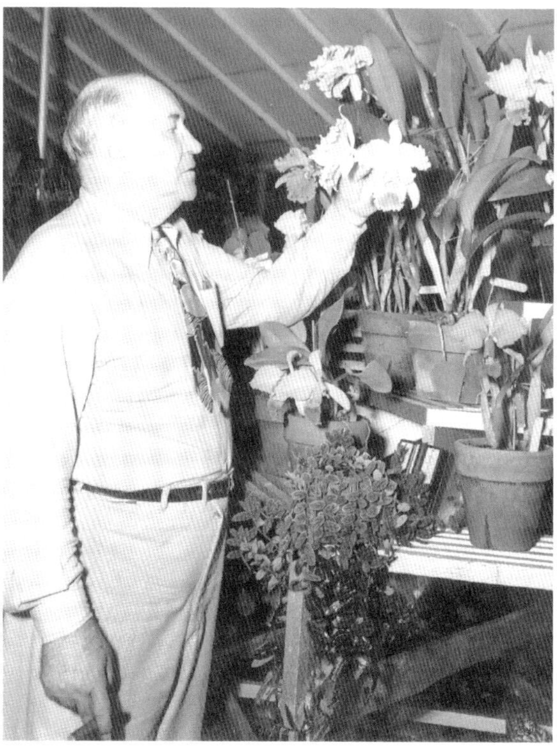

Robert H. Gore Sr., Editor of the *Fort Lauderdale News*

Born in Kentucky, Robert Gore Sr. started in the newspaper business as a cub reporter. By 1916, he was the editor and publisher of the *Terre Haute Post*, and he introduced accident insurance as a way to increase subscriptions. After this program went nationwide, Gore became a multimillionaire. In 1921, he went into the insurance business full-time in Chicago. While trying to sell insurance in Fort Lauderdale, Gore decided to purchase the *Fort Lauderdale News* for $75,000. In 1933, President Roosevelt named him governor of Puerto Rico. This was short-lived, and Gore soon returned to Fort Lauderdale and purchased the Wil-Mar Hotel skeletal frame and developed it into the Governors Club Hotel. As the editor of the *News*, he held sway on many local issues until he sold the newspaper for $18 million in 1963. Gore loaned the city $350,000 in 1949 so that they could complete the purchase of the Bahia Mar Yacht Basin. He was also fascinated with orchids and opened Gore Nursery. Through hybridization, Gore introduced the first all-red orchid in the industry.

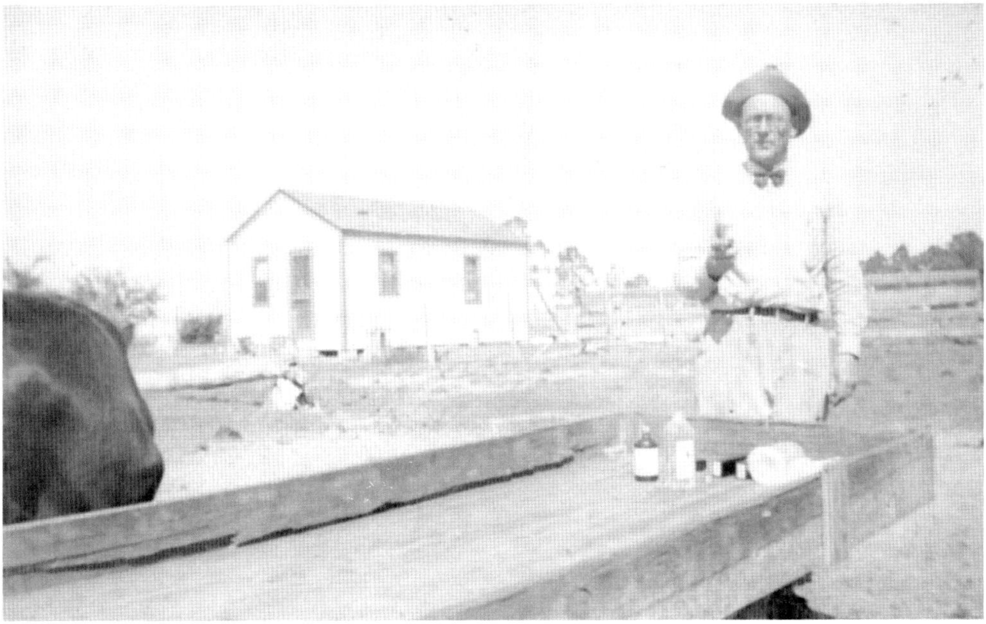

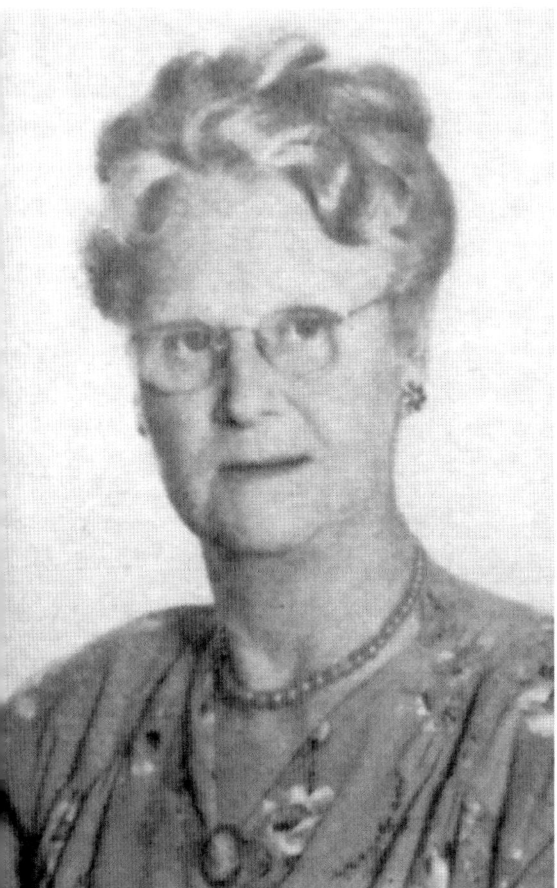

Dr. Daniel L. Campbell, Veterinarian and First City Health Inspector

After serving as a lieutenant in the Veterinarian Reserve Corps of the US Army during World War I, Dr. Daniel Campbell arrived in Fort Lauderdale in 1923. He established his practice and was hired by the Southeastern Packing Company as a food inspector. Campbell became the city's first health inspector in 1924, serving for two years before going back into private practice. He remained in Fort Lauderdale until 1963.

Dr. Anna Darrow (Doc Anner), First Woman Doctor

Anna Darrow graduated with honors from the Chicago School of Medicine in 1909. That same year, her and her husband Roy moved to Florida. Darrow scored a 98 percent on her medical exam and was the second woman doctor to be licensed in Florida. The Darrows opened their practice in Tantie in 1911, with Roy running the office and Anna making the house calls. The Darrows moved to Fort Lauderdale in 1924. Roy passed away in 1926, but "Doc Anner" continued her practice until she retired in 1949.

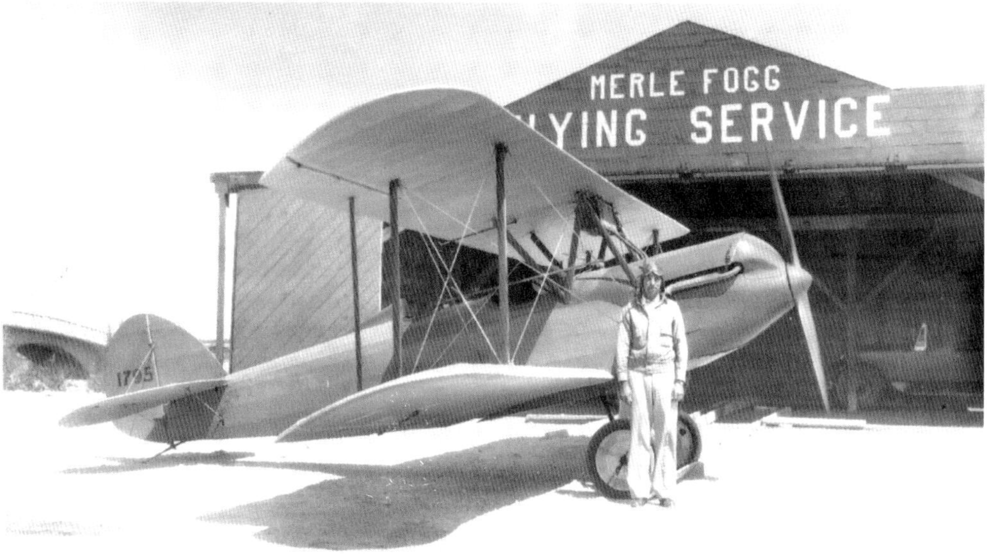

Merle L. Fogg, Pioneer Aviator and Flying Service Owner

Born in Maine, Merle Fogg was a World War I Army veteran, who had an engineering degree from the University of Maine. In 1922, he came to Clearwater, Florida, where he learned to fly. After barnstorming for about a year, Fogg returned to Maine. In 1925, he arrived in Fort Lauderdale as a pilot for Tom Bryan's seaplane. Fogg also established a small airfield along Las Olas Boulevard and opened Broward County's first commercial flying service. From there, he gave flying lessons, sightseeing tours, performed aerial surveys, and flew people around the state. Fogg would fly over the Everglades to drop messages to hunting parties and was the first man to land an airplane in the Bahamas. In 1928, he was killed during a student landing at West Palm Beach. The following year, the city dedicated Merle Fogg Field to him. Today, the site is the Fort Lauderdale–Hollywood International Airport.

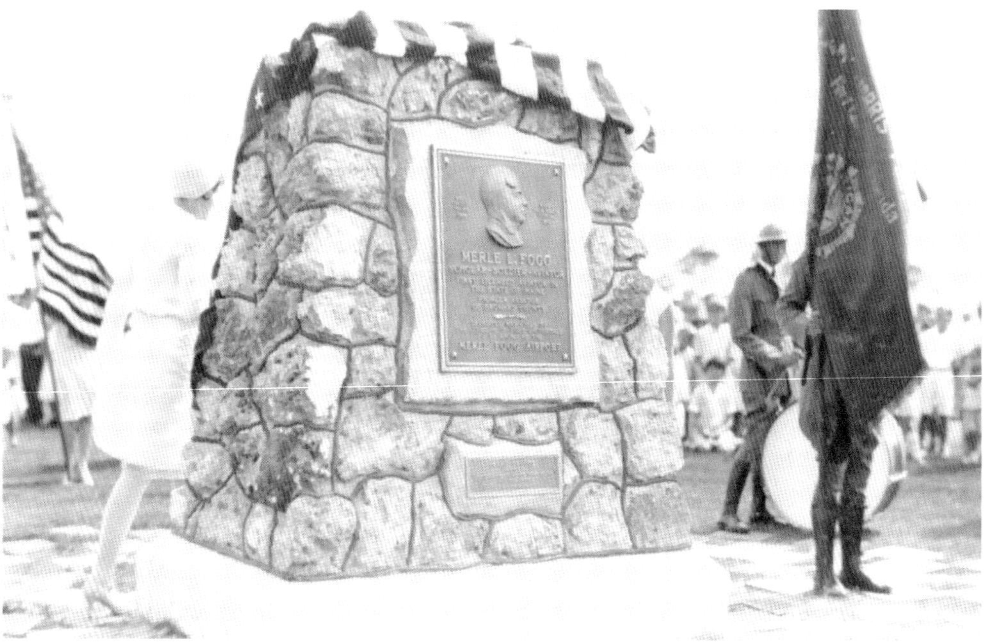

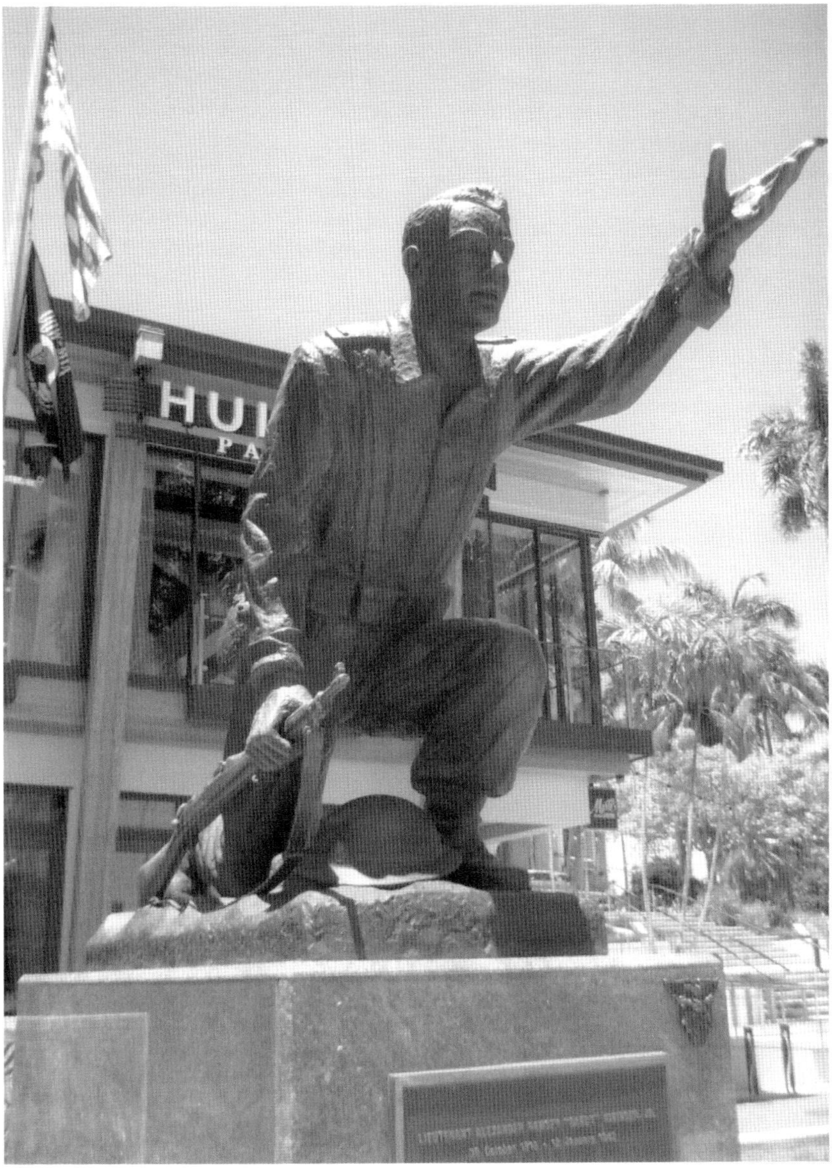

Alexander "Sandy" Nininger Jr., First Medal of Honor Recipient in World War II
Born in Georgia in 1918, Sandy Nininger moved to Fort Lauderdale in 1927 with his family. His father owned the Sunset Theatre, and Sandy worked as an usher. A 1937 graduate of Fort Lauderdale High School, Sandy played football, baseball, and basketball. He was a charter member of the Key Club in 1936 and organized the effort to aid high school athletics by helping to form the Dad's Club. Nininger graduated with honors from West Point in 1941 and requested assignment in the Philippines. On January 12, 1942, Second Lieutenant Nininger was killed in action after leading a 10-man counterattack during the Battle of Bataan. For his efforts, he was awarded the first Medal of Honor in World War II. In 1946, Key Club International established the Sandy Nininger Medal to recognize high school students who distinguish themselves. A park at Fort Knox, Kentucky, the main street at Fort McPherson, Georgia, and a cargo ship were all named in his honor. In 2001, the State Veteran's Nursing Home in Pembroke Pines was dedicated to Nininger. (Photograph by the author.)

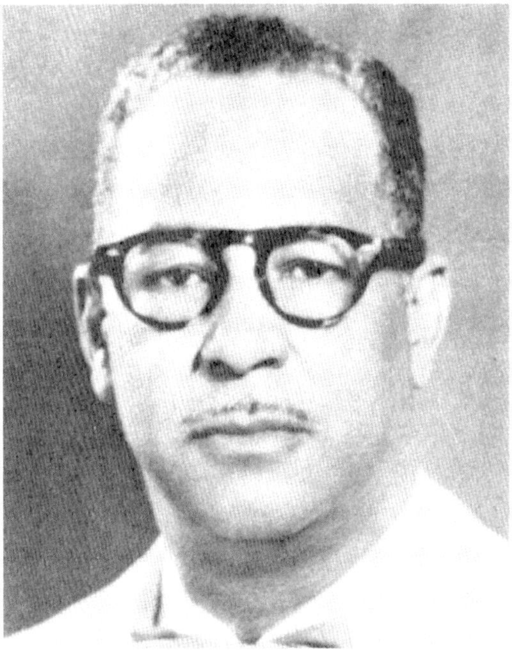

Dr. James L. Bass, First Black Dentist

A 1926 graduate of Meharry Medical College (Tennessee), Dr. James Bass came to town in 1938. He treated both black and white patients. Bass was the first African American to head the Florida State Tuberculosis and Respiratory Disease Association. He pushed for better health care and education for the black community. Bass helped found Provident Hospital and create the Northwest YMCA. As a philanthropist, he helped many black students go to college. In 1979, Fort Lauderdale dedicated a park in his honor, making him the first African American to be so honored by the city. (Courtesy of the African-American Research Library and Cultural Center.)

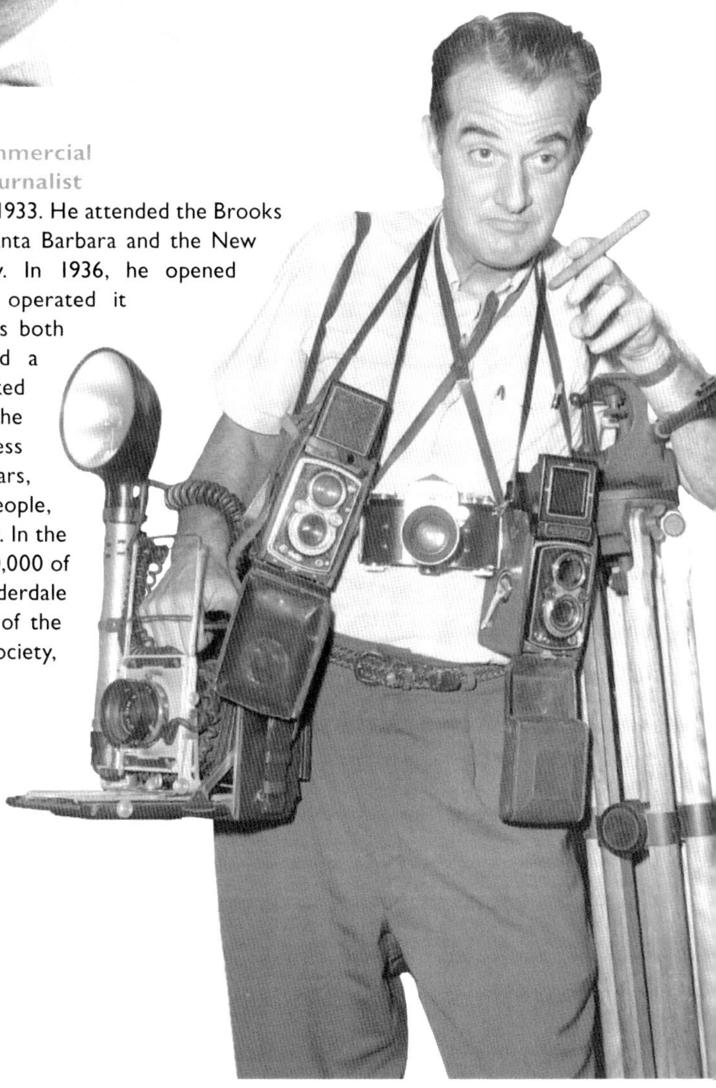

Gene Hyde, Longtime Commercial Photographer and Photojournalist

Gene Hyde moved to town in 1933. He attended the Brooks Institute of Photography in Santa Barbara and the New York School of Photography. In 1936, he opened Gene Hyde Associates and operated it for 45 years. Hyde worked as both a commercial portraitist and a photojournalist. Hyde worked for the *Fort Lauderdale News*, the *Miami Herald*, and United Press International (UPI). For 60 years, he documented the places, people, and events of Broward County. In the 1980s, Hyde donated over 180,000 of his negatives to the Fort Lauderdale Historical Society. (Courtesy of the Fort Lauderdale Historical Society, Gene Hyde Collection.)

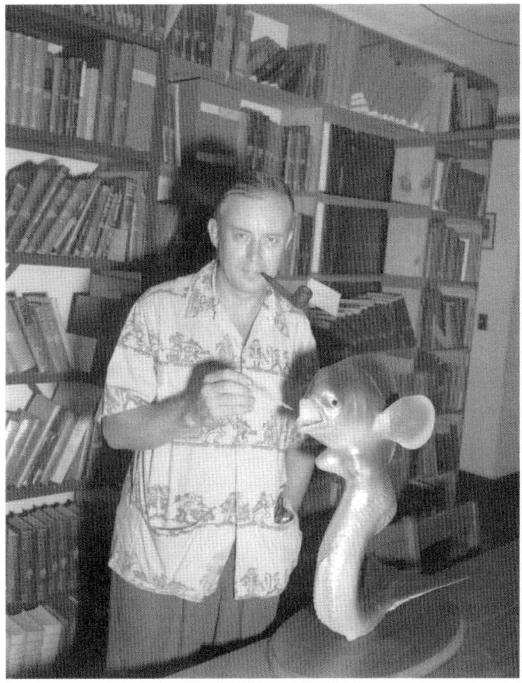

Joseph T. Reese, Fish Taxidermist

Growing up in Oklahoma, Joseph Reese learned how to stuff the animals that he caught or killed. He apprenticed under taxidermist Guy Rush, learning how to do mounts for museums. In 1937, Reese vacationed in Florida and was appalled by the crudeness of mounts turned out by most marine taxidermists. He came to Fort Lauderdale in 1938 and started J.T. Reese Taxidermy, which grew into one of the nation's largest taxidermy establishments. Specializing in skin mounting, it is estimated that Reese mounted most of the 3,500 species of fish in Florida. (Courtesy of the Fort Lauderdale Historical Society, Gene Hyde Collection.)

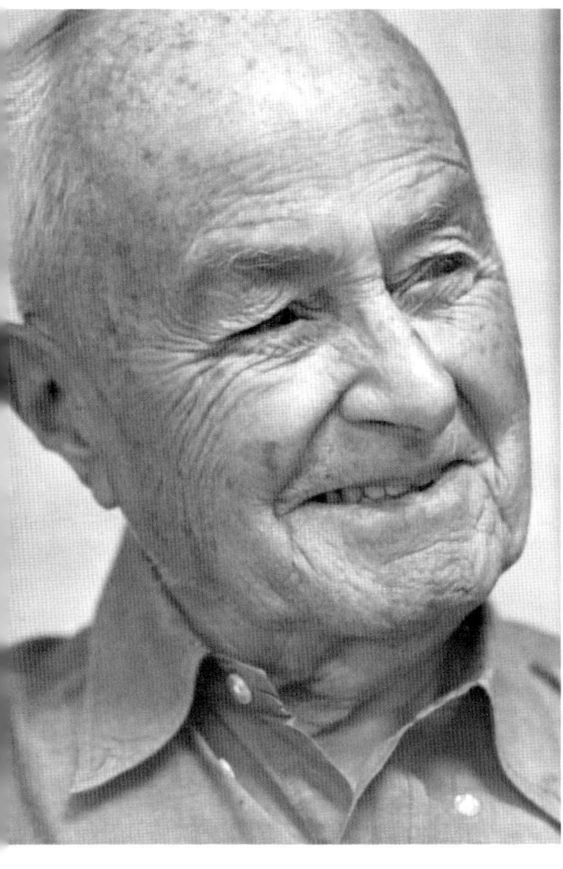

Wesley W. Stout, *Fort Lauderdale News* Columnist

Wesley Stout began his newspaper career at age 18 with the *Wichita (KS) Beacon*. He worked for various newspapers over the next 15 years. Stout started working for the *Saturday Evening* Post in 1922, and in 1936 he was made the editor, a position he held until 1942. Stout came to Fort Lauderdale in 1950 and began writing *The Beachcomber* column in 1952 for the *Fort Lauderdale News*. He published over 4,800 columns in 19 years regarding the historical background and development of the city.

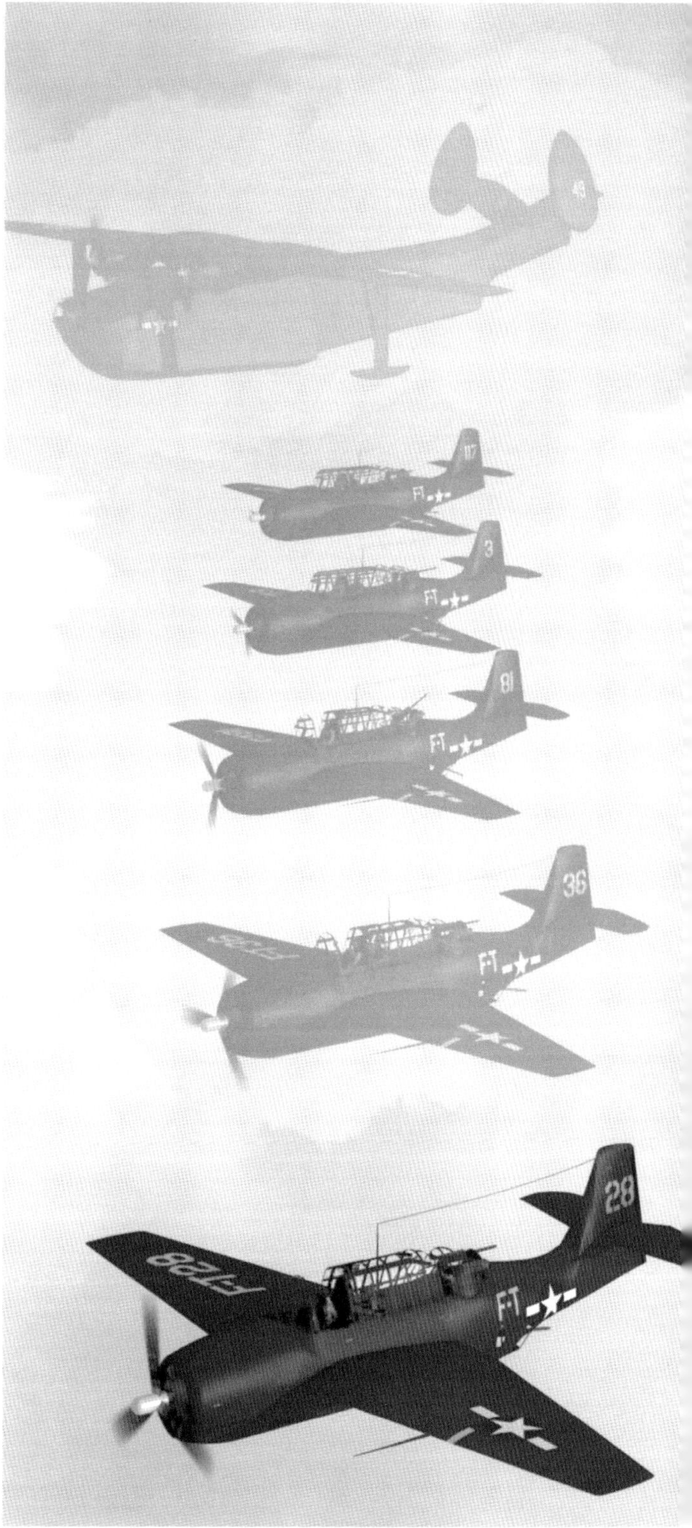

Flight 19, The Lost Patrol
On December 5, 1945, five US Navy TBM Avenger torpedo bombers took off from Naval Air Station Fort Lauderdale for a training mission to the Bahamas. Led by flight leader Lt. Charles Taylor, the planes were to fly east to the Bahamas for low-level bombing exercises, then turn northwest, flying over Grand Island before turning southwest to return to Fort Lauderdale. After the bombing run and turning northwest, Lieutenant Taylor reported that the compasses were malfunctioning and that they seemed to be lost. Transmissions from Taylor indicated that he thought he was over the Florida Keys, and the flight made course corrections based on that. Flight 19 was never seen or heard from again. It is presumed that they crashed in the open ocean, somewhere east of Brevard County.

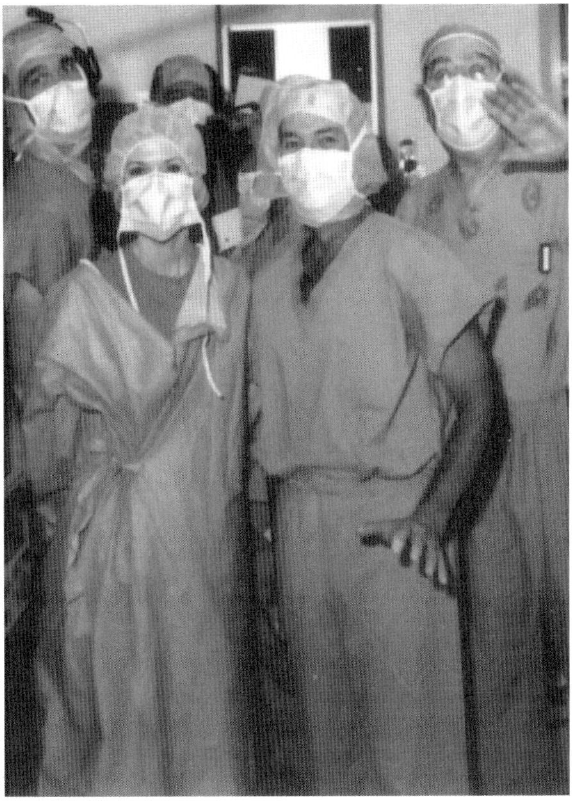

Dr. Edward Cayia (far right), First Board-Certified Anesthesiologist at Holy Cross Hospital
Dr. Edward Cayia graduated from Loyola University with a degree in anesthesiology in 1948 and completed his residency at Cook County Hospital in Chicago. During the Korean War, Cayia served as chief of anesthesiology at the 343rd General Hospital in Koizumi, Japan. In 1956, he moved to Fort Lauderdale and became the first board-certified anesthesiologist at Holy Cross Hospital. Cayia retired in 1989. The Cayia family founded New River Studios in 1983. Artists such as Miami Sound Machine, Jimmy Buffet, Cyndi Lauper, and INXS recorded there. (Courtesy of the Cayia family.)

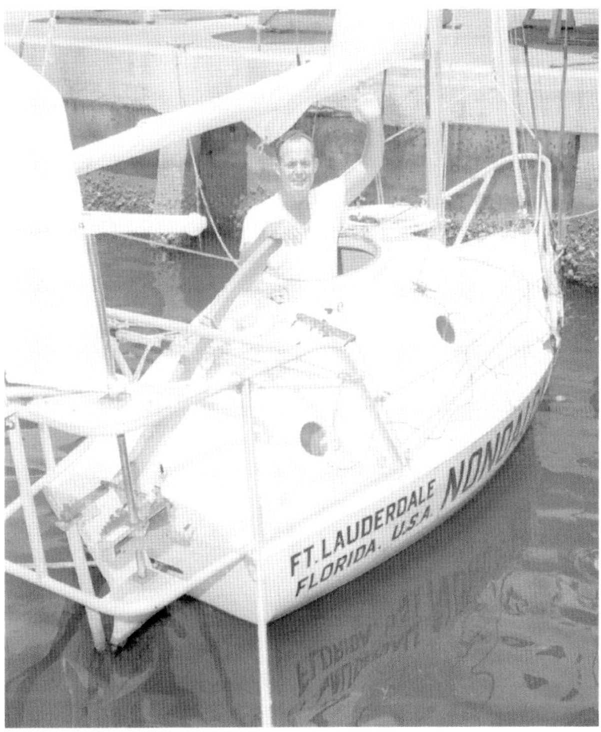

William Verity, Irish Monk St. Brendan Sailing Expedition
Inspired by the *Kon-Tiki* expedition, William Verity set out to prove that it was possible for the Irish monk St. Brendan to have crossed the Atlantic to Florida and Mexico in 550 AD. He built the 12-foot *Nonoalca* and, in 1966, sailed from Fort Lauderdale to Fenit, Ireland. It took him 65 days. In 1969, Verity did the reverse trip from Ireland to the Bahamas in the 20-foot *St. Brendan*, thus proving his theory. (Courtesy of the Fort Lauderdale Historical Society, Gene Hyde Collection.)

BIBLIOGRAPHY

INDEX

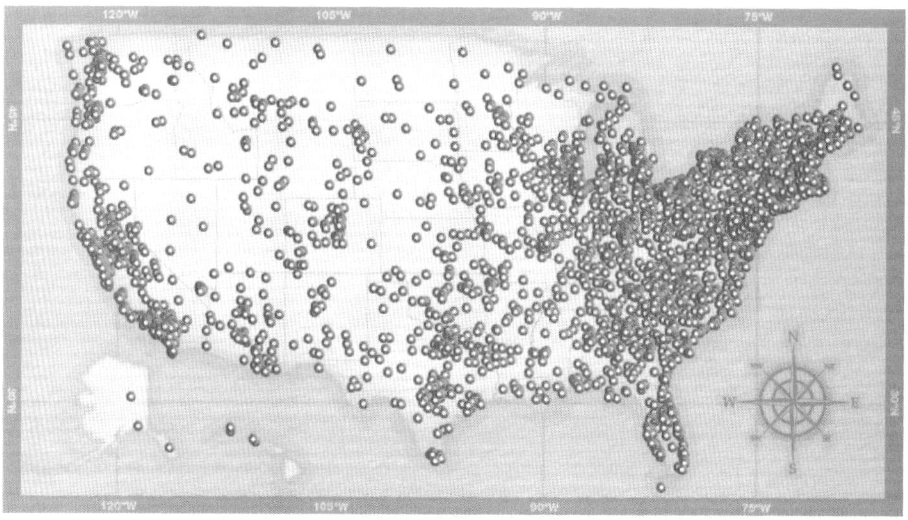